COMPUTER TECHNOLOGY FOR HIGHER EDUCATION

VOLUME TWO
The Indian Experience

COMPUTER TECHNOLOGY FOR HIGHER EDUCATION

Volume One	:	**An Overview**
Volume Two	:	**The Indian Experience**
Volume Three	:	**The Canadian Experience**

COMPUTER TECHNOLOGY FOR HIGHER EDUCATION

A Design Model for a Computerizing University

Volume II
The Indian Experience

Sarla Achuthan
Binod C. Agrawal
Vimal P. Shah
R.P. Soni
S.R. Thakore

Concept Publishing Company, New Delhi 110059 (India)

ISBN-81-7022-466-7 (Set)
ISBN 81-7022-468-3 (Vol II)

First Published 1993

Published and Printed by
Ashok Kumar Mittal
Concept Publishing Company
A/15-16, Commercial Block, Mohan Garden
NEW DELHI-110059 (India)
Phones: 5554042, 5504042

PREFACE

It was a unique opportunity to work on this collaborative research project with senior colleagues, Shri S. R. Thakore, Dr. Vimal Shah, Dr. Binod Agrawal and Dr. Sarla Achuthan as a team in India and Dr. D. Chandler, Dr. Barbara Kaltz, Dr. Murray Knutilla, Dr. Brien Maguire and Dr. W. Stahl in Canada, who dedicated themselves for more than three years to the project. During this span, we received assistance and cooperation from Dr. M. T. Ahmed, Dr. Sarukeshi and Dr. Man Mohansingh of Aligarh, Bharathiar and North Eastern Hill University respectively. Dr. J. L. Handoo of CIIL, Mysore readily accepted to work on the language aspect of the project. For the activities at Ahmedabad, assistance provided by the Regina training participants and the staff of Rollwala Computer Centre is commendable. Timely logistic support from Shastri Indo Canadian Institute and the financial assistance by University Grants Commission and Canadian International Development Agency made it possible to reach this stage in the project. Digital Equipment India Limited whole heartedly accepted our request and donated the MicroVax-II system for the project activities. The support received from Space Applications Centre as well as Development and Educational Communication Unit, especially in the early stage of the project, generated enough confidence for pursuing the mission established by both the teams. The continuous forbearance and warmth of Dr. Larry Symes and the initiative of Dr. Rolland Miller during formative stage, were simply remarkable. We kept on moving on a progressive path because of emotional backing of Prof. Ambubhai Desai, Ex-Pro-Vice Chancellor and Prof. N. V. Vasani, Pro-Vice Chancellor who assumed office in August 1992. The Indian team wishes to place on record its gratitude to all these individuals and organizations.

This volume is the second in the series which covers in detail, the experiences of the team members on the project. The Chapters 1 and 2 were written by Dr. Binod Agrawal, 3 by Dr. Vimal Shah and Dr. Binod Agrawal jointly, 4 by Dr. Vimal Shah, 5 and 6 by Dr. Sarla Achuthan and 7 and 8 by Mr. R. P. Soni. Appendix-A and Appendix-B were prepared jointly by all the members of the Indian team. Appendix-C was prepared by Mr. R. P. Soni.

Lastly, we are extremely grateful to Dr. M. N. Desai, Vice Chancellor who not only accepted the initial proposal from University of Regina for collaboration, but personally visited the University of Regina and assessed the potential benefits, the project may bring to India with its multiplier effect. His continuous backing resulted into the establishment of Computer Training and Applications Laboratory (COMTAL) on the campus of Gujarat University.

R. P. Soni
Project Director

PREFACE

[illegible]

[illegible]

[illegible]

[illegible]

TABLE OF CONTENTS

CHAPTER 1

INTRODUCTION

1. Background

The historical documentation of an international collaborative project can be an important and rewarding experience. It gives insights into the problems, frustrations, and joys of intercultural experiences in dealing with educational institutions, governments, scholars and cultural meanings of communications between collaborative institutions. The collaborative research project between Gujarat University in India and University of Regina in Canada, is a case in point.

To begin with, there is no one single title to the collaborative project. While the Indian segment of the collaborative project is entitled as "Application and Social Impact of Computer Technology in Higher Education" the Canadian title of the project is "A Design Model for a Computerizing University". It is no accident that the two teams could not find a common title for the collaborative project. In more than one ways, the difference in the titles of the collaborative project reflects the differences in the preoccupations, expectations and perceptions of the two research teams. Hence, although a conscious decision was taken by both research teams to keep the titles of the collaborative project different, the core objectives and activities of both the projects were common, and the process of mutual consultation and endeavor to gear the project programmes was continuous and mutually rewarding.

In this Chapter, an effort will be made to narrate the evolution of the project as seen by the Indian team over a period of eight years since 1984, when this project was conceived in Canada during one of the Shastri Indo-Canadian Institute Board meetings held at Regina, Saskatchewan, hosted by the University of Regina. Besides members of the Institute and University, the Indian High Commissioner [P. K. Fabian] and a representative of the Government of Saskatchewan were in attendance. An idea grew out of the interaction that Canada and India, which have so much in common, also share some common questions and problems, ranging from soil salinity to the educated unemployed, most of which are directly related to universities. Could not a university in Saskatchewan and a counterpart institution or institutions in India collaborate on researching one of these common questions ? Attention soon focussed on computer technology. It was the Indian High Commissioner who first underlined the critical significance of this issue and urged its possible consideration, in the light of its current importance for both nations. Things moved swiftly from there, and the project was born under the title: "The Social Impact of High Technology on Higher Education in Saskatchewan and in An Appropriate Area in India." (Miller 1987:5). This project proposal was prepared by Dr. Roland E. Miller, Luther College, University of Regina in April 1985.

This was followed by a seminar in June 1985 held at Montreal, which was attended by Dr. Gunwant Shah, South Gujarat University and the members of University of Regina. In this seminar, many ideas about the social impact of high technology in higher education were discussed. This meeting was most auspicious for the project, as the University Grants Commission approved Rs. 50,000 for holding a seminar at Surat in 1986 entitled "Computers in Indian Universities". The collaborative project proposal began to take some shape and the Regina team started consultations with Indian and Canadian agencies. While recalling the genesis of the project, Miller (1987:6) reported that "The Shastri Indo-Canadian Institute rendered a sponsoring and coordinating service. The University of Regina provided encouragement and gave scholarly and financial resources, the Government of Saskatchewan provided support, the International Development Research Centre granted aid for preliminary investigations as well as for Canadian participation in this Seminar; in India, the Ministry of Education and the University Grants Commission provided assistance through the formation of an Expert Committee and direct assistance towards the conduct of this Seminar, the Indian Space Research Organization graciously hosted a team from Regina, and the University of South Gujarat generously and unstintingly contributed its resources and energy by serving as the venue and host of our Seminar". The initial Regina proposal was discussed in India by Education Secretary, Government of India, Chairman, University Grants Commission, Expert Group under the Chairmanship of Dr. Iqbal Narain, the then Member-Secretary of the Indian Council of Social Science Research in 1986.

In early 1985, Professor Asis Gupta (later Resident Director, Shastri Indo-Canadian Research Institute, New Delhi) also made efforts in this direction and persuaded Dr. Binod C. Agrawal, Indian Space Research Organization, Ahmedabad, to participate and also to help design the study. On December 30, 1985, the Regina team submitted a proposal to the International Development Research Centre (IDRC) for support. The proposal had three components for financial support: (i) a travel grant to enable the University of Regina team to visit India for identifying research issues, and collaborative institutions and to carry out discussions regarding a seminar to be held at South Gujarat University, Surat, some time in November/December 1986, (ii) a travel grant to the Canadian team to attend the proposed seminar in Surat, and (iii) support to the proposed collaborative project. This project proposal was prepared by Dr. Roland E. Miller (Part One) and Dr. Bruce F. MacDonald, Principal Researcher (Part Two), with the assistance of the members of the coordinating committee and the research scholars of the University of Regina.

2. Regina Team Exploratory Visit

The University of Regina constituted a four-member research team, which, supported by a travel grant from IDRC, visited India from December 30, 1985 to January 16, 1986. The team consisted of Dr. L. R. Symes, Associate Project Director, Dr. B. F. MacDonald, Principal Researcher, Dr. R. B. Maguire, Computer Science Researcher, and Dr. W. A. Stahl, Social Science Researcher.

The Regina team was assisted by the officials of the Shastri Indo-Canadian Institute, New Delhi. Not much had happened at the South Gujarat University for developing the project proposal when Regina team was in India.

The Regina team visited seven universities, two research institutes and one research organization, in the Western and the Southern regions of India. In Ahmedabad, the Regina team met at the Space Applications Centre (SAC) of the Indian Space Research Organization (ISRO), where SAC scientists including Dr. Binod Agrawal along with faculty members of Gujarat University and the Indian Institute of Management, Ahmedabad, discussed various aspects of the proposed project. The response from the members present at the meeting was positive and some action began to take place in Ahmedabad, but the Indian side was very much in the mood of "wait and watch".

2.1 Surat Seminar

Subsequently an Indo-Canadian joint seminar was held on February 11-14, 1987, at the South Gujarat University, Surat, to bring out research issues and to refine the project goals of both sides. The Canadian team was headed by the President of the University of Regina, Professor L. I. Barber. The participants of the seminar included a number of scholars from various universities, institutes and organizations from within India and Canada, who also presented papers at the seminar. The papers and discussions at the seminar led to identification of the research issues and project activities concerning pedagogy and computer introduction in higher education. Since the Indian Space Research Organization was reluctant to act as a collaborating institution in India, the question of collaboration was once again discussed. Mr. S. R. Thakore, Consultant, University Grants Commission and coordinator of the computer teaching programme in Gujarat University suggested that Gujarat University might act as a collaborating institution which can enlist the assistance of Indian Institute of Management and Indian Space Research Organization, both located in Ahmedabad. It was suggested that Gujarat University will submit a proposal for financial support to the University Grants Commission and the University of Regina will submit a proposal for financial support to CIDA. Upon completion of the Seminar, the Canadian team met in Delhi to refine the statement of project goals and to propose future plans. They also met Secretary, UGC and Secretary, ICSSR and other officials of the UGC in Delhi, and apprised them of the progress of project formulation activities.

The other points discussed and agreed between the Regina team and the Indian participants are of crucial importance for a comprehensive understanding of the project formulation and its execution. Earlier, "The project envisioned two research teams, one in India and one in Saskatchewan, independently but interactively researching the same key issues. The prominent words in the terms of reference were: comparative, reciprocal, cooperative"

(Miller 1987:6). These points were further elaborated and equality as the first and the foremost principle of collaboration was accepted. Equality of participation in operational terms meant that both teams will be equal partners in the project formulation and its execution The second aspect of equality involved sharing of cost of project by both teams from their respective countries. It is because of this reason that eventually both teams submitted separate research proposals for support in their respective countries. So, in India a clear reference was made about the proposal of the University of Regina while submitting the proposal to the University Grants Commission for the financial support. The University of Regina team incorporated the Indian research proposal in its proposal for support to Canadian International Development Agency (CIDA). Further, equality in project participation was reflected, in the way travel expenses along with local hospitality were to be met by each team.

The second principle of collaboration was based on sharing of research experiences while pursuing the country specific plans of research action. In operational terms, both research teams were to pursue their respective plans of action while continuously sharing and exchanging the findings of their research work. This meant periodic exchange of information, joint meetings, and exchange of documents.

Not much happened in the remaining period of 1987, as the expert group set up by the UGC could not meet to take a final decision in this regard. In order to facilitate further detailing of the project proposal, the Regina team proposed the visit of the Indian team to Regina in the early part of 1988. The visit could not take place however, the Shastri Indo-Canadian Institute Advisory Committee discussed the project proposal in Canada.

3. Shaping of the Collaborative Project

The university of Regina team took initiatives to accelerate the process of preparing project proposals on both sides. In May-June 1988, Prof. R. Miller and Prof. L. R. Symes made the first formal contact with Gujarat University and discussed the proposal at length with Prof. M. N. Desai, Vice Chancellor of Gujarat University and other faculty members of the university. As a result, Prof. M. N. Desai formally wrote to Prof. L. I. Barber, President of the University of Regina. Prof. Desai wrote:

> On the basis of the deliberations in our meeting as well as subsequent consideration by the faculty of university, I am glad to state that we are interested in collaborating with your university in such a collaborative research endeavor. I am sure such a collaborative arrangement will help both universities in developing a mutually beneficial arrangement in this endeavor of immense importance.

The letter sowed the seed for shaping the collaborative project and gave a firm and definite direction. This meeting also added an additional and significant idea to the project. It was in this meeting that Mr. S. R. Thakore mooted the idea of setting up an experimental computer laboratory on the lines of academic staff colleges to carry out experimentations and develop suitable pedagogical module for computer applications in different disciplines of higher education. Gujarat University faculty sought the active assistance of the University of Regina team in acquiring computer hardware for this purpose as well as support for software and training material.

3.1 Scope of the Project and its Submission

In the May-June 1988 meeting, Professor Miller and UGC official also suggested the enlargement of the scope of the project. This meant national representation on a selective basis. After deliberations, it was decided to include three universities representing three regions of the country apart from Gujarat University, Ahmedabad in the West, in the study. Professor A. Qadeer, Aligarh Muslim University, Aligarh from North, Dr. Man Mohan Singh, North Eastern Hill University, Shillong from North-East and Professor Sarukesi, Bharathiar University, Coimbatore from South were selected for participation in conducting the baseline survey. In this way, the total scope of the project proposal from the Indian side became national in character.

While the Gujarat University submitted its proposal to the University Grants Commission in the last week of July 1988, the University of Regina submitted its proposal to Canadian International Development Agency(CIDA) in October 1988. Both these proposals, while complementary to each other had country specific elements that reflected the research concerns of each team. In the final proposal, training figured as an important component of the project on both sides. On October 3, 1988, the University Grants Commission approved the Gujarat University proposal including financial support, but with some modifications subject to final clearance by the Government of India.

3.2 Gujarat Team Visit to Regina

In the early part of 1989, CIDA approved the University of Regina proposal along with financial support. In this respect, the University of Regina project segment of the collaborative project came into being and was inaugurated, but the Indian segment was yet to be cleared by the Government of India for final sanction. Notwithstanding this technical problem, the University of Regina team began to operationalize the project and in order to detail out the common areas of research invited the Indian team for a two week meeting in Regina. This meeting was attended by Mr. S. R. Thakore, Dr. Binod C. Agrawal, Mr. R. P. Soni, Dr. Vimal P. Shah, and Dr. Sarla Achuthan. In addition, Prof. Sarukesi of Bharathiar University as a member of the collaborative institution, attended the Regina meeting held in August 1989. During this meeting, the progress of the project on both sides was reviewed, and the future plans of action were decided and common areas of investigation identified. Both the teams discussed at length the possible sources for acquiring computer hardware for the proposed Gujarat University Computer Laboratory.

As a result of this meeting, both sides initiated actions on the proposed objectives in the respective countries. Since Dr. Miller had left the Regina University on an extended leave, Prof. Larry R. Symes took over the responsibility as Project Director from the University of Regina, Regina. Mr. R. P. Soni, who co-ordinated the initial activities for the Indian team, assumed responsibility as Project Director from Gujarat University, Ahmedabad, India. These two project leaders in consultation with the members of the teams, worked out the mode of project operations, communications and review. It may be mentioned that the Indian team still did not then have the full clearance though the project was eventually cleared within a couple of months thereafter. Once the clearance was obtained, both teams began work on the project.

4. Objectives of the Study and its Importance

The objectives of the project evolved as a result of several rounds of discussions and recommendations made during the Surat Seminar. Also the individual team members indicated their special research interest while defining the objectives of the project. Lastly, keeping in view the original proposal of the Regina team, the following objectives of the project were defined:

1. To conduct a survey of the available computer facilities in the institutions of higher education and research in Gujarat (West), Tamil Nadu (South), Uttar Pradesh (North) and Meghalaya (North-East).

2. To examine the use of computers in processing the data related to students' admission, performance in examination, management information system and accounting by the universities in Gujarat.

3. To set up a Computer Laboratory in Gujarat University, to develop computer-based modules for pedagogical methods in different disciplines and to examine by controlled experiments the effectiveness of using computer technology in the classroom environment.

4. To train university and college teachers participating in the orientation programmes of the Academic Staff Colleges being established by the UGC.

5. To develop a replicable model of a university using computer technology in training, research, examination and management information systems.

6. To cooperate and collaborate with the University of Regina in carrying out the necessary comparative researches, experiments, training and evaluation of the project mentioned above.

Each of the project objectives were further refined and elaborated while carrying out the project in India.

5. Project Execution

In 1989, in all earnest, the Indian team began to work after they returned from Regina in August 1989. The first task was to carry out the baseline survey in Gujarat, Tamil Nadu and Uttar Pradesh and the North Eastern region. The instruments were prepared and sent to participating institutions for data collection. It was agreed among the participating institutions that they will write their individual reports which would be integrated in the final report at Ahmedabad. The results of first preliminary analyses were presented at a joint review meeting held at Ahmedabad in August 1990 in which both teams were present. Based on the discussion, it was agreed that future research activities must include the evaluation of training programmes and longitudinal studies, if possible. It was thought essential especially as to how the social impact of computers can be evaluated in a comparative perspective. Both teams felt that clarity on this issue will help a great deal in the final design model. Further, initial common understanding of the concept of social impact would be helpful in providing uniformity, continuity and comparison of the design model evolved by both teams. In this review meeting, a series of joint research proposals were worked out by both teams. A significant addition to the project was a proposal jointly prepared by Dr. J. L. Handoo and Dr. Barbara Kaltz in the area of Computer Assisted Language Learning. Thus, both sides began to work on several research projects prepared and agreed during the August 1990 meeting.

The Project Director Dr. L. R. Symes visited Ahmedabad in April-May 1991, at the time of the first computer training course organized at COMTAL for Mathematics college teachers of Gujarat. This course was coordinated by Dr. Sarala Achuthan. Dr. Symes was impressed with the work of the trainees and complemented his Indian colleagues for their first successful training programme. During this review, an outline of the design model prepared by the Canadian team was discussed. In this meeting, keeping in view the limitations of survey results, it was decided to prepare at least twelve case studies on the history, growth and development of computer education in the four regions of India. In these case studies, the historical development of computing facilities, various computer applications and reasons leading to particular computer applications were descriptively analyzed. A report entitled "Computer Scenario of Higher Education in India : Selected Case Studies, 1992" was prepared in April 1992.

Six months later, Professor Symes visited Ahmedabad in connection with the formal inaugural function of the Computer Training and Applications Laboratory (COMTAL) on December 11, 1991. During this visit, consultations and meetings were held to review the progress of the project between May to December 1991. Also, a number of actions were initiated to achieve the project goals within the time frame agreed earlier. The proposed August 1992 meeting at Regina, and 1992 third Regina training was discussed in detail. A most important decision taken during this meeting was to send about fifty per cent women for training to Regina in 1992 programme. Accordingly, five out of 12 participants were women in 1992 Regina training. Along with the 1992 training team, three completed draft reports were sent to Regina namely, "Computer Scenario of Higher Education in India" (1992), "Computer Scenario of Higher Education in India : Selected Case Studies" (1992), and "Pedagogy of Computer Training in Higher Education of India : An Evaluative Study" (1992). These draft reports, proved useful for shaping the future reports to be prepared for the final design model on both sides.

As agreed, an integrated report entitled "Application and Social Impact of Computer Technology in Higher Education : Evolving a Design Model for Computerizing University in India" (1992), was prepared by the members of the Indian team, in response to the draft of "Design Model" sent by the Canadian team in June 1992. The exchange of these two reports provided the background and basis for proposed August 1992 meeting at Regina. The project review meeting was held for two weeks in August 1992 in Regina. All the five members of the project team from India attended this review meeting in which the two draft reports exchanged earlier were discussed in great detail by both teams. One of the major aims of these discussions was to draw common findings from both reports. In doing so, both teams wanted to overview the main findings and make recommendations for design model. During these two weeks, individual authors of the chapters from both sides sat together to bring out major recommendations from their chapters. These recommendations were refined during several group meetings. At the end of the meeting, draft report in the form of "An Overview" was circulated. It was further agreed that this draft report will be edited by Dr. David Chandler of the Canadian team and the same will be circulated for final approval to all members before its printing. The same was carried out by the Regina team and the entire overview report was faxed to the Indian team after which it was finalized for publication. In this meeting, both teams agreed to bring out three volumes of the final reports containing an overview of the design model jointly authored by both the teams in Volume I. In Volume II the Indian Experience, and in Volume III the Canadian Experience was to be reported.

Since the inception of the project and especially after 1989 visit of the Indian team to Regina, periodic reviews were held both in Ahmedabad and

Regina, individually and jointly as indicated earlier. All these review meetings were documented in the form of minutes duly signed by both project directors. These minutes contained future action plans of research, agreed decisions, milestones achieved, new action items, and suggestions for midway corrections and exchange of experiences with the idea of incorporating them for future action.

6. Setting up of Computer Training and Applications Laboratory (COMTAL) at Ahmedabad

It is necessary to document the way Prof. Larry R. Symes and the Regina team worked for setting up a Computer Training and Applications Laboratory (COMTAL) at Gujarat University. It is important because COMTAL would continue to be a training facility even after the completion of the project. It must be recalled that the Gujarat University team mooted this idea way back in 1988 and sought help of the Regina team. Since then Prof. Larry R. Symes along with other members of the Regina team began preliminary talks with major computer companies such as IBM, Digital Equipment Corporation and other Canada-based companies to "gift" or "donate" computer for this project. When the Indian team visited Regina in August 1989, a series of meetings were held with the help of the Regina team, between the Indian team and the computer companies at Regina. In these meetings the Indian team indicated the utility of such a laboratory for expanding the computer education in India at the university level. They also tried to impress upon the Regina team vital role such a facility will play in achieving the broad goals of the collaborative project.

Accordingly, the year 1989 assumed significance in setting up COMTAL. Prof. Symes and members of his team visited India to further define the required hardware configuration. Concurrently, he got in touch with the top management of Digital Equipment Corporation, Boston, USA. The negotiations were vigorously pursued by Prof. Symes and once again he came to India to meet Mr. Mike Shah Managing Director, Digital Equipment India. These discussions and negotiations finally fructified, and Digital Equipment India (DEIL) agreed to gift a MicroVax-II computer system. The battle, however, was not over yet as there were a number of problems even in giving an outright gift by Digital India to Gujarat University. Once again Prof. Symes got into action and the Indian side also remained in touch with Digital Equipment India. The combined efforts of both the teams saw a computer installed in Ahmedabad. Presently, the system is fully operational and maintained by Digital Equipment India under a maintenance contract.

6.1 Training Activities in Ahmedabad and Regina

Computer training formed an important component of the project on both sides. Three training programmes having 12 participants each year were organized by the University of Regina. All participating and assisting institutions sent trainees to the University of Regina between 1990 to 1992. One trainee from CIIL Mysore participated in the training programme conducted at Regina in 1991. The training team was accompanied by a group leader who was a member of the Indian research team.

The first training programme was conducted in Ahmedabad at COMTAL for the teachers of Mathematics from April 15 to May 10, 1991. That programme was well received by the participants. Encouraged by this, the project team conducted separate training programmes for teachers of Economics, Social Sciences, Physics, Statistics, Chemistry and Library Science. All these training programmes were of four weeks' duration. Each programme had fifteen to sixteen participants. Each participant completed a small project in their discipline in the use of the computer. Moreover, COMTAL also provided computer training to teachers who came for orientation or refresher courses in different subjects in Gujarat University, as a part of Academic Staff College Training Programme. No doubt these training programmes have helped a great deal to the participants.

7. Participating and Assisting Institutions

The original project proposal envisaged that Gujarat University will have the prime responsibility of implementing the project having five team members. These included four faculty members of the Gujarat University, namely, R. P. Soni, Vimal P. Shah, Sarala Achuthan and S. R. Thakore (now Consultant, University Grants Commission) and Binod C. Agrawal, Indian Space Research Organization. Three Universities representing South, North and North- Eastern regions were identified as participating institutions.

Bharathiar University, Coimbatore in South, Aligarh Muslim University, Aligarh in North, and North-Eastern Hill University, Shillong in North-Eastern region. The main responsibility of these universities were to participate in the base line survey for data collection, analysis and individual report writing. The Regina team having a language faculty on the team it became imperative to have a similar person in the Gujarat team. After careful consideration and some negotiations, Professor J. L. Handoo of Central Institute of Indian Languages, Mysore was invited by the Gujarat team to assist the project. Dr. Handoo and Dr. Kaltz since then started working on the language segment of the project.

In this respect, the Gujarat University research team was supported apart from three universities, by Indian Space Research Organization, Ahmedabad and Central Institute of Indian Languages, Mysore. The participation of these institutions were identified in two areas. First, in carrying out the project work in India and second, participation in three six weeks training programmes organized by University of Regina between 1990 to 1992. Also, it was expected that these institutions will participate in the deliberations of the project. Professor Sarukesi, Bharathiar University attended first Regina meeting in August 1989 whereas Professor Handoo attended meetings held at Ahmedabad along with representatives of Aligarh, Coimbatore and Dr Man Mohan Singh (Shillong). While inputs have been taken from all participating institutions in the final preparation of the design model, the main responsibility for the preparation of all reports remained with the Gujarat team.

8. Summary

In the introductory chapter, the evolution of the project has been discussed highlighting the efforts made by both the teams. Special mention has been made about the efforts made by the Regina team to set up Computer Training and Applications Laboratory (COMTAL) at Gujarat University. The project objectives and additional research work done by the Gujarat team have been highlighted. In the last section, the participation of other institutions in the project has been discussed.

- Contributed by Binod C. Agrawal

References

Miller, Roland E

Genesis of the Project. Paper presented at the Seminar on Computers in Indian Universities, February 11-14, 1987 held at South Gujarat University, Surat, Gujarat, India.

CHAPTER 2

METHODOLOGY

In the previous chapter the history and objectives of the project were discussed. In this chapter, an attempt will be made to describe broadly the methodology followed in three major studies undertaken for this project. The objectives of the project evolved after several rounds of discussions and keeping in view the interest of the individual team members. During the course of time, each of the project objectives were further refined and elaborated[1].

One of the major research objectives was to examine the availability, use and application of computers in higher education and its social impact. This required a study of economic, social, technological and educational aspects of the issues concerning the use and application of computer in higher education. The baseline survey was designed to achieve this objective keeping in view the existing knowledge about computer use in the country. Accordingly the objectives of the survey were evolved.

1. Objectives of the Survey

1. To review the growth of computer facilities in institutions of higher learning.

2. To examine the current status of computer technology in the educational institutions. This involves preparation of an inventory of available hardware, software, manpower, training programmes and courses concerning computers, extent of use of computer in administrative services and pedagogical activities. It includes identification of problems and constraints in the use of computer technology.

3. To study future plans regarding computer expansion/acquisition.

4. To identify the perceptions, opinions and attitudes of faculty regarding the social impact of computer use in higher education.

5. To assess the training needs for computer use in administrative, pedagogical and research activities and the software requirements thereof.

---

1 The description of the methodology followed in various studies conducted by Gujarat University team has been directly taken from the three draft reports namely (1) Computer Scenario of Higher Education in India (1992), (2) Computer Scenario of Higher Education in India : Selected Case Studies (1992) and (3) Pedagogy of Computer Training in Higher Education of India : An Evaluative Study (1992) prepared by Sarala Achuthan, Binod C Agrawal, Vimal P Shah, R P Soni and S R Thakore (all team members). In the text they are referred to as Survey (1992) Case Study (1992) and COMTAL Training (1992).

2. Sampling

At the time of the baseline survey in 1990, there were 156 universities (including deemed universities), about 100 research and training institutions and about 6,500 colleges in India. Given such a large number of universities and institutions of higher education, it was decided to select four regions in the country for this survey. Besides Gujarat University in the West, Bharthiar University in the South, Aligarh Muslim University in the North and North-Eastern Hill University in the North-Eastern region representing four geographical regions were selected for the survey. It was left to each of the participating universities to demarcate the geographical boundary for the purpose of its baseline survey.

Gujarat University research team decided to conduct the baseline survey to cover the geographical boundary of Gujarat State. There were 10 universities, 24 research and training institutions and 305 affiliated colleges in Gujarat. It was, therefore, decided to include in the sampling all the 10 universities, 17 research and training institutions and 305 affiliated colleges.

To identify the perception, opinions and attitudes of the teachers and research faculty regarding the social impact of computer use in higher education, a sampling frame of all heads of departments in various universities of Gujarat was prepared and a random sample of 78 heads of departments was selected. In addition, to study whether the perception of the faculty members belonging to rural areas was different from that of urban areas, 34 heads of departments of different colleges (other than the principals) of urban areas and 20 heads of departments of different colleges of the rural areas (other than the principals) were selected on a random basis. The rural as well as the urban samples thus obtained, represented a wide spectrum of different disciplines.

In the case of Aligarh Muslim University, the research team decided to conduct the survey in the state of Uttar Pradesh. The Union Territory of Delhi was also included in the sampling frame for this purpose. As Uttar Pradesh is a very large state its entire coverage was found to be difficult, particularly in view of the limitations of time and resources. Therefore, important institutions generally located in the major cities were included in the sample consisting of 21 universities, 480 colleges and 11 institutes.

Bharathiar University research team selected the state of Tamil Nadu for data collection. For this purpose the educational and research institutions were classified into four groups, namely universities, colleges, research institutes and training colleges. The sample consisted of 120 institutions selected from all the four groups located within the state of Tamil Nadu.

3. Data Collection Instrument

The data collection instrument was divided into three parts according to the nature of information sought.

Part-I was designed to seek information on the broad features of the institution. This part was intended to be filled in by the administrative head of the institution. It included questions pertaining to organizational structure, objectives, affiliation, courses offered, humanpower availability, general policies, ownership or access to computers, future plans of acquisition or expansion of computer facility, training requirements in the use of computers, etc. Most of the questions were close-ended; only the question concerning objectives, policies, etc. were open-ended. As the organizational structure and the activities of the universities, institutes and colleges varied, three sets of Part-I questionnaire were devised so as to suit them.

Part-II of the questionnaire was meant to collect information regarding the computer facilities available in the institutions of higher education. Therefore, it was intended to be filled in by the head of the computer centre. The broad items included in this part concerned history and growth of computer facilities, funding pattern, details about hardware, software, humanpower, user group, major uses and their areas, maintenance practices, and constraints and problems in running the computer related activities.

Part-III of the questionnaire was meant to identify the reasons for no or inadequate use of computers in higher education and to understand the perception, opinions and attitudes of the academic community regarding different aspects of using computer technology. It was observed that though there are many institutions having computer facility, its use was limited. With all the potential of the computer, not many faculty used it as much as they could or should. A list of 12 reasons for no or inadequate use of computer was prepared and the respondents were asked to rate each reason on a three-point scale (very certain, fairly certain and doubtful). The next section included 30 statements concerning general opinion regarding the role and impact of computers in higher education and society as a whole. The respondents were asked to rate these statements on a five point scale ranging from strongly agree to strongly disagree. In addition, background information of the respondents such as age, sex, professional experience, qualification, were also sought.

The draft questionnaire was pretested on a purposively selected sample of ten respondents. Each of the three parts of the questionnaire was pretested by personal interviews with heads of institutions, heads of computer centres and faculty members. Based on the comments received, minor modifications were made in some questions. However, no major changes in the items were found necessary. Based on the pretesting, it was estimated that Part-I would require around 30 minutes, Part-II around 45 minutes and Part-III around 10 minutes. Keeping the objectives of the survey in mind, this was considered reasonable. The questionnaires are given in Appendix-A.

4. Data Collection

Considering the large number of institutions and the respondents to be included in the sample, it was planned to collect the data through "mail questionnaire method" in the first instance and then to follow it up with personal contacts and interviews as and when necessary. In the first week of November 1989 the questionnaires accompanied by a forwarding letter explaining the genesis of the project, with a request to fill in the questionnaires were mailed to all educational institutions in Gujarat. Same was also done in the case of Tamil Nadu. However, due to some unavoidable circumstances in Uttar Pradesh questionnaires were mailed in the first week of May 1990.

A great deal of efforts in the form of reminders and personal follow-up had to be made to obtain the data. The follow-up was made on a continuous basis. This required three reminders in the case of Gujarat, one in Uttar Pradesh, and one in Tamil Nadu.

In the first instance, in Gujarat only 34, 30 and 48 questionnaires of part I, II and III respectively were received by mid-December 1989. As the response to the first wave mailed questionnaire was quite low, another request as reminder letter was mailed to all non-respondents on December 22, 1989. In this effort, 68, 5 and 92 part I, II and III questionnaires were received. The second reminder was sent on February 1, 1990. This was followed by personal contacts. In this effort, 60, 11 and 62 Part I, II and III questionnaires were respectively received. Thus, three waves spread over a period of about four months of data-collection resulted into a fairly acceptable response rate in a mail-questionnaire study.

While most of the respondents filled in all the three parts of the questionnaire, some returned only one or two parts duly filled. This was largely true in the case of colleges that did not have any computer facility. The blank parts of the questionnaire have been excluded from the data analysis. This partly explains the relatively large difference in the response rate of part I and part III as compared to the response rate of part II questionnaire.

In case of Uttar Pradesh and Delhi, in all 550 questionnaires of all three parts were mailed to 21 universities, 480 colleges and 11 institutes. In spite of the best efforts only 98 questionnaires were received. The lowest response was from the colleges. It is evident that the overall response, in Uttar Pradesh and Delhi even after several attempts, has not been an encouraging one. So, it became imperative to send reminders and to make personal requests. But this could not be taken up on the scale it was done in case of Gujarat.

In Tamil Nadu questionnaires were sent by post to 120 institutions. Responses were received only from 19 institutions. In addition, Part II questionnaires were sent to 217 individual faculty members but only 42 replies were received. Most of these responses were incomplete. Hence, during December 1989, January-February 1990 investigators were sent to the concerned institutions for collection of the data. In this respect the response has been better in Tamil Nadu as compared to Uttar Pradesh but not as good as in case of Gujarat.

5. Selected Case Studies

After the compilation of survey, both Gujarat University and University of Regina teams felt that an indepth understanding of computer use and introduction in higher education required further efforts. Translated into action, it was decided to collect qualitative, descriptive data from selected universities, and research institutions through indepth interviews of key persons. For this purpose, case study approach was followed.

The following objectives were defined for the case studies.

5.1 Objectives of the Case Studies

1. To understand the introduction, growth and use of computer in the institutions of higher learning.
2. To identify the problems in the introduction of computers.
3. To find how the problems have been tackled.
4. To sketch the present computing environment and use.
5. To understand the decision making process and management of change with thc introduction of computers.
6. To project the future of computer use.

5.2 Data Collection for Case Study

Data collection for the case studies involved both structured and unstructured instruments. The three part structured instruments prepared for survey was broadly used. But in this case, the data were collected through personal interviews of the concerned individuals. In addition, detailed data were collected from the selected individuals and from the heads of the computer centres. For this purpose, members of the research team from Ahmedabad visited each institution. In many places secondary data were collected about the history of the institution and of computer introduction. Both institutional and faculty perspectives were taken into account while collecting first hand data. Case histories of individuals who acted as "champions" of computerization and were largely responsible for the introduction of computer in that institution were noted down. Seventeen case studies were completed, majority being located in Western India. Most of the institutions selected for case study were having computer for at least ten years. These case studies reflected the process and use of computerization in the country. Based on these 17 case studies, generalization and conclusions have been drawn for the final volume.

6. Evaluation of Computer Training

In order to assess the impact of computer training programmes organized at COMTAL, a structured pre and post questionnaire was administered to all participants before and after the training respectively. Two sets of attitude questions identical to the one used during the base line survey were incorporated in the impact evaluation questionnaire. The first twelve items pertained to reasons for inadequate use of computer. The second thirty items pertained to role and impact of computer in society as a whole. The data were collected from all the 104 participants of seven training course. It must be mentioned that the broad social sciences methodology of evaluation and technology assessment was followed in the project.

As some of the items in the questionnaire were negatively worded for the purpose of analysis the scale was reversed. The mean difference of pre and post was compared. It was assumed that if the results were in the positive direction it will show favorable change of attitude of the participants towards computer after the training.

7. Analysis

Each part of questionnaire had quantitative as well as qualitative responses. Using the Data Base Management Package, the quantitative and qualitative data were stored in computer, and necessary procedures were carried out for data validation, data editing and consistency checks.

Quantitative data were analyzed using descriptive and inferential statistics. Simple to complex statistical models have been used to unfold the latent features of the data. The detail regarding the operational definition of the sample as well as composite variables are given in the subsequent chapters where these have been used. The qualitative data were first summarized item-wise, and then the observations emerging from the summaries were pulled out. These observations have been incorporated, discussed and interpreted in appropriate places in this volume. Same holds true for the analysis of the case studies and the evaluation of the computer training.

8. Summary

This chapter provides detailed description of the research methods followed in this project. Methodology used in each of the three major studies along with the objectives have been separately discussed. Also the method of analysis has been provided at the end of the chapter.

Contributed by Binod C. Agrawal

CHAPTER 3

THE UNIVERSITY AND THE INDIAN SOCIETY

Education is concerned with learning. Learning is the process of acquiring knowledge or skills by instruction, study or experience; in this broad sense, learning is a life-long process. Education refers to the method by which a society attempts to direct and accelerate the learning process of its members. Formal education refers to schooling—an organized system of enrollment (selection), specified instructional programme spread over a period of time, examination (evaluation) and certification.

The independent India has pursued, right from the early years, the philosophy and approach of a planned programme of development in different spheres of life. It launched its first Five Year Plan in 1951-52; the eighth Five Year Plan is now under way. Till the Sixth Five Year Plan, education was taken to be a social service rather than an input in the development process. The emphasis has since changed whereby education is considered pivotal in social and economic development of the country through development of human resources (India 1991:84-86). The faith of the government in the role of education for development seems to have been based on the functionalist orientations and the forward link that education has, first, with occupation and earnings, and, eventually, with the stratification system that is slowly moving from the caste-based to a mixture of caste- and class-based criteria. While the functionalists have viewed the educational system as offering opportunities to individuals for mobility, the conflict theorists have generally stressed the role of structured inequality that helps the already privileged sections to continue to obtain a disproportionately large share of benefits from the expanding and developing educational facilities. In order to examine the feasibility of introducing computer as an aid in teaching, research, administration and other relevant spheres of higher education, it is necessary to describe briefly the overall picture of the educational development in India since its Independence as well as the major problems and challenges in this regard.

1. Education and Society

The educational system in India evolved as a result of an ancient tradition of education handed over from generation to generation for several millennia and its encounter with British Educational System in the nineteenth century, and Islamic tradition of education brought earlier and intensified during the 14th and the 17th century due to the rise of Mughal empire (for details, see Gupta, 1988). The present educational system as it is prevalent in the country is a legacy of British education with some influence of North-American tradition of higher education. The rise and expansion of higher education in independent India has been on the lines of British higher education with a few indigenous innovations to respond to socio-cultural needs of the contemporary society. Ghosh and Talbani (1989 : 2) summarize the social implications of the British educational system at the time of India's independence in 1947.

> At independence, India inherited an educational system with great educational disparities between males and females, upper and lower classes and urban and rural populations. The colonial system of downward filtration prevented the development of a broad educational base. This was due to several socio-economic factors: limited economic development, a feudal agricultural society which was hierarchical and inegalitarian, social handicaps, which prevented women from education, caste discrimination which prevented lower castes from being educated, and isolation in the remote and hill areas which led to the educational backwardness of tribal people.

Keeping in consonance with the constitutional rights of the individual citizens which guaranteed equality of status, opportunity and freedom from discrimination, the law makers viewed education as a means to achieve these goals. In a country full of historical disparities among various regions and communities, education was also seen as a vehicle to bring about justice, liberty, equality and fraternity among the citizens of a multilingual, multireligious and multiethnic country, especially after the partition of the country on the basis of religion. Education in this respect was conceived as an instrument of social change for future egalitarian society though perception varied a great deal among various sections of the Indian society in this regard.

Gore (1982 : 3) summarizes the varying perceptions of British education in the following words:

> Among Indians some looked upon the new [British] system of education as the channel to secure governmental jobs and such other positions of bureaucratic authority as were open to Indians. But there were others who primarily saw the new system of education as a way of introducing young Indians to the new knowledge of science, and there were still others who hoped that the new education at the college level with its emphasis on the study of nineteenth century liberal philosophies would open new vistas of thought and philosophy and help promote social reform within the country.

These perceptions continue to exist to a large extent in independent India. The efforts to correct these perceptions have had limited success. On the contrary, education by some is seen as the only means of economic prosperity and upward social mobility beyond the boundaries of India. It is no accident that, in the post-independent period, a large praportion of the migrants to North America is largely confined to persons having professional, technical and liberal higher education in search of better economic opportunities. These developments in no way have deterred the educational planners and the leaders of the country to affirm their belief that education would liberate the nation—the people of India from the age old bondage of inequality and would lead towards an egalitarian democratic society. It is this kind of belief that has made education the responsibility of both Central (Federal) and State (Provincial) Governments.

Today, in India, primary education and secondary education is mandatory in almost all states of the country and is provided free of cost. The college education is open for all, and in some states it is free for women. Special efforts with some success have been made through positive discrimination by reserving seats for educationally and economically weaker communities referred to as Scheduled Castes and Scheduled Tribes and other backward communities to provide equal opportunities for education. These progressive measures have had socio-political backlashes from time to time in the country, leading to social unrest, political upheavals and discontent. Scholars, educators and political leaders continue to discuss mechanisms for bringing about equality of opportunity at all levels of education. These efforts have borne some fruits through increased participation of both poor and rich, men and women in acquiring higher education in almost all disciplines.

One of the most striking features of all these efforts can be seen through a growing number of students seeking admission in the institutions of higher learning in the country. This has had remarkable influence on the management and administration of higher education across the country. This has also forced educational planners and administrators to look for new means of providing higher education like open university and distance education. Administrative reforms, new methods of examination and use of computers for admission, result preparation, and research have taken new roots in the entire educational system of the country.

1.1 The Educational System

Prior to 1976, education was exclusively the responsibility of the State Governments; the Central Government was concerned with only certain areas like coordination and determination of standards in technical and higher education. But, following a constitutional amendment in 1976, education has now become a concurrent responsibility of the Central and the State Governments.

There has been a tremendous expansion of the facilities for education at all levels in independent India. In 1951, there were 209,671 primary/junior basic schools, 13,590 middle/senior basic schools and 7,288 high schools/higher secondary schools. As of 1989, there were, in all, 550,700 primary/junior basic schools, 143,747 middle/senior basic schools and 76,119 high schools/higher secondary schools (Table 1). With a view to providing opportunities to children with special talent or aptitude to proceed at a faster pace, *National Policy on Education 1986,* envisaged setting up of co-educational residential schools, called Navodaya Vidyalayas in each district numbering more than 400; 261

TABLE 1 Educational Institutions : 1989-90

				COLLEGE FOR		
	PRIMARY	MIDDLE	SECON DARY/ HIGHER SECONDARY	GENERAL EDUCA- TION	PROFES- SIONAL EDUCA- TION	UNIVERSI- TIES
MAJOR STATES						
ALL INDIA	550700	143747	76119	4755	891	184
ANDHRA PRADESH	47216	5827	6366	403	86	17
ASSAM	28875	5703	3137	179	15	3
BIHAR	52181	12530	4006	552	31	11
GUJARAT	13103	16794	5021	227	57	10
HARYANA	4922	1321	2266	119	22	4
KARNATAKA	23538	16318	5062	403	132	9
KERALA	6812	2892	2547	132	31	6
MADHYA PRADESH	65897	13453	3449	448	37	12
MAHARASHTRA	38796	18145	10071	571	189	18
ORISSA	39593	9396	4695	232	30	5
PUNJAB	12357	1413	2740	171	26	4
RAJASTHAN	30022	8600	3642	138	41	9
TAMILNADU	29491	5651	4949	209	71	15
UTTAR PRADESH	74275	14549	5946	414	24	25
WEST BENGAL	50827	4179	6804	302	62	11
OTHER STATES						
ARUNCHAL PRADESH	1101	241	108	4		1
GOA	996	118	361	14	4	1
HIMACHAL PRADESH	7522	1101	1037	39	4	3
JAMMU & KASHMIR	8712	2320	1097	27	9	3
MANIPUR	2771	443	393	33	4	1
MEGHALAYA	4162	685	298	23	1	1
MIZORAM	1084	522	185	13	1	
NAGALAND	1286	343	124	16	1	
SIKKIM	512	127	68	1		
TRIPURA	2043	437	428	13	2	1
UNION TERRITORIES						
ANDAMAN & NICOBER	186	42	63	1	1	
CHANDIGARH	43	31	70	12	2	2
DADRA & NAGAR HAVE	120	41	11			
DAMAN & DIU	43	20	19	1		
DELHI	1851	397	1043	52	6	11
LAKSHADWEEP	19	4	11			
PONDICHERRY	344	104	102	6	2	1

SOURCE :- Centre for Monitoring Indian Economy, Bombay : Basic Statistics relating to Indian Economy. Vol. 2, Sept. 1991.

such Navodaya Vidyalayas were already set up during the Seventh Five Year Plan. There are several other schemes in vogue for (a) vocationalisation of secondary education, (b) improvement of science education in schools, (c) environmental orientation to school education, and (d) open schools to provide an alternative or second chance for education and opportunity to school drop-outs, housewives, unemployed or working adults to avail of continuing education.

The pre-primary schools are relatively small in number, and are run by private managements, and mostly cater to the better-off population in the urban areas. The primary schools are largely state-financed and run by the local bodies (village panchayats, municipalities and municipal corporations); in addition, there are private, primary schools recognized by the state, and located mostly in urban areas. Education in classes I to VIII in all Government/local bodies and aided schools in most of the states and union territories is free.

It may be noted in this connection that out of a total of 530,176 villages (habitations) in the country with a population of 300 or more persons, 23 per cent habitations do not have facilities for primary education in their habitation, 17 per cent habitations have such facilities within a distance of upto one km. from the habitation, and 6 per cent habitations do not have such facilities within a distance of even upto one km. from the habitation. Obviously, in such a situation the children living in such habitations are least likely to enroll for primary education. In addition, there are deficiencies in the elementary school system due to single-teacher schools, absenteeism of teachers who live in a distant place, non-availability of separate rooms for different classes, and so on.

Apart from the government, most of the secondary and higher secondary schools are run by private organizations or trusts/societies duly registered for the purpose under the state laws and receiving grant-in-aid from the state governments. The National Council of Educational Research and Training (NCERT), established in 1961, acts as a principal agency for academic advice to the Ministry of Human Resource Development, Government of India, in matters pertaining to formulation and implementation of policies and programmes for qualitative improvement of school education.

Similarly, there were only 27 universities, 53 teachers training colleges and 542 colleges in 1951. There are now ten Central Universities, 136 universities functioning under the State Acts, and 28 institutions (including 5 Indian Institutes of Technology) declared as Deemed Universities, ten institutions of national importance, and 48 research institutions. There are 17 Regional Engineering Colleges, 5 Indian Institutes of Management and several specialized institutions of higher education and research in the country. There are 4,755 colleges for general education and 891 colleges for professional education affiliated to various universities. There are 840 approved polytechnics (including 62 polytechnics for girls) that offer middle-level diploma courses in engineering, technology, and management. The Indira Gandhi National Open University, established in 1985, and many state universities provide facilities for a variety of programmes for distance education.

1.2 Structure of Universities and Institutes of Higher Learning

One of the major achievements of the nineties has been the acceptance of a uniform policy of higher education. Now the undergraduate programme of three years after twelve years of primary, secondary and higher secondary education, popularly known as 10+2+3, has been accepted in the country. It has taken several decades in independent India for its acceptance. Even today, one cannot say with certainty that the three year undergraduate programme is fully operational throughout the country.

The higher education in India comes under the purview of university education. The beginning of the university education goes back to the mid-nineteenth century when three universities, namely, Bombay, Calcutta and Madras, were set up in 1857 in three British colonial Presidencies of India. These universities were transplanted on the Indian soil on the lines of London University which was then a purely examining and a non-teaching body. Since then, there has been a slow but steady growth of higher education in the country. For convenience, the university expansion can be divided into two major phases. The first phase consists of higher education in British India covering the period between 1857 and 1947, which was very slow as the total number of universities established during this period does not go beyond 17, whereas the second phase of expansion in independent India after 1947 is phenomenal. In less than 45 years, there has been a more than ten-fold expansion reaching to about 190 universities. In British India, there were three types of universities, namely unitary (teaching within the campus), affiliating (largely responsible for conduct of examination of the colleges within its jurisdiction) and federal constituent colleges or institutions having organic association and sharing of administrative responsibilities of the university as a whole. In independent India "...several changes have taken place in this classification and otherwise. The concept of federal university which implied teaching work in cooperation with its colleges, stands altered...A certain amount of mixing up of the various types has also taken place. Many of the unitary universities have some affiliated colleges now; and the North-Eastern Hill University, Shillong has been planned from the very beginning as a teaching and affiliating university. Similarly, a large number of affiliating universities have established teaching departments of their own." (Shukla 1983 : 160).

Almost all universities and institutions of higher learning are supported by either central or state governments or both. In this respect, they are referred to as central universities or state universities. The University Grants Commission (UGC) is the national agency charged with the responsibility to take appropriate measures for promotion and coordination of university education and determination and maintenance of standards of teaching, examination and research in universities. The Central universities, deemed universities and the institutions of national importance get 100 per cent grant for their maintenance and developmental programmes from the Central

Government and/or the UGC. The state universities and colleges get maintenance grants from their state government. The UGC allocates special developmental grants to the state universities and colleges generally with a stipulation that the respective state governments will take over, after a certain period, the full responsibility of the recurring component of the developmental grant.

Central universities like Aligarh Muslim University and North-Eastern Hill University are directly supported by University Grants Commission. Similarly, the state universities like Gujarat University and Bharathiar University are supported by their state government as well as the University Grants Commission. Both these kinds of universities have one common link — University Grants Commission (UGC), "...a statutory autonomous organization under the act of Parliament to enable the central government to discharge its constitutional responsibility..." (Shukla 1983 : 186). In addition, there are many similar institutions which are governed by separate councils and boards like agricultural universities, medical institutes and management institutes, enjoying the status of deemed universities.

The national agencies like the Indian Council of Social Science Research (ICSSR) and the Indian Council of Historical Research (ICHR), give annual maintenance grants and specific developmental grants to the various research institutions, some of which also receive some maintenance grants from their state governments. Thus, for an introduction of any new programme of development in the universities and institutions of higher learning, the Central Government plays a very crucial role through UGC and national funding agencies like the ICSSR and the ICHR.

2. Administration of Universities

All universities are headed by a Vice Chancellor, as its chief executive, reporting to the Chancellor. It has been observed that irrespective of the type of university/institution of higher learning "...the internal structure and purpose of administration is more or less the same in all the general universities. There are three main authorities of such a university, namely, the court or senate, the executive council or syndicate, and the academic council. Their composition, powers and functions are laid down by the act under which the university has been established and the statues under the act" (Shukla 1983 : 160).

The court or senate consists of a cross section of academics and community leaders or professionals, donors, and former students. The deliberations of this body enables to identify the needs and requirements of the public and means of meeting them. The executive council or syndicate in most of the universities is the principle executive body. "It provides sanction for actions by vice-chancellor. It is a small body with not more than about twenty members. The vice-chancellor is its Chairman. The pro-vice-chancellor or rector, if the university has one, is an ex-officio member" (Shukla 1983 :

162). In addition to these three most important bodies, there are some other important committees and councils like the faculty, the academic council, boards of studies of varies subjects, the student welfare council, the finance committee, the selection committees, the admission committee, the examination committees, the sports committee and the building committee. These committees may vary from university to university. The vice-chancellor or his/her nominee is generally the chairperson of each of these committees or bodies (see for detail Shukla 1983 : 158-200). Over a period of time many scholars, administrators and vice-chancellors have indicated that the "traditional structure" suggested here for internal administration of the universities is somewhat out of date and does not work. Hence, from time to time reforms have been suggested and implemented with little success. The process of internal reflection and retrospection continues even today to bring about an efficient, effective and harmonious university structure to achieve its educational goals.

2.1 Gujarat University - A Case

The structure of a university can be illustrated through an example. Gujarat University established in 1949 after separation from the Bombay University is a teaching and an affiliating university having over 121 affiliated colleges, seven recognized institutions and ten university schools having several departments in each. These schools were set up few years after the creation of the university — the latest, Seth A.G. Charity Trust School of Law was founded in 1977.

Courses Offered

Gujarat University offers Bachelor's and Master's degrees in Arts, Commerce and Science disciplines. It has also Bachelor's and Master's degrees in Library Sciences, Education and Labour Welfare, along with Development Communication. The faculty of engineering offers Bachelor's and Master's degrees of engineering in about a dozen subjects like Civil, Mechanical, Electrical, Chemical, Textile, Instrumentation and Control, Electronics and Communication Engineering. These courses are offered at the L. D. Engineering College and other colleges affiliated to Gujarat University. Faculty of Law offers Bachelor's and Master's degrees, Diploma in Labour Laws and Practice, and Diploma in Taxation Laws and Practice. In the faculty of medicine, both degree and diploma courses are offered at Bachelor's and Master's levels and super specialization (DM/MCH). Also, nursing diploma, and specialized post-graduate diploma in a variety of medical sciences are offered. Master's degrees for non-medical graduates are also offered in the fields like anatomy, physiology, pharmacology and medical microbiology and helminthology. In addition, Bachelor's and Master's degrees in Pharmacy and

Dental Sciences along with post-graduate diploma in Space Sciences are also offered.

Other courses include certificate, diploma and Master's degree in computer applications, post-graduate diploma in clinical and community psychology and in counseling psychology. Another special feature of the university is the Master's degree programme in Physical Education. The University also offers courses in Business Management at Master's level. Recently introduced courses include Master of Environmental Science. In addition, the University offers M.Phil and Ph.D. degree programmes in several subjects. There is, however, no component of courses for Ph.D. The students pursue their Ph.D. research work under the guidance of the teachers recognized as Ph.D. guides by the university. The total number of students in Gujarat University as of 1990-91 was 1,03,000. Since then, the number has increased.

Structure

The university is headed by Vice-Chancellor who reports to Chancellor. The Chancellor of the University is Governor of Gujarat State. The Vice-Chancellor is appointed for a three year term. The university has a court (Senate), an Executive Council and various faculty committees to look after the university's academic matters including courses to be offered, teaching, research and planning. The Vice-Chancellor is assisted by Pro-Vice-Chancellor. The Registrar of the university heads the administration and assists Vice-Chancellor in the management of the university affairs. Being an affiliated university, conduct of examinations is an extremely important activity which is looked after by the Controller of Examinations. In order to provide a fair representation of affiliated college teachers on various committees, councils, executive council and court/senate, regular elections are held on term basis and a few members are nominated on senate, councils/committees. It must be mentioned that university enjoys a great deal of autonomy in academic matters, though there are occasional incidents of indirect political pressures being exerted in the arena of appointments, admissions, disciplinary matters related to students, university teaching and nonteaching staff, and in the recognition of new colleges and courses. A detailed analysis of university autonomy was documented by Dongerkery (1967) indicating a similar situation in mid-sixties in Osmania University.

Gujarat University represents a very complex organization, autonomous in character but not free from external push and pull having to administer its own teaching and research departments, postgraduate centres and affiliated colleges. In more than one way, Gujarat University being a State University is closely linked with the state official machinery. The ups and downs in the political scenario in the state also affect the day to day working of the university. For example, the state policy of reserving seats for the admission of Scheduled Castes and Scheduled Tribes or reservation of jobs directly influence the socio-political climate of the university. In this respect, Gujarat University is a thriving organic entity within the larger social system of the state. Since its inception, media of instruction has been a point of discussion, though both English and Gujarati are now accepted as media of instruction for teaching, research and administration.

3. Educational Achievements

The strides made by independent India have been phenomenal, if one looks at the quantitative growth, as indicated earlier, in every field of higher education. But if the same figures are juxtaposed on the growing population mosaic, it becomes a modest achievement.

3.1 Literacy

The Directive Principles of the State Policy, as enshrined in the Indian Constitution, set the goal of ensuring free and compulsory primary education for all children upto the age of 14 years. India does not seem anywhere near achieving its coveted basic goal of universal literacy, although India has made steady progress from the crude literacy rate of 16.67 per cent in 1951 to an adjusted literacy rate of 52.07 per cent for the population above seven years in 1991 (Table 2). During the past 45 years, its population increased from 361 million in 1951 to 843.9 million in 1991. One of the direct results of the failure on the front of universalization of elementary education has been a large number of illiterates in the country. In absolute terms, the number of illiterate persons aged seven years and above is estimated to be 404.8 million in 1991. A detailed classification of the 5 per cent sample data of the 1981 Census showed that a half of India's population in the age-group 15-35 years was illiterate; further, 74.3 per cent of the rural females as against 18.46 per cent of the urban males in this age-group were illiterate. India has, therefore, launched various programmes aimed at providing motivation, special assistance, and financial and other resources for a speedy eradication of illiteracy. For example, the non-formal education programme aims at providing education to children who do not/cannot attend school due to some reasons, children from habitations without school, school drop-outs, girls who cannot attend whole day schools and working children. The National Literacy Mission aims at imparting functional literacy to about 80 million illiterates in the age-group 15-35 years by 1995 and supports several thousand Adult Education Centres under the Central Scheme of Rural Functional Literacy Project (RFLP) and the State Adult Education Project (SAEP).

Further, wide differences have been observed in the literacy rates, by gender, in rural-urban areas, by state and scheduled caste and scheduled tribe population. Also, there are wide differences in the literacy rates, by gender, rural-urban areas, state and scheduled/other population. In 1951, among the major states, Kerala with 41 per cent literate population was at the top of the literacy pyramid while Rajasthan

TABLE 2 Literacy Rates :1951,1961,1971,1981,1991. (Per cent)

STATES	MALES					FEMALES					PERSONS				
	1951	1961	1971	1981	1991	1951	1961	1971	1981	1991	1951	1961	1971	1981	1991
ALL INDIA	25	40	39	(H)56	(1)64	8	15	19	(H)30	(1)39	17	28	29	(H)44	(1)52
ANDHRA PRADESH	20	35	33	47	56	7	14	16	24	34	13	25	25	36	45
ASSAM	(C)27	(C)44	(D)37		62	(C)8	(C)20	(C)19		44	(C)18	(C)33	(D)29		53
BIHAR	21	35	31	47	53	4	8	9	17	23	12	22	20	32	39
GUJARAT	32	49	46	65	73	13	23	25	38	49	23	36	36	52	61
HARYANA	(B)	35	37	58	68	(B)	11	15	27	41	(B)	24	27	44	55
KARNATAKA	29	42	42	59	67	9	17	21	33	44	18	30	32	46	56
KERALA	50	65	67	88	94	32	46	54	76	87	41	55	60	82	91
MADHYA PRADESH	16	32	33	48	57	3	8	11	19	28	10	21	20	32	43
MAHARASHTRA	31	49	51	70	75	10	20	26	41	51	21	35	39	56	63
ORISSA	27	40	38	56	62	5	10	14	25	34	16	25	26	41	49
PUNJAB	(A)21	41	40	56	64	(A) 9	21	26	40	50	(A)15	32	34	48	57
RAJASTHAN	14	28	29	45	55	3	7	8	14	21	9	18	19	30	39
TAMILNADU	32	52	52	68	75	10	21	27	40	52	21	36	39	54	64
UTTAR PRADESH	17	32	32	47	55	4	8	11	17	26	11	21	22	33	42
WEST BENGAL	34	47	43	60	67	12	20	22	36	47	24	35	33	49	58

Table 2 Contd.

STATES	MALES					FEMALES					TOTAL PERSONS				
	1951	1961	1971	1981	1991	1951	1961	1971	1981	1991	1951	1961	1971	1981	1991
OTHER STATES															
ARUNCHAL PRADESH		15	18	35	51		2	4	14	29		9	11	26	41
GOA	(F)30	(F)45	(F)54	76	85	(F)17	(F)26	(F)35	55	68	(F)23	(F)35	(F)45	66	77
HIMACHAL PRADESH	13	38	43	64	75	2	11	20	38	52	8	25	32	51	64
JAMMU & KASHMIR		20	27	44			5	9	20			13	18	33	
MEGHALAYA	(E)	(E)	34	47	52	(E)	(E)	25	37	45	(E)	(E)	29	42	48
MIZORAM	(E)	(E)	(E)	79	84	(E)	(E)	(E)	69	78	(E)	(E)	(E)	74	81
NAGALAND	15	27	35	59	66	6	13	19	40	56	10	20	27	50	61
MANIPUR	21	54	46	64	73	2	19	20	35	49	11	36	33	50	61
SIKKIM	13	22	29	53	64	1	5	10	27	47	7	14	20	42	57
TRIPURA	22	35	40	61	70	8	12	21	38	50	16	24	31	50	60
UNION TERRITORIES															
ANDAMAN & NICOBER	34	49	52	70	80	12	25	31	53	66	26	40	44	63	74
CHANDIGARH	(B)	63	67	79	83	(B)	43	54	69	74	(B)	55	62	74	79
DADRA & NAGAR HAVE	6	18	22	45	52	2	5	8	20	26	4	12	15	33	39
DAMAN & DIU	(G)	(G)	(G)	74	86	(G)	(G)	(G)	47	61	(G)	(G)	(G)	60	74
DELHI	43	70	64	79	83	32	51	48	63	68	38	62	56	72	76
LAKSHADWEEP	36	42	56	81	87	5	13	31	55	71	15	27	44	68	79
PONDICHERRY		59	57	77	84		29	35	53	66		44	46	65	75

NOTE :- (A) Included Haryana & Chandigarh. (B) Included in Punjab. (C) Included Mizoram and Meghalaya. (D) Included Mizoram. (E) Included in Assam. (F) Included Daman and Diu. (G) Included under Goa. (H) Excludes Assam. (1) Excludes Jammu & Kashmir.

SOURCE:- Centre for Monitoring Indian Economy, Bombay: Basic Statistics relating to Indian Economy. Vol. 2, Sept 1991.

with only 9 per cent literate population was at its bottom. While their ranks in the 1991 literacy pyramid remain the same, the differences have accentuated over the years—only 39 per cent literate population in Rajasthan against 91 per cent in Kerala in 1991. Similarly, although the crude female literacy rate increased from 8 in 1951 to 39 in 1991, the gender differences have increased from 17 percentage points in 1951 to 25 percentage points in 1991; this indicates that the gains from the expanding facilities for education have accrued more to men than to women. The rural-urban differences in literacy are also of the same magnitude, and the combined output of the gender and rural-urban differences is quite alarming, namely, in 1991 25.4 per cent of rural women were literate while 69.3 per cent of urban men were literate.

A detailed classification of the 1991 Census for the scheduled caste and tribe population is not yet available, but the earlier Census data show a distinct trend of the lowest level of literacy among the tribal population, and the highest level of literacy among the non-scheduled caste/tribe population. The glaring differences in literacy can be gauged from 1981 Census. In 1981 even after 30+ years of planned programmes of development, only 6.8 per cent of the scheduled tribe women living in rural areas could read and write as against 68.5 per cent of the non-scheduled caste/tribe men living in urban areas.

Given the democratic ideology and concern for providing equal opportunities to all citizens since Independence, the central and state governments in India have launched, several programmes of assistance to motivate the scheduled castes and the scheduled tribes to obtain education. A certain quota (generally in proportion to their population) is also reserved for them for admission in educational institutions and for jobs in the government and government-aided agencies. Education and reservation of jobs have been looked upon as major instruments for improving the socioeconomic conditions of these weaker sections.

Literacy is only a crude indicator of the educational development of India's population. The number of students being enrolled at different levels and in different types of education, their ratio in terms of the population in the corresponding age-groups, and the percentages of the population who have been able to complete the various levels of education are some of the other indicators of the educational development.

3.2 Enrollment

There has been a steady increase in the enrollment of students at all levels of education. The total number of students enrolled in all types and levels of education increased almost six fold from those enrolled in 1950-51 to those in 1988-89. For example, the percentage of the students enrolled in classes I to V in the population in the age-group 6-11 years increased from 42.6 per cent to 99.56 per cent in 1988-89, similar percentages of the students enrolled in classes (a) VI and VII and (b) IX-XI/XII in the population in the corresponding age-groups of 11-14 and 14-17 years increased from 12.7 per cent and 5.3 per cent to 56.95 per cent and 25.3 per cent, respectively (GOI, India 1991 : 89). There are, however, serious problems of drop-outs and stagnation, especially at the primary level of education. The drop-out rate from classes I to V for 1986-87 (the ratio of the number of students enrolled in class I in 1982-83 minus those in class V in 1986-87 to the number of students in class I in 1982-83) is estimated to be 43.6 per cent. In general, the drop-out rates are higher for girls, rural areas, scheduled castes/tribes, and others belonging to socioeconomically deprived families.

TABLE 3 Growth of Entrolment for General Education by Courses/ Stages and Collegiate Level (Standard) 1950-5i to 1984-85

YEAR	STAGES/COURSES							
	P.U.C./INTERMEDIATE		GRADUATE		POST-GRADUATE		DOCTORATE	
	BOYS	GIRLS	BOYS	GIRLS	BOYS	GIRLS	BOYS	GIRLS
1951	194921	26416	75032	16636	14401	2127	1051	139
1961	381384	76517	235633	63379	36873	9215	3879	768
1962	368824	77021	281950	80715	40945	10763	4178	779
1963	380751	84605	318961	96480	41827	12191	4318	861
1964	409381	97215	347989	113384	43369	13751	4599	1028
1965	430102	105670	404271	144961	47057	15624	5090	1217
1966	490654	132988	455787	170120	52659	18553	5446	1405
1967	551896	146822	514838	198087	56784	20866	5720	1397
1968	612423	164522	608215	236288	65828	25786	6570	1488
1969	672922	177940	725111	273498	74711	29395	7717	2002
1970	728645	207751	850210	316894	82842	34071	7722	2113
1971	798248	222354	911900	347772	87730	38397	7658	2461
1972	956693	270964	924288	365071	98390	40164	8183	2593
1973	1028918	293025	963307	396632	108215	44533	9246	3043
1974	703948	246238	907691	347183	171675	47882	9214	3069
1975	1113593	352364	973283	440551	123672	52354	9870	3615
1976	1142870	361959	956744	452000	123365	53248	10221	3677
1977	1173941	366238	1309210	510514	149071	59497	11944	4340
1978	1155152	340201	1360153	533803	146380	58698	16089	6203
1979	1208575	342466	1408489	586304	160520	65530	18582	7055
1980	1247385	348204	1336421	556653	170363	71162	16770	6939
1981	798356	278876	1435578	602646	172150	76367	16805	7572
1982	727543	256805	1443177	663190	168577	76470	16857	7966
1983	1631049	574464	1482487	637995	192739	88224	17402	7536
1984	1473060	501234	1602079	678792	199862	93738	17807	7985
1985	1660085	590992	1787427	789288	215646	102556	19729	8893

SOURCE:- Government of India, Ministry of Human Resources Development : A Handbook of Educational and Allied Statistics, 1987.

The growth of enrollment at the university from 1951 to 1985 can be examined from Table 3. There has been a steady increase in the enrollment of boys as well as girls at all levels of higher education. Although the gender differences in enrollment still persist to a great extent, a trend of decline in the differences is quite apparent. The available statistics regarding the enrollment, in the various stages of higher education, of all students as well as those belonging to the Scheduled Castes and Scheduled Tribes for the year 1988-89 are shown, by gender, in Table 4. It is apparent that the share of the Scheduled Caste and Scheduled Tribe students, inspite of the various schemes for financial and other assistance as well as the provision for reservation of seats in admission, in benefiting from the expanding facilities for higher education is still much lower than their proportionate population.

Without going into a detailed examination of the other indicators of educational development, it may be noted that while all sections of the population have benefited to a certain extent from the expanding facilities and opportunities for education since Independence, there are considerable differences, by state, gender, rural-urban areas and Scheduled Castes and Scheduled Tribes categories of population, in the various indicators of educational development. In fact, such differences are accentuated at the higher levels of education. It is not surprising to find differences in the educational development of people in India; this is true of other countries also. One of the most consistent findings in literature has been that there are significant differences by gender, rural-urban residence and family socioeconomic conditions, in the educational and occupational achievements of individuals, all over the world. Such a situation has been a key factor in the system of social stratification of all modern societies. The relevant question is not whether there are such differences in the educational development of different segments of the population but whether there is a trend towards bridging the differences or towards an increase in the differences.

In all fields of higher education, there has been an all round expansion to break the elitist and restrictive approach to higher education. A great deal of debate has gone on the issue whether higher education should be restricted to a few in order to improve the quality of higher education. As education is seen as a means of social mobility, jobs and economic prosperity, it has been difficult for policy makers to have a restrictive approach towards higher education. No doubt, it has helped enlarge the base of higher education in the country. But, this expansion has also led to lowering of educational standards which is decried by the educationists throughout the country. Some think it has created a serious crisis in the university education leading to undesirable implications for higher education as a whole. The university and colleges have been referred to as places of holding youth from entering the employment market. In this respect, university and colleges are playing the role of baby sitting.

In spite of these comments discussed earlier it must be indicated that colleges and universities are overflowing and a large number of students are not able to secure admission for higher education. There is a stiff competition to get admission in any professional and technical institution. This has led to growth of a large number of private tutorial and coaching colleges to prepare students for competitive examinations at every step of educational ladder. Also, it has created conditions for unfair means for achieving high grades in examinations. At the same time, exceptions apart, the rate of passing in most universities and colleges do not even cross fifty per cent especially in the faculties of arts, science and commerce.

4. Problems of Education

Reading any publication on Indian education will convince a reader how it suffers from multiple problems. It will depress the person beyond belief. The question is why so? One of the possible answers relates to the high expectations and not so high achievements in an ever growing country. Secondly, the educational planners are not able to meet the education needs of the country. Any analysis of spatial distribution of colleges and universities will leave no doubt that the institutions of higher learning are by and large an urban phenomenon. In the last 45 years, though there has been some reduction in regional imbalances in educational opportunities and access to educational institutions, still large parts of Indo-Gangetic plains are scarcely touched by the fruits of higher education or for that matter any education.

The regional variations can be clearly seen in the enrollment figures at the elementary stage of education in India as shown in Table 2. Nine out of 25 major states, including two most populous states like Uttar Pradesh and Bihar, are far below the national average. While in these states, the enrollment figures barely touch fifty per cent, in the other states they range from 60 per cent to 90 per cent in 1981 census. Same can be said about differences between urban and rural areas. Many felt that educational planning has an urban bias. One of the most glaring differences between men and women can be found in the Indian education. "If we were to identify one section which is the most deprived from the point of view of education, it is women, it is girls," said Rajiv Gandhi, the then Prime Minister of India in April 1986. (Ghosh and Talbani 1989 : 38). The most deprived are rural females who are least educated. Also there is a colossal wastage as a result of a very high drop out rate in the educational system. Ghosh and Talbani (1989 : 9) reported that "Of 100 enrolled in class I only 23 reach class VIII. Fiftynine per cent of students enrolled in higher education drop out or fail, while a large number of those who pass get the "third division". In this way, Indian education suffers from enormous problems needing a fresh approach to solve some of the problems. Computer applications in university administration may provide solutions to some of these problems.

Generally, there is a state-wide examination at the end of the primary, secondary and higher secondary stages held by the statutory bodies designated for the purpose in each state. One consequence of the dependence of the different types of schools on the local bodies/state governments and the statewide examination at the end of the primary, secondary and higher education has been a fixed course curricula and prescribed text-books for the students at all levels and throughout the state. There are many state-level School Text-book Boards that publish text-books prescribed for the various levels of school education. Thus, the Indian system of school education does not provide for any flexibility; it does not give any freedom to the teacher and the individual school to structure the course curricula; this rules out any possibility of innovative and/or experimental approaches in the pedagogy unless the same is imposed from above or approved by the appropriate authority at the state level.

As compared to the school system, the system of higher education does provide for more freedom in structuring the course curricula and choice of the teaching/learning material. In theory, the universities are autonomous; the academic bodies of the university decide the content and procedure for the courses and examinations which are common for all colleges/institutions affiliated to or recognized by it. While the freedom and flexibility provided by the university system seem to be used by the central universities and institutions of higher learning, the general observation is that most of the state universities are very slow in initiating or adopting any new or innovative programme, partly because of its financial dependence on the state government and also because of the nature of management and the type of the students that most of its affiliated colleges serve. The centralized system of course curricula, prescribed text-books and examination has led to an examination-oriented functioning of the system of education. The importance attached to the performance in examinations and certification rather than interest, aptitude and relevant skills as the major criteria for recruitment by the government and the public sector organizations and the prevailing incidence of unemployment among the educated play a supporting role in this regard. The performance in the examination rather than acquisition of knowledge seems to have become the primary goal of the students, their parents, the teachers, and others concerned with the educational system. The phenomena of private tuitions, coaching classes, and copying and corruption in mass centralized examinations adversely affect the functioning of the educational system.

5. National Policy on Education, 1986

The National Policy on Education 1986, considers higher education "at the apex of the educational parameters" and envisages the use of computers in several aspects of college and university education and management. The overriding importance of computer education derives from the realization on the part of policy makers that "as computers have become important and ubiquitous tools, a minimal exposure to computers and a training in its use will form part of professional education" (National Policy on Education, 1986 : 17). Further, policy-makers have recognized that "modern communication technologies have the potential to by pass several stages and sequences in the process of development encountered in early decades" (National Policy on Education, 1986 : 22). In other words, the use of computers in education was perceived as one of the essential means for the achievement of larger national goals within a finite duration. Hence, training and teaching requirement related to computer education was fully emphasized. It also mentioned that the multiple use and applications of computer in higher education was of crucial importance.

Although, the introduction of computer in the university system began a decade ago, computer still play a minor or insignificant role in most college classrooms other than those of computer courses, and that too in a limited sphere as discussed in next chapters. The remarkable growth of hardware industry is poorly matched by the levels of academic training and practical experience of the average user.

Colleges and universities and other academic institutions are caught unawares by the sudden national demand for trained humanpower, since sufficient teaching faculty to train the students are simply not available. There seems to be a vacuum in the field of computer teaching and training. The poor quality of teaching coupled with inadequate exposure to practical or hands-on experience in computer use has disappointed many students.

TABLE 4 Enrolment by Stages/Classes, by Scheduled Castes/Tribes (1988-89)

DEGREE	TOTAL			SCHEDULE CASTES			SCHEDULE TRIBES		
	BOYS	GIRLS	TOTAL	BOYS	GIRLS	TOTAL	BOYS	GIRLS	TOTAL
PH.D/D.SC/D.PHIL	18686	9129	27815						
M.A	127886	78227	206113	17683	3687	21370	3612	1282	4894
M.SC	46903	23517	70420	2537	886	3423	375	141	516
M.COM	68049	15252	83301	4863	743	5606	1008	95	1103
B.A/B.A (HONS)	937990	599419	1537409	120026	33070	153096	32437	13236	45673
B.SC/B.SC(HONS)	469504	269963	739467	29837	12156	41993	4501	1420	5921
B.COM/B.COM(HONS)	937990	599419	1537409	40522	8481	49003	9427	1786	11213
B.E/B.SC ENGG/B.ARCH	469504	269963	739467	12230	1439	13669	2393	162	2555
B.ED/B.T	52092	40563	92655	5602	1973	7575	1472	632	2104
M.B.B.S	55213	29051	84264	4878	2327	7205	1571	614	2185
INTERMEDIATE/JUNIOR COLL	1798536	641421	2439957	199909	42638	242547	20606	5177	25783
PRE-DEG COURSE/PRE-UNI(2)	169614	145651	315265	16108	14582	30690	9730	7541	17271
PRE-UNI (1)	2827	897	3724	182	73	255	15	6	21

SOURCE: Government of India, Ministry of Human Resources Development : Selected Educational Statistics, 1989-90, 1991

TABLE 5 Literacy Level by Sex, Rural Urban Residence and Caste/ Tribe 1961-1981

	RURAL AREAS			URBAN AREAS			ALL AREAS		
	1961	1971	1981	1961	1971	1981	1961	1971	1981
ALL									
TOTAL	19.00	23.70	29.70	47.00	52.40	57.40	24.00	29.50	36.20
MALES	29.10	33.80	40.80	57.50	61.30	65.80	34.40	39.50	46.90
FEMALES	8.50	13.20	18.00	34.50	42.10	47.80	13.00	18.70	24.80
SC									
TOTAL	8.90	12.80	18.50	21.70	28.60	36.60	10.30	14.70	21.40
MALES	15.10	20.00	27.90	32.20	38.90	47.50	17.00	22.40	31.10
FEMALES	2.50	5.10	8.50	10.00	17.00	24.30	3.30	6.40	10.90
ST									
TOTAL	8.20	10.70	14.90	22.40	28.80	37.90	8.50	11.30	16.40
MALES	13.40	16.90	22.90	30.40	37.10	47.60	13.80	17.60	24.50
FEMALES	2.90	4.00	6.80	13.50	19.60	27.30	3.20	4.90	8.00
OTHER									
TOTAL	22.30	27.80	34.20	49.70	55.10	60.40	27.90	33.80	41.30
MALES	33.70	38.50	46.10	60.20	64.30	68.50	39.40	44.50	52.30
FEMALES	10.40	15.90	21.70	37.20	44.90	51.20	15.60	22.20	29.40

SOURCE :- Vimal P. Shah and Tara Patel, Social Context of Tribal Education, Concept Publishing Co., New Delhi 1984.
Pravin Visaria, Anil Gumber and Leela Visaria, School Enrolment, Attendence, Drop-outs and Literacy in Western India : Some Data on Levels and Determinants, Working Paper Series No. 41 : Gujarat Institute of Area Planning, March, 1992.

Contributed by Vimal P. Shah and Binod C. Agrawal

References

A Handbook of Educational and Allied Statistics, Government of India, Ministry of Human Resources Development, 1987.

Centre for Monitoring Indian Economy, Bombay, Basic Statistics Relating to Indian Economy. Vol.2, September 1991.

Dongerkerey, S.R., University Autonomy in India. Bombay: Lalvani Publishing House, 1967.

Ghosh, Ratna and A.S. Talbani. Educational Policy in India: Its Evolution and Content. Montreal: Administrative and Policy Studies in Education, McGill University, 1989.

Gore, M.S., Education and Modernization in India. Jaipur: Rawat Publications, 1982.

Gupta, Ram Chandra, Whither Indian Education. Delhi: B.R. Publishing Corporation, 1988.

India 1991, A Reference Annual, Research and Reference Division, Ministry of Information and Broadcasting, Government of India. Delhi: Ministry of Information and Broadcasting, 1992.

National Policy on Education, 1986. New Delhi: Ministry of Human Resource Development.

Selected Educational Statistics, 1989-90, Government of India, Ministry of Human Resources Development, New Delhi, 1991.

Shah, Vimal P and Tara Patel, Social Contexts of Tribal Education. Delhi: Concept Publishing Company, 1984.

Visaria, Pravin, Anil Gumber and Leela Visaria, Ministry of Human Resources Development, Working Paper Series No. 41. Ahmedabad: Gujarat Institute of Area Planning.

References

[illegible], [illegible] Statistics, [illegible] Government of India, [illegible]

Centre for [illegible] Studies, [illegible] Survey, [illegible] New Delhi, [illegible]

Bhattacharya, [illegible], [illegible] in India, [illegible], 1982.

Gibbs, [illegible] and A.S. Wallace, [illegible], Chicago, [illegible] University, 1961.

Gore, M.S., Urbanization and Modernization in India, Bombay: Popular Prakashan, 1968.

Gupta, Ram Chander, [illegible] in India, [illegible], 1986.

India, [illegible], Reference [illegible], New Delhi: [illegible] Information and Broadcasting, [illegible]

National [illegible] Education [illegible], New Delhi: Ministry of Human Resource Development.

[illegible], Government of India, Ministry of [illegible] Development, [illegible], 1991.

[illegible], [illegible] Urbanization, [illegible], 1991.

CHAPTER 4

OPINIONS AND ATTITUDES OF FACULTY MEMBERS

1. Introduction

There are several factors influencing the introduction and use of computer in higher education. These factors can be grouped into four broad categories:

(a) availability of financial and computer-related resources (hardware, software, and technical-support staff),

(b) the educational system and pedagogy,

(c) socio-cultural setting of the society, and

(d) opinions and attitudes of the decision-makers regarding the role and impact of computer on the educational system and the society at large.

In the Indian system of higher education, the faculty constitutes a key segment of the decision-makers involved in policy-formulation, planning, and implementation of the pedagogical process. Awareness of the faculty members regarding areas and activities that are amenable to computer application, their willingness to put in extra effort and time to acquire relevant technical skills for computer use, and their perception of likely implications of computer use on students as well as themselves, the educational process, and the society at large can indicate the scope and feasibility of introducing and using computer in higher education. As mentioned earlier, the Part II of the questionnaire was designed to elicit opinions of the respondent faculty members regarding (a) reasons for many educational/research institutions not using computer as much as they could use in higher education, and (b) role and impact of computer use in higher education.

The survey was conducted by Gujarat, Bharthiar and Aligarh Muslim universities in their respective region. There was a considerable difference in the response rate achieved by the three universities. The sample of 369 faculty members, whose opinions and attitudes are analyzed in this chapter, is composed of 54.7% from Gujarat, 18.7% from Tamil Nadu and 26.6% from Uttar Pradesh. For simplicity, the respondent faculty members are referred to in this chapter as GU, BU and AMU sub-samples, respectively. In view of the difference in the size of the three sub-samples, the background characteristics of the respondents are shown separately for each sub-sample in Table 1.

TABLE 1 Background Characteristics of Respondents

	GU	BU	AMU	TOTAL
1. GENDER				
MALE	87.1	66.7	90.8	84.3
FEMALE	12.9	33.3	9.2	15.7
N	202	69	98	369
2. AGE(YEARS)				
<=30	10.7	29.0	16.3	15.7
31-40	11.7	24.6	27.6	18.4
41-50	31.0	21.7	30.6	29.1
>=51	46.7	24.6	25.5	36.8
N	197	69	98	364
3. TYPE OF INSTITUTION				
UG COLLEGE	16.3	39.1	–	16.3
UG&PG COLLEGE	57.4	49.3	–	40.7
PG DEPT	13.9	2.9	36.7	17.9
RES & TRG INST	12.4	7.2	58.1	23.6
OTHERS	–	1.4	5.1	1.7
N	202	69	98	369
4. ED. QUALIFICATIONS				
BACHELOR'S DEG	6.9	2.9	2.0	4.9
MASTER'S DEG	50.0	56.5	35.7	47.4
M.PHIL.	4.5	13.0	7.1	6.8
PH.D.	36.1	26.1	53.1	38.8
D.SC.	2.5	1.4	2.0	2.2
N	202	69	98	369
5. DESIGNATION				
LECTURER (AST PRF)	25.2	39.1	39.8	31.7
READER (ASSO PRF)	5.0	1.4	17.3	7.6
PROFESSOR	10.9	11.6	22.4	14.1
HEAD OF DEPT	16.8	15.9	8.2	14.4
HEAD OF COL/INST	42.1	31.9	12.2	32.2
N	202	69	98	369

	GU	BU	AMU	TOTAL
6. EXPERIENCE				
(A) UG TEACHING				
<=10 YRS	46.5	42.0	42.9	44.7
11-20 YRS	16.8	23.2	17.3	18.2
21-30 YRS	25.2	27.5	28.6	26.6
>=31 YRS	11.4	7.2	11.2	10.6
(B) PG TEACHING				
<=10 YRS	52.0	76.8	58.2	58.3
11-20 YRS	25.7	17.4	21.4	23.0
>=21 YRS	22.3	5.8	20.4	18.7
(C) RESEARCH				
<=10 YRS	74.8	89.9	57.1	72.9
11-20 YRS	13.4	7.2	21.4	14.4
>=21 YRS	11.9	2.9	21.4	12.7
N	202	69	98	369
7. FACULTY/SUBJECT				
NOT MENTIONED	1.0	7.2	4.1	3.0
AGRICULTURE	3.5	1.4		2.2
ARTS-LANG	12.4	10.1	5.1	10.0
ARTS-SOC	18.3	11.6	18.4	17.1
ARTS-MATHS	1.0	–	–	.5
COMM-LANG	1.0	–	–	.5
COMM-SOC	3.5	–	–	1.9
COMM-MATHS	1.5	–	–	.8
COMM-ACC	6.4	–	1.0	3.8
COMM-BANK	1.5	–	1.0	1.1
COMM COMP	2.5	–	–	1.4
COMM-MANAG	2.5	–	–	1.4
COMPUTER	1.5	18.8	–	4.3
EDUCATION	5.0	–	3.1	3.5
EDUC-LANG	2.5	–	–	1.4
EDUC-SOC	1.0	–	–	.5
EDUC-MATH	1.5	–	–	.8
ENGINEERING	3.0	7.2	22.4	8.9
HOME SCIENCE	1.0	–	–	.5
LAW	4.5	1.4	–	2.7
MANAG-SOC	.5	–	–	.3
MANAG-MANAG	1.0	1.4	–	.8
MEDICAL	3.0	2.9	9.2	4.6
PHARMACY	1.0	1.4	–	.8
SCI-LANG	.5	–	–	.3
SCI-SOC	1.0	–	2.0	1.1
SCI-MATHS	9.9	24.6	10.2	12.7
SCI-COMP	.5	4.3	7.1	3.0
SCI-NATURAL	7.9	7.2	16.3	10.0
N	202	69	98	369

	GU	BU	AMU	TOTAL
8. PAST/FUTURE USE OF COMPUTER				
NOT USED AND DOES NOT DESIRE TO USE	13.9	7.6	42.7	20.3
NOT USED BUT DESIRES TO USE	48.0	39.4	2.1	34.3
NO FORMAL TRNG BUT HAS USED	32.2	28.8	46.9	35.4
HAS OBTAINED FORMAL TRNG	5.9	24.2	8.3	9.9
N	202	66	96	364

2. Background Characteristics

The female respondents constitute only 15.7% of the sample. About two-thirds of the respondents are 40+ years old. More than a half of the respondents work in colleges. About 47% respondents have obtained a post-master's research degree. About 60% respondents hold the rank as professor or head of department/institution. All of them have some experience of teaching at the post-graduate level. While all of them have some research experience, the span of research experience of about three-fourths of the respondents is of less than ten years. All faculties and groups of subjects are represented among the respondents.

2.1 Differences in Background Characteristics

There are, however, considerable differences in the background characteristics of the three sub-samples. The range of percentages of female respondents is from 9.2% (AMU) to 33.3% (BU). The proportion of older faculty members is the highest in GU sub-sample and the least in BU sub-sample. There is a preponderance of the respondents working in research and training institutions in AMU sub-sample but BU sub-sample has a very small proportion of those working in research and training institutions. This is presumably a reason for AMU sub-sample consisting of 35% respondents with a Ph.D. or a D.Sc. degree as well as a large proportion of those having 11+ years of research experience. While the distribution of the respondents in terms of their faculty and subject is fairly wide spread in the total sample, BU and AMU sub-samples are concentrated in fewer faculties/subjects.

In absence of any independent secondary source of the relevant data, it is not possible to judge the extent to which the sub-samples of respondents in this baseline survey are representative of all faculty members in their respective region. However, their distributions in terms of gender, age, educational qualifications, designation, teaching/research experience, type of institution, and faculty/subject indicate that GU sub-sample constitutes a fair cross-section of the faculty members working in the various affiliated colleges, university departments, and research institutions in Gujarat State, but the other two sub-samples have somewhat skewed distributions in regard to certain background characteristics.

3. Experience of Using Computer and Interest in Using Computer in Future

Since we are interested in eliciting opinions of the faculty members regarding the use of computer in higher education, it is necessary to examine whether they have ever used computer in the past, and whether they would like to use computer in future. Only about 10% respondents have obtained a certificate/diploma/degree in computer science and application. In addition, about one-third of the respondents have used computer in the past. Another one-third of the respondents have not used computer in the past but they desire to use computer for teaching/research/reporting purposes in future. Thus, while 80% respondents have either some experience of using computer in the past or desire to use computer in future, the remaining 20% respondents have neither used computer in the past nor do they desire to use it in future. It should, however, be noted that from among those who have not used computer in the past, a very large proportion of GU and BU respondents desire to use computer in future but 90% of such AMU respondents do not desire to use computer in future.

4. Reasons for No/Inadequate Use of Computer

Computer facilities are not very widely available at present in all institutions of higher education. Even when some of them do have, to a certain extent, computer facilities for a long time, it is observed that there is quite an underutilization of available computer facilities. Such a situation raises an important question, namely, what are the reasons for many educational/research institutions not using computer as much as they could or should? In order to elicit opinions of the respondents in this regard, the respondents were given a set of 12 statements and requested to indicate their opinions on a three- point scale (1:doubtful, 2:fairly certain, and 3:very certain). The response rate for each of these statements varies from 86.9% to 91.9%. While the pattern of responses to these statements throws some light on the respondents' opinions regarding different reasons, it is necessary to find out the factors underlying the opinions of the respondents. For this purpose as well as for parsimony, factor-weighted composite measures of the respondents' opinions were developed. Using pairwise correlation coefficients and the method of principal components analysis, the opinions of the respondents were factor-analyzed. A four-factor structure was obtained. These factors explained a total of 50.1% variance in the responses to the twelve statements. The factor-matrix was orthogonally rotated according to varimax criterion. In order to build composite measures of variables, the software package provides for an option which produces the best set of coefficients for the variables in such a way that the correlation between the variables and the hypothetical factor is maximum. Using this option, the factor scores of all the items on the respective factors were obtained. Then, a constant was added to the total score on each factor obtained by each respondent so as to remove the negative scores.

The factors and their component items having a loading equal to or greater than 0.40 are given in Table 2. The percentages of the respondents in each category of all items (arranged according to their factor-weight on the respective factor) are shown separately for each sub-sample in this table. The mean score of the respondents on each item is also shown separately for each sub-sample in this table.

There are four underlying factors concerning the respondents' opinions regarding the reasons for many educational/research institutions not using computer as much as they could or should. For convenience, these factors are labeled as (i) Fear of Loss of Power (FEAR), (ii) Need For Change (CHANGE), (iii) Computer Use Not Required (CUNR), and (iv) High Cost (COST).

4.1 Fear of Loss of Power

The first factor concerns the decision-makers and the kind of fear they might have due to computer use. It is composed of five items. About one-third to one-half of the respondents are certain that fear due to loss of power, role change, problems in adjustment, and reduction in the power of the decision-makers are reasons for no or inadequate use of computer. The mean scores on these five items vary from 1.44 to 1.68, but the mean scores of GU sub-sample on all these items are the lowest among the three sub-samples. This shows that GU respondents are more doubtful than the others about the FEAR factor being the reason for no or inadequate use of computer.

4.2 Need for Change

The CHANGE factor comprises of four items concerning the need for reorganization of the educational system, need for change of work habits, ignorance about the potential use of computer, and a lack of technical skills required for computer use. About 75% to 80% respondents are certain that changes in the educational system and work habits required for computer use and a lack of technical skills and ignorance about the potential use of computer constitute important reasons for no or inadequate use of computer. The mean scores on these four items very from 2.11 to 2.46, but the mean scores of GU sub-sample on three of the four items are higher than those of the other two sub-samples.

Table 2 Opinions Regarding Reasons for Many Educational/Research Institutions not Using Computer As Much As They Could Or Should

	%Very Certain (3)	%Fairly Certain (2)	%Doubtful (1)	Mean	N
FACTOR 1: Fear of Loss of Power (FEAR):					
7. Fear of loss of power since all the information will be centralised. (.767)*					
GU	10.5	14.0	75.6	1.35	172
BU	16.7	30.0	53.3	1.63	60
AMU	11.2	38.2	50.6	1.61	89
TOTAL	11.8	23.7	64.5	1.47	321
6. Fear of role change. (.765)*					
GU	8.1	23.8	68.0	1.40	172
BU	9.8	34.4	55.7	1.54	61
AMU	12.2	26.7	61.1	1.51	90
TOTAL	9.6	26.6	63.8	1.46	323
4. Feeling that those who work with computer have a hold over others because of their specialized knowledge. (.571)*					
GU	10.9	16.1	73.0	1.38	174
BU	14.3	34.9	50.8	1.64	63
AMU	14.3	14.3	71.4	1.43	91
TOTAL	12.5	19.2	68.3	1.44	328
10. Reduction in the importance or power of some people who are taking decisions. (.545)*					
GU	14.0	23.4	62.6	1.51	171
BU	19.7	27.9	52.5	1.67	61
AMU	25.3	30.8	44.0	1.81	91
TOTAL	18.3	26.3	55.4	1.63	323
12. Changes in the social and cultural environment due to computer and the problems to adjust with these changes (.478)*.					
GU	15.2	31.5	53.4	1.62	178
BU	21.3	23.0	55.7	1.66	61
AMU	24.7	32.3	43.0	1.82	93
TOTAL	19.0	30.1	50.9	1.68	332

	%Very Certain (3)	%Fairly Certain (2)	%Doubt-ful (1)	Mean	N

FACTOR 2: Need For Change (CHANGE):

8. Computer requires change of work habits.(.673)*

GU	42.9	35.0	22.0	2.21	177
BU	22.6	37.1	40.3	1.82	62
AMU	40.2	38.0	21.7	2.19	92
TOTAL	38.4	36.3	25.4	2.13	331

9. Introduction of computer may require reorganization of the educational system. (.597)*

GU	50.3	29.6	20.1	2.30	179
BU	40.3	33.9	25.8	2.14	62
AMU	51.1	30.9	18.1	2.33	94
TOTAL	48.7	30.7	20.6	2.28	335

3. Ignorance about the potential use of computer.(.578)*

GU	41.8	33.5	24.7	2.17	182
BU	29.7	37.5	32.8	1.97	64
AMU	35.5	38.7	25.8	2.10	93
TOTAL	37.8	35.7	26.5	2.11	339

1. Lack of technical skill and expertise for the use and maintenance of computer. (.535)*

GU	63.2	27.5	9.3	2.54	182
BU	50.8	38.1	11.1	2.40	63
AMU	53.8	25.8	20.4	2.33	93
TOTAL	58.3	29.0	12.7	2.46	338

FACTOR 3: Computer Use Not Required (CUNR) :

5. Teaching/training does not require computer technology. (.825)*

GU	12.8	18.0	69.2	1.44	172
BU	15.0	28.3	56.7	1.58	60
AMU	5.4	12.0	82.6	1.23	92
TOTAL	11.1	18.2	70.7	1.40	324

	%Very Certain (3)	%Fairly Certain (2)	%Doubt-ful (1)	Mean	N
11. Fear that computer may go wrong and mistakes may not be detected. (.594)*					
GU	5.6	23.5	70.9	1.35	179
BU	6.5	30.6	62.9	1.44	62
AMU	8.7	17.4	73.9	1.35	92
TOTAL	6.6	23.1	70.3	1.36	333
FACTOR 4: High Cost (COST):					
2. High cost of hardware, software and maintenance (.937)*					
GU	48.1	36.5	15.5	2.33	181
BU	52.3	32.3	15.4	2.37	65
AMU	38.0	43.5	18.5	2.20	92
TOTAL	46.2	37.6	16.3	2.30	338

* Indicates the factor-weight of the item on the respective factor.

4.3 Computer Use Not Required

Only about 30% respondents are certain about two items constituting the CUNR factor, namely, teaching/training does not require computer technology, and fear that computer may go wrong and mistakes may not be detected. The mean scores on these items are the lowest among all items. However, the mean scores of BU sub-sample on these two items are somewhat higher than those of the other two sub-samples.

4.4 High Cost

The last factor is composed of only one item. About 84% respondents consider high cost of hardware, software and maintenance as a reason for no or inadequate use of computer. The differences in the mean scores of the three sub-samples on this item are very small.

4.5 Relationship Between Respondent Characteristics & Opinions

In order to examine the independent as well as overall strength of the relationships between the respondents' background characteristics and the factors underlying their opinions, multiple classification analysis (MCA) and multiple regression analysis were carried out. For MCA, it was necessary to reduce the number of categories of some independent variables. We have, therefore, dichotomized seven variables, namely, educational qualifications, designation, type of institution, age, and number of years of under-graduate, post-graduate and research experience. For consistency, the same variables are used in the multiple regression analysis.

The grand means of the dependent variables (scores on the four factors) and the deviation values adjusted for the independent variables are given in Table 3. The regression coefficients in standard form (beta), multiple correlation coefficients (Rs) and the proportions of variance explained by all independent variables together (R-square) are also shown in this table.

Table 3 Multiple Classification Analysis showing Deviation Values adjusted for Independent Variables

Independent Variables		N	Dependent Variables			
			F1 FEAR	F2 CHANGE	F3 CUNR	F4 COST
1.	Sub-sample					
1	GU	147	-0.10	0.10	-0.01	-0.03
2	BU	52	0.27	-0.29	0.24	0.10
3	AMU	30	0.04	0.03	-0.38	-0.03
	Beta		0.16	0.16	0.18	0.05
2.	Past/Future Use of Computer					
1	Not used; does not desire to use	32	0.10	0.02	0.00	0.25
2	Not used but desires to use	90	-0.13	0.11	0.03	-0.05
3	No formal training but has used	81	-0.04	-0.16	0.12	0.04
4	Formal training in computer	26	0.45	0.09	-0.49	-0.25
	Beta		0.18	0.12	0.19	0.13
3.	Gender					
1	Male	189	0.02	-0.02	-0.02	-0.06
2	Female	40	-0.08	0.09	0.10	0.31*
	Beta		0.04	0.04	0.05	0.14
4.	Ed. Qualifications					
1	BA-MA	120	0.01	0.05	0.05	0.12
2	M.Phil+	109	-0.01	-0.05	-0.05	-0.13
	Beta		0.01	0.05	0.05	0.12
5.	Experience:					
(a)	Under-graduate					
1	<= 10	112	0.01	-0.03	-0.04	0.14
2	10+ Years	117	-0.01	0.03	0.04	-0.14
	Beta		0.01	0.03	0.04	0.14

Independent Variables		N	Dependent Variables F1 FEAR	F2 CHANGE	F3 CUNR	F4 COST
(b) Post-graduate						
1	<= 10	141	0.08	-0.11	-0.03	0.06
2	10+ Years	88	-0.12	0.18	0.05	-0.10
	Beta		0.10	0.14	0.04	0.08
(c) Research						
1	<= 10	83	0.01	-0.01	0.05	0.09
2	10+ Years	146	-0.05	0.03	-0.15	-0.30
	Beta		0.03	0.01	0.09	0.17
6. Age						
1	< 40 YRS.	94	-0.07	-0.03	0.00	-0.30
2	> 40 YRS	135	0.04	0.02	0.00	0.17
	Beta		0.05	0.02	0.00	0.23
7. Designation						
1	Lecturer/Reader	176	-0.01	-0.08	0.15	-0.07
2	Prof./Head	53	0.00	0.05	-0.10	0.05*
	Beta		0.01	0.06	0.13	0.06
8. Type of Institution						
1	UG College	150	-0.04	-0.04	-0.03	-0.03
2	PG & Res Inst.	79	0.08	0.08	0.06	0.06
	Beta		0.06	0.06	0.05	0.05
Total Population (Grand Mean)		229	1.54	2.40	1.63	2.54
Multiple R			0.292**	0.288**	0.256	0.331**
Multiple R-squared			0.085	0.083	0.066	0.110

* Differences in the unadjusted means of the categories of this variable are statistically significant at 0.05 level.

** Multiple R is statistically significant at 0.05 level.

The magnitude of the multiple R varies from 0.256 for the CUNR factor to 0.334 for the COST factor; three of the four multiple Rs are statistically significant. All of the background characteristics used in this study explain a total of 6.6% to 11.0% variance in the respondents' scores on the four factors. An examination of the standardized regression coefficients shows that the sub-sample, Past/Future Use of Computer and post- graduate teaching experience have a fairly higher independent effect than that of the other independent variables on the respondents' scores on the FEAR and CHANGE factors. The deviation values adjusted for independent variables show that BU respondents, those with a formal training in computer, and those with less than ten years of post-graduate teaching experience are more certain than their counterparts that the fear of loss of power and role change is a reason for no or inadequate use of computer. They are also more doubtful than the others that the need for reorganization of the educational system and change of work habits is a reason for no or inadequate use of computer. The sub-sample, past/future use of computer and designation show a fairly higher independent effect on the respondents' scores on the CUNR factor. There is a substantial difference between BU and AMU respondents in this regard. While BU respondents are most certain, AMU respondents are most doubtful about this reason. Those with a formal training in computer and those holding a rank of a professor/ head are also most doubtful about this reason. The independent effects of gender and designation on the COST factor are statistically significant. The female respondents and those holding a high rank are more certain than the others that high cost of computer hardware, software and maintenance is a reason for no or inadequate use of computer.

5. Role and Impact of Computer Use

During the last two decades, there has been a steady increase in the use of computers in India, particularly in large commercial, industrial and governmental organizations as well as institutions of higher education. Until the beginning of the eighties, computer facilities were available only in a relatively small number of universities and research institutions wherein their use was generally limited to research, accounting, and examination-related functions. But now, due to conscious efforts of the educational planners, many colleges and even some high schools have installed micro-computers that provide an introductory exposure of computer to students. Many universities offer short-term or long-term certificate/diploma/degree courses in computer programming and application. The central and state governments as well as the national funding agencies like the University Grants Commission provide finance to their grant-in-aid institutions for installation and use of computers. The National Policy on Education, 1986, envisages the use of computer in several aspects of university education and management. Computer as an educational tool and as a service facility within the educational system is not a questionable proposition. But, in addition to the problem of availability of necessary financial and other computer-related resources, there are many issues concerning the pedagogical use of computer and its likely impact on the educational system as well as the society at large. Such issues concern several aspects of the educational process—motivation to students to learn and quality of their learning; productivity and creativity of students, researchers and teachers; mechanisms for the selection and training of students as well as evaluation of performance; bridging or widening of the gap among the students in terms of their gender, rural-urban environment, and class background, demand and supply of trained manpower in society, and so on.

5.1 Opinions of Faculty

In order to elicit opinions of the faculty members regarding the above issues, 30 statements concerning the role and impact of computer use in higher education were included in the questionnaire. The respondents were requested to indicate their opinion regarding each statement on a five-point scale (strongly disagree, disagree, no opinion, agree, and strongly agree). The response rate for these statements varies form 95% to 98% . The range of "no opinion" responses is form 4.2% to 36.8%; only four statements were marked "no opinion" by more than 25% respondents, and additional eight statements were marked "no opinion" by 20% to 25% respondents. Agreement of the respondents to 16 of the 30 statements indicate their positive opinion concerning the role and impact of computer use in higher education while that to the remaining statements indicate their negative opinion in this regard. Keeping in view the direction of each statement, the positive opinions were scaled from 1 (strongly disagree) to 5 (strongly agree) and the negative opinions were scaled from 5 (strongly disagree) to 1 (strongly agree). In order to find out the factors underlying the opinions of the respondents, factor-weighted composite measures were developed. For this purpose, we followed the same procedure as described earlier in regard to their opinions concerning no or inadequate use of computer. A nine-factor structure was obtained. These factors explained a total of 55.3% variance in the responses to the thirty statements.

The factors and their component items having a loading equal to or greater than 0.40 for the respondents' opinions are given in Table 4. The percentages of the respondents in each category of all items (arranged according to their factor-weight on the respective factor) are shown separately for each sub-sample in this table. The mean score of the respondents on each item is also shown separately for each sub-sample in this table. For convenience, these factors are labeled as (i) Quality of Learning (QLTY), (ii) Gender Gap (G-GAP), (iii) Employment (EMP), (iv) Rural-Urban Gap(R-U GAP),(v) Improvement in Admission, Evaluation and Administration (IMP), (vi) Costly and Adverse Effects (COST), (vii) Help Weaker Sections (WS), (viii) Dependence on Machines (DEP), and (ix) Threat to Workers and Teachers (THRT).

There is a very good homogeneity in the clustering of the items into different factors. The items indicating a positive opinion regarding the role and impact of computer in higher education and society are included into four factors, namely, QLTY, IMP, WS and EMP. Similarly, the items indicating a negative role and impact of computer are also grouped into four factors, namely, G-GAP, R-U GAP, COST and THRT. The ninth factor, DEP, has one negative and another positive item, but the latter has a negative loading on the factor. In the case of three items which have a loading equal to or greater than 0.40 on two factors, the pattern of homogeneity in clustering of items continues. It should be noted that the responses to negatively worded items were coded as 1 for strongly agree to 5 for strongly disagree, and therefore a mean score higher than 3 would indicate a positive opinion of the respondents in regard to negatively worded items also.

Table 4 Opinions Regarding Role and Impact of Computer

	% Strongly Agree (5)	% Agree (4)	% No Opinion (3)	% Dis-Agree (2)	% Strongly Disagree (1)	Mean	N
FACTOR 1: Quality of Learning (QLTY):							
2. Computer can help achieve higher quality of learning.(.732)							
GU	38.7	46.1	10.5	4.7	–	4.19	191
BU	43.5	47.8	5.8	2.9	–	4.32	69
AMU	49.5	38.1	9.3	2.1	1.0	4.33	97
TOTAL	42.6	44.3	9.2	3.6	.3	4.25	357
19. Computer will increase creativity of the teachers, researchers and students. (.668)							
GU	30.6	46.1	10.9	11.4	1.0	3.94	193
BU	33.8	51.5	8.8	4.4	1.5	4.12	68
AMU	30.9	57.7	6.2	5.2	–	4.14	97
TOTAL	31.3	50.3	9.2	8.4	.8	4.03	358
5. Computer motivates students.(.579)							
GU	24.2	43.8	12.4	17.5	2.1	3.71	194
BU	31.9	43.5	8.7	14.5	1.4	3.90	69
AMU	22.9	54.2	13.5	8.3	1.0	3.90	96
TOTAL	25.3	46.5	12.0	14.5	1.7	3.79	359
1. Computer can help to increase productivity in the educational process.(.569)							
GU	49.2	42.6	5.1	2.6	.5	4.37	195
BU	47.1	45.6	5.9	1.5	–	4.38	68
AMU	49.5	40.2	5.2	3.1	2.1	4.32	97
TOTAL	48.9	42.5	5.3	2.5	.8	4.36	360
4. Computer helps to lay the foundation of basic education.(.488) (also in F7: .437)							
GU	14.2	32.6	24.7	25.8	2.6	3.30	190
BU	13.2	38.2	22.1	26.5	–	3.38	68
AMU	12.5	28.1	25.0	27.1	7.3	3.12	96
TOTAL	13.6	32.5	24.3	26.3	3.4	3.27	354
12. Computer will bring about a revolution in the pedagogy of higher education.(.424)							
GU	20.3	46.9	17.2	13.0	2.6	3.69	192
BU	21.7	59.4	15.9	2.9	–	4.00	69
AMU	25.8	55.7	11.3	4.1	3.1	3.97	97
TOTAL	22.1	51.7	15.4	8.7	2.2	3.83	353

	% Strongly Agree (5)	% Agree (4)	% No Opinion (3)	% Dis-Agree (2)	% Strongly Disagree (1)	Mean	N
FACTOR 2: Gender Gap (G-GAP):							
28.* Computer will widen the gap between men and women.(.731)							
GU	3.1	2.1	14.5	57.5	22.8	3.95	193
BU	1.5	3.0	10.6	54.5	30.3	4.09	66
AMU	1.0	2.1	9.4	54.2	33.3	4.17	96
TOTAL	2.3	2.3	12.4	56.1	27.0	4.03	355
13.* Computer can be used only in science and technical education.(.552)							
GU	5.2	10.4	4.7	54.9	24.9	3.84	193
BU	4.4	7.4	5.9	51.5	30.9	3.97	68
AMU	4.1	8.2	2.1	51.5	34.0	4.03	97
TOTAL	4.7	9.2	4.2	53.4	28.5	3.92	358
11.* Introduction of computer is just a "political game" for higher education. (.447)							
GU	2.6	4.7	12.5	46.9	33.3	4.04	192
BU	4.5	3.0	15.2	40.9	36.4	4.02	66
AMU	3.1	4.2	14.6	38.5	39.6	4.07	96
TOTAL	3.1	4.2	13.6	43.5	35.6	4.04	354
FACTOR 3: Employment (EMP):							
24. Adoption of computer will create new jobs.(.729)							
GU	12.4	57.7	15.5	12.4	2.1	3.66	194
BU	19.4	49.3	13.4	16.4	1.5	3.69	67
AMU	15.5	55.7	13.4	14.4	1.0	3.70	97
TOTAL	14.5	55.6	14.5	13.7	1.7	3.68	358
27. Computer studies will ensure a higher paying jobs. (.533)							
GU	14.0	55.4	21.2	8.3	1.0	3.73	193
BU	19.1	47.1	20.6	10.3	2.9	3.69	68
AMU	10.5	55.8	17.9	15.8	–	3.61	95
TOTAL	14.0	53.9	20.2	10.7	1.1	3.69	356
30.* Adoption of computer will lead to loss of jobs.(.500)							
GU	4.6	23.7	24.2	38.1	9.3	3.24	194
BU	1.5	26.9	14.9	35.8	20.9	3.48	67
AMU	2.1	17.7	19.8	45.8	14.6	3.53	96
TOTAL	3.4	22.7	21.3	39.8	12.9	3.36	357

	% Strongly Agree (5)	% Agree (4)	% No Opinion (3)	% Dis-Agree (2)	% Strongly Disagree (1)	Mean	N
6. Computer can prevent social isolation. (.467)							
GU	6.8	14.1	37.2	36.1	5.8	2.80	191
BU	9.2	21.5	36.9	27.7	4.6	3.03	65
AMU	5.3	18.9	35.8	33.7	6.3	2.83	95
TOTAL	6.8	16.8	36.8	33.9	5.7	2.85	351
FACTOR 4: Rural-Urban Gap (R-U GAP):							
9.* Computer will widen the gap between rural and urban students. (.757)							
GU	16.0	29.4	13.4	33.0	8.2	2.88	194
BU	16.7	31.8	13.6	28.8	9.1	2.82	66
AMU	15.6	31.3	13.5	35.4	4.2	2.81	96
TOTAL	16.0	30.3	13.5	32.9	7.3	2.85	356
21.* Computer will widen the gap between rich and poor students(.746)							
GU	8.8	17.5	25.8	38.1	9.8	3.23	194
BU	9.0	35.8	16.4	34.3	4.5	2.90	67
AMU	7.2	27.8	26.8	28.9	9.3	3.05	97
TOTAL	8.4	23.7	24.3	34.9	8.7	3.12	358
29.* Those with power in the university make all major decisions about computer.(.551)							
GU	10.5	32.1	35.3	17.4	4.7	2.74	190
BU	14.9	28.4	29.9	16.4	10.4	2.79	67
AMU	15.6	44.8	21.9	15.6	2.1	2.44	96
TOTAL	12.7	34.8	30.6	16.7	5.1	2.67	353
FACTOR 5: Improvement in Admission, Evaluation and Admn. (IMP):							
16. Introduction of computer will lead to fair and equitable admission and evaluation.(.730)							
GU	26.8	58.4	10.0	3.7	1.1	4.06	190
BU	24.2	59.1	10.6	4.5	1.5	4.00	66
AMU	36.8	46.3	8.4	8.4	–	4.12	95
TOTAL	29.1	55.3	9.7	5.1	.9	4.07	351
15. Computer will help improve university administration.(.642)							
GU	37.1	59.3	1.5	1.5	.5	4.31	194
BU	46.3	41.8	9.0	1.5	1.5	4.30	67
AMU	41.2	50.5	2.1	6.2	–	4.27	97
TOTAL	39.9	53.6	3.1	2.8	.6	4.30	358

	% Strongly Agree (5)	% Agree (4)	% No Opinion (3)	% Dis-Agree (2)	% Strongly Disagree (1)	Mean	N
17. Computer is neutral for learning by men and women.(.472)							
GU	33.0	51.3	10.5	4.7	.5	4.12	191
BU	52.2	44.8	3.0	–	–	4.49	67
AMU	51.6	38.7	8.6	1.1	–	4.41	93
TOTAL	41.6	46.7	8.5	2.8	.3	4.26	351
FACTOR 6: Costly and Adverse Effects (COST):							
8.* Development of computer based pedagogical modules are very time consuming and costly and hence not worth the efforts (.602)							
GU	7.3	15.5	30.1	38.9	8.3	3.25	193
BU	6.1	16.7	27.3	42.4	7.6	3.29	66
AMU	2.1	20.8	32.3	33.3	11.5	3.31	96
TOTAL	5.6	17.2	30.1	38.0	9.0	3.28	355
14.* Introduction of computer will increase malpractice in the examination and admission of higher education.(.575)							
GU	3.7	14.2	16.3	48.9	16.8	3.61	190
BU	4.4	17.6	13.2	41.2	23.5	3.62	68
AMU	11.5	12.5	15.6	36.5	24.0	3.49	96
TOTAL	5.9	14.4	15.5	44.1	20.1	3.58	354
18.* Computer will adversely affect students' analytical abilities.(.572)							
GU	6.9	29.1	14.8	41.3	7.9	3.14	189
BU	6.1	18.2	22.7	43.9	9.1	3.32	66
AMU	12.5	17.7	13.5	44.8	11.5	3.25	96
TOTAL	8.3	23.9	16.0	42.7	9.1	3.21	351
FACTOR 7: Help Weaker Sections (WS):							
3. Computer can help to individualize instructions to the needs of particular students.(.558)							
GU	23.6	45.5	20.4	9.9	.5	3.82	191
BU	31.8	43.9	18.2	6.1	–	4.02	66
AMU	31.6	30.5	28.4	8.4	1.1	3.83	95
TOTAL	27.3	41.2	22.2	8.8	.6	3.86	352
7. Computer can help the students of weaker sections by repeated exposures.(.515)							
GU	15.3	42.9	22.2	16.4	3.2	3.51	189
BU	23.9	43.3	14.9	16.4	1.5	3.72	67
AMU	11.3	35.1	23.7	26.8	3.1	3.25	97
TOTAL	15.9	40.8	21.2	19.3	2.8	3.48	353

	% Strongly Agree (5)	% Agree (4)	% No Opinion (3)	% Dis-Agree (2)	% Strongly Disagree (1)	Mean	N
10. Computer will reduce the gap between poor and better standard universities.(.495)							
GU	9.5	32.3	20.6	28.0	9.5	3.04	189
BU	14.7	39.7	19.1	23.5	2.9	3.98	68
AMU	12.5	30.2	29.2	24.0	4.2	3.23	96
TOTAL	11.3	33.1	22.7	26.1	6.8	3.16	353
FACTOR 8: Dependence on Machines (DEP):							
20.* Computer will make humans machine-dependent.(.725)							
GU	9.4	43.2	19.8	25.5	2.1	2.68	192
BU	22.4	43.3	7.5	20.9	6.0	2.45	67
AMU	15.6	41.7	17.7	21.9	3.1	2.58	96
TOTAL	13.5	42.8	16.9	23.7	3.1	2.61	355
22.* Computer is an expensive toy.(.416) (also in F2: .489)							
GU	12.9	36.6	12.9	32.0	5.7	2.81	194
BU	20.9	20.9	10.4	31.3	16.4	3.02	67
AMU	14.4	27.8	12.4	32.0	13.4	3.02	97
TOTAL	14.8	31.3	12.3	31.8	9.8	2.91	358
25. University administrators implement computerization to make their jobs easier.(-.547)							
GU	16.7	58.9	9.9	13.5	1.0	3.77	192
BU	22.4	55.2	10.4	9.0	3.0	3.85	67
AMU	24.5	58.5	8.5	6.4	2.1	3.97	94
TOTAL	19.8	58.1	9.6	10.8	1.7	3.84	353
FACTOR 9: Threat to Teachers and Workers (THRT):							
26.* Computer can represent a threat to workers' health.(.819)							
GU	2.6	7.8	26.6	51.6	11.5	3.62	192
BU	1.5	16.4	32.8	29.9	19.4	3.49	67
AMU	3.1	15.6	17.7	41.7	21.9	3.64	96
TOTAL	2.5	11.5	25.4	44.8	15.8	3.60	355
23.* Introduction of computer in pedagogy will become a threat to teachers.(.476) (also in F2: .475)							
GU	1.6	13.5	22.9	51.0	10.9	3.56	192
BU	4.7	7.8	23.4	48.4	15.6	3.63	64
AMU	2.2	3.2	16.1	64.5	14.0	3.85	93
TOTAL	2.3	9.7	21.2	54.2	12.6	3.65	349

Figures within parentheses indicate the factor weights of the items on the respective factors.

* Indicates items with a negative direction scored as 1 to 5 for the responses "strongly agree" to "strongly disagree," respectively.

5.2 Quality of Learning

The Quality of Learning factor is composed of six items. About 72% to 91% respondents are of the opinion that computer will help achieve higher quality of learning, motivate students, increase creativity and productivity of students, teachers and researchers, and bring about a revolution in the pedagogy of higher education. The mean scores of these items vary from 3.79 to 4.36. One of the items (computer helps to lay the foundation of basic education) is included in two factors, QLTY and WS, with a loading of .488 and .437, respectively. About 46% respondents agree with this statement, and its mean score is 3.27.

5.3 Gender Gap

The three items of the G-GAP factor indicate a negative impact or a restricted role of computer in higher education. More than 80% respondents do not agree with the opinion that computer will widen the gap between men and women, or that computer can be used in science and technical education only, or that introduction of computer is just a "political game" for higher education. The mean score of each of these items is about 4.0.

5.4 Employment

Three items concerning the impact of computer use on employment opportunities constitute another factor. A little over two-thirds of the respondents agree with the statements that adoption of computer will create new jobs and that computer studies will ensure higher paying jobs. And, a half of the respondents disagree with the statement that adoption of computer will lead to loss of jobs. Most of the respondents are either undecided or disagree with the statement that computer can prevent social isolation. The mean scores of these four items, constituting the EMP factor, vary from 2.85 to 3.69; this indicates a fairly positive perception of the impact of computer on employment opportunities.

5.5 Rural–Urban Gap

There is a mixed opinion among the respondents regarding widening of the gap between rural and urban students or between rich and poor students due to computer use in higher education. The statement that those with power in the university make all major decisions about computer is also included, along with these two items, in the R-U GAP factor. The mean scores on these items vary from 2.67 to 3.12.

5.6 Improvement in Admission, Evaluation, Admission

Another factor indicating a positive role and impact of computer concerns improvement in admission, evaluation and administration due to introduction of computer. About 84% to 94% respondents agree with the statement that introduction of computer will lead to fair and equitable admission and evaluation, that computer will help improve university administration, and that computer is neutral for learning by men and women. The mean scores of these items vary from 4.07 to 4.30.

5.7 Cost

The COST factor is composed of three items indicating that use of computer is not worth the necessary efforts and costs, and concerns fear regarding likely malpractices in admission and examination as well as adverse effects on students' analytical abilities. About 47% to 64% respondents disagree with these statements. The mean scores of these items vary from 3.12 to 3.58.

5.8 Help Weaker Sections

Computer can help to individualize instructions to the needs of particular students and, presumably therefore, it can help the students of weaker sections. About 57% to 69% respondents agree with these statements. Two other statements (computer helps to lay the foundation of basic education, and computer will reduce the gap between poor and better standard universities) are included in this factor. This suggests that individualization of instructions and repeated exposures that can become possible due to computer use will not only help the students of weaker sections but also lay the foundation of basic education, and maybe thus reduce the gap between poor and better standard universities.

5.9 Dependence on Machines

The DEP factor, is composed of three items. About 56% respondents are of the opinion that computer will make humans machine-dependent. The mean score of this item is the lowest among all. While about 46% respondents consider computer as an expensive toy, about 42% respondents do not think so. This item is included in two factors, G-GAP and DEP, with a loading of .489 and .416, respectively. About three-fourths of the respondents agree with the statement that university administrators implement computerization to make their jobs easier; this item has a negative loading on this factor.

5.10 Threat to Teachers

Sometimes doubts have been expressed that introduction of computer in pedagogy will become a threat to teachers and that workers' health may be jeopardized in the physical environment created for computer use. More than 60% respondents do not share such doubts.

It should be noted that the differences in the mean scores of the three sub-samples in regard to various items are not much; most of the differences are within a range of -0.2 to +0.2 from the mean of the total sample.

6. Background Characteristics and Opinions of Faculty

In order to examine the independent as well as overall strength of the relationships between the respondents' background characteristics and the factors underlying their opinions regarding role and impact of computer in higher education and society, multiple classification analysis and multiple regression analysis were carried out. For this purpose, we followed the same procedure as described earlier. The grand means of the dependent variables (scores on the nine factors), the deviation values adjusted for the independent variables, regression coefficients in the standard form (beta), multiple regression coefficients(Rs) and the proportions of variance explained by all independent variables together (R-square) are shown in Table 5.

The magnitude of the multiple R varies from .227 for the EMP factor to .343 for the G GAP factor. Five of the nine multiple Rs are statistically significant. All of the background characteristics used in this study explain a total of 5.2% to 11.8% variance in the respondents' scores on the nine factors.

With regard to the respondents' scores on three factors (EMP, IMP, and DEP), there are very small or modest differences in the deviation values adjusted for the independent variables. This is also reflected in the respective standardized regression coefficients. This means that none of the background characteristics of the respondents considered here has any substantial independent effect on their opinions concerning these three factors. Similarly, two of the independent variables (post-graduate teaching experience and research experience) do not have any significant independent effect on the respondents' opinions regarding any of the nine factors. Further, although there are relatively large differences in the factor scores of the three sub-samples, we do not find any specific pattern in this regard.

Focussing our attention on the remaining cells of Table 5, several observations should be made. First, examining the values of deviation from the grand means adjusted for the independent variables, it is found that Past/ Future Use of Computer shows relatively large differences in the respondents' opinions concerning various factors. In general, those who have used computer in the past and/or desire to use computer in future have more favorable opinions regarding the various types of role and impact of computer in higher education and society than those who have not used computer in the past or

Table 5 Multiple Classification Analysis showing Deviation Values adjusted for Independent Variables

Independent Variables	N	F1 QLTY	F2 G-GAP	F3 EMP	F4 R-U GAP	F5 IMP	F6 COST	F7 WS	F8 DEP	F9 THRT
		Dependent Variables								
1. Sub-sample			**							
1 GU	164	0.02	-0.12	0.03	0.03	-0.05	-0.07	-0.09	0.04	0.01
2 BU	53	-0.17	0.33	0.05	-0.26	0.22	0.13	0.14	-0.09	0.13
3 AMU	29	0.21	0.09	-0.26	0.31	-0.12	0.15	0.26	-0.05	-0.31
Beta		0.11	0.18	0.09	0.16	0.13	0.10	0.14	0.06	0.12
2. Past/Future Use of Computer		**					**			
1 Not used;does not desire to use	37	-0.41	-0.19	-0.13	0.10	-0.05	-0.15	-0.10	-0.21	-0.12
2 Not used but desires to use	101	-0.15	0.07	-0.13	-0.11	0.00	0.04	-0.01	-0.03	-0.08
3 No formal training but has used	84	0.26	0.09	0.16	0.01	-0.07	0.17	0.02	0.15	0.21
4 Formal training in computer	24	0.37	-0.31	0.17	0.27	0.31	-0.52	0.12	-0.09	-0.20
Beta		0.28	0.13	0.15	0.12	0.12	0.20	0.06	0.12	0.15
3. Gender								**		
1 Male	210	-0.04	0.05	0.04	0.05	0.04	0.03	-0.06	0.02	0.00
2 Female	36	0.24	-0.30	-0.24	-0.26	-0.23	-0.18	0.33	-0.10	0.00
Beta		0.10	0.12	0.10	0.11	0.11	0.07	0.14	0.04	0.00
4. Ed. Qualifications		**								
1 BA-MA	128	0.15	0.10	0.06	-0.04	-0.04	0.03	0.03	-0.12	0.02
2 M.Phil+	118	-0.16	-0.11	-0.07	0.04	0.05	-0.04	-0.04	0.13	-0.02
Beta		0.16	0.11	0.07	0.04	0.05	0.03	0.04	0.13	0.02
5. Experience:										
(a) Under-graduate		**	**					**		**
1 <= 10 years	112	-0.21	0.24	-0.13	-0.02	-0.06	-0.01	0.18	-0.09	-0.20
2 10+ years	134	0.18	-0.20	0.11	0.02	0.05	0.01	-0.15	0.08	0.17
Beta		0.20	0.21	0.12	0.02	0.06	0.01	0.17	0.08	0.17

Table 5 Contd.

Independent Variables	N	F1 QLTY	F2 G-GAP	F3 EMP	F4 R-U GAP	F5 IMP	F6 COST	F7 WS	F8 DEP	F9 THRT
		Dependent Variables								
(b) Post-graduate										
1 <= 10 years	147	0.01	-0.06	0.09	0.02	0.09	0.00	-0.02	-0.07	0.01
2 10+ years	99	-0.02	0.09	-0.13	-0.03	-0.13	0.01	0.04	0.11	-0.02
Beta		0.02	0.07	0.11	0.03	0.12	0.00	0.03	0.09	0.01
(c) Research										
1 <= 10 years	190	0.02	-0.03	0.03	-0.03	-0.04	-0.05	0.02	0.00	-0.03
2 10+ years	56	-0.08	0.12	-0.12	0.10	0.13	0.18	-0.08	0.01	0.11
Beta		0.04	0.06	0.06	0.06	0.08	0.09	0.05	0.00	0.06
6. Age								**		
1 < 40 years	81	0.16	0.10	-0.11	0.22	-0.08	0.03	-0.30	0.17	0.11
2 > 40 years	165	-0.08	-0.05	0.05	-0.11	0.04	-0.02	0.15	-0.08	-0.05
Beta		0.12	0.07	0.08	0.15	0.06	0.02	0.21	0.12	0.07
7. Designation								**		**
1 Lecturer/Reader	98	-0.11	0.09	0.02	-0.11	-0.11	0.01	-0.18	-0.06	-0.21
2 Prof./Head	148	0.07	-0.06	-0.02	0.07	0.07	-0.01	0.12	0.04	0.14
Beta		0.09	0.07	0.02	0.09	0.09	0.01	0.15	0.05	0.16
8. Type of Institution					**					**
1 UG College	164	-0.06	-0.05	-0.07	0.16	-0.02	0.05	0.08	0.00	-0.19
2 PG & Res Inst.	82	0.11	0.10	0.13	-0.32	0.04	-0.10	-0.16	0.01	0.37
Beta		0.08	0.07	0.10	0.22	0.03	0.07	0.12	0.00	0.25
Total population(Grand Mean)	246	3.68	3.34	2.87	2.91	4.42	3.82	3.10	3.40	3.04
Multiple R		0.341*	0.343*	0.227	0.290*	0.246	0.228	0.310*	0.239	0.317
*Multiple R-squared		0.116	0.118	0.052	0.084	0.060	0.052	0.096	0.057	0.101

** Differences in the unadjusted means of the categories of this variable are statistically significant at 0.05 level.
* Multiple R statistically significant at 0.05 level.

do not desire to use it in future. However, the respondents who have a formal training in computer science/application seem to have considerable reservations or negative opinions regarding three factors, namely, G-GAP, COST and THRT. This probably collaborates the proverbial epigram that the taste of the pudding is in eating it.

Second, the faculty members with less than ten years of teaching experience at the under-graduate level hold less favorable opinion than those who have more than ten years of such experience; this pattern is, however, reversed in the case of two factors (G-GAP and WS). Also, the respondent's gender, age and educational qualifications have substantial independent effects on the WS factor; females, those who are 40+ years old, and those who hold the rank of a professor/head have a more favorable opinion regarding the WS factor than their counterparts.

Third, the female respondents and those working in post-graduate departments or research institutions have some concern regarding widening of the rural-urban and rich-poor gap due to computer use in higher education.

Fourth, the respondents working in undergraduate colleges, those who have less than ten years of undergraduate teaching experience, and those who hold the rank of a lecturer/reader perceive computer as presenting a threat to teachers and workers' health more than their counterparts.

Finally, while we find modest independent effects of different background characteristics on the factors underlying the respondents' opinions concerning the role and impact of computer in higher education and society, it must be noted that only fourteen of the standardized regression coefficients are statistically significant.

7. Concluding Remarks

The opinions of the respondent faculty members regarding the role and impact of computer use in higher education and society are generally positive and favorable. A majority of them believe that computer use will (a) help achieve higher quality of learning, (b) improve admission, evaluation and administrative procedures, (c) increase employment opportunities, and (d) help weak students by individualization of instructions and repeated exposures. Some of them have no doubt certain reservations concerning pedagogical use of computer in higher education and its assumed positive impact on students' ability or have negative opinions indicating fear of widening of the rural-urban gap, increase in machine-dependence and malpractices due to computer use.

The feasibility and success of any plan for pedagogical use of computer in higher education will depend, to a great extent, on willingness, ability and attitudes of the faculty members. This study suggests that more than a half of the faculty members are likely to have never used computer in the past but a fairly large proportion of them do desire to use computer for teaching/research/reporting purposes. There is, therefore, an imminent need to organize computer training programmes for the faculty.

The cost of computer hardware, software and maintenance is perceived by a large majority of the respondent faculty members as a major factor for no or inadequate use of computer. An equally important perceived reason in this regard is the CHANGE factor (concerning the need for reorganization of the educational system, the need for change of work habits, ignorance about the potential use of computer and a lack of technical skills required for computer use) which also points out that adequate computer training programmes for the faculty will go a long way in reducing the phenomenon of no or inadequate use of computer even when computer facilities are available.

Contributed by Vimal P. Shah

Coordinator: Vinod P. Shah

CHAPTER 5

COMPUTERS IN TEACHING

1. Introduction

In India, significant developments in the use of computers have taken place in the industrial and the commercial sectors. Computers have wide applications in educational sectors also. It is essential that the educational sector, specifically the higher education segment, adopts and integrates computers in its system to improve quality and productivity. The computer, with its versatility, accelerates one's ability to solve many problems related to teaching, research and administration that are encountered in higher education. This study was undertaken in order to sketch the current state of computer penetration, its use, application and its impact on higher education. This chapter reviews the impact of computers on teaching.

2. Computer as a Discipline and Computer as a Tool

The role of computers in teaching has more than one facet. One of them is that it is an object of study in its own right as a discipline. Second could be as a tool for teaching. The former role is vocational and the latter one is pedagogic. Out of these, the oldest and strongest is vocational where investment has been substantial. This is necessary as advances and uses in computer technology assume a good manpower of computer professionals. Moreover, there is need to train people from other disciplines so that they can use the technology in their profession. As computers are pervading every aspect of life computer knowledge is essential for professionals in most fields. Eventually it is in the process of becoming like arithmetic that every one should have some acquaintance with.

2.1 Computer as a Discipline

If one were to ask, "what effects do the computer have on higher education?", the foremost answer would be that it has emerged as a separate discipline; that is, educational programmes leading to different degrees of computer proficiency have been introduced very widely by various educational institutions in the country. Infact a decade ago whenever computers were introduced in any educational institution, its primary goal was to devise a variety of courses in computer competence. Then comes a secondary use of computers in research , administration and teaching. Thus teaching about computer can be viewed in two phases: 1) Developing a pool of computer professionals and 2) Developing a generation of computer users.

2.1.1 Computer Professionals' Phase

This phase has received a lot of attention from all corners, such as the government, institutions of higher learning and other agencies. One of the foremost formal courses for computer science in the country was started by the Indian Statistical Institute in 1962. In the late 60s' Indian Institutes of Technology (Bombay and Madras) introduced computer courses as elective under electrical engineering. Till early 70s computer courses were offered as a part of an engineering curriculum. Later it was imparted as a specialisation course in only national institutions like the Indian Institutes of Technology, the Indian Institute of Science and Regional Engineering Colleges, that too in limited areas, computer Hardware and Software. In the 80s, courses on computer sciences, engineering and applications were introduced in several universities and institutions with the encouragement and support of the central and state governments. At present there are five types of computer courses.

1. Certificate Courses in Programming (CCP).

2. Diploma in Computer Application (DCA) and Master in Computer Application (MCA).

3. Bachelors and Masters programmes in Computer Science. (B.Sc. & M.Sc.)

4. Bachelors and Masters programmes in Computer Engineering/Technology (B.E./B.Tech. & M.E./M.Tech.)

5. Doctoral Programme in Computer Science (Ph.D.).

The basic goal of the above courses is to generate manpower of the levels of programmers, system analysts, computer engineers etc. for the industry.

In India the seventies and eighties can be considered as the initial period of computer science and computer application development phases, which were experienced around the sixties in North America. Most of these courses had the objective "to develop computer professionals". The status of computer education in Gujarat as observed from the baseline survey is given in Table 1.

Computer programming papers were introduced in Gujarat University at the under-graduate level of science and commerce faculties in the year 1983. The courses conducted at some of the other institutions, where case studies were developed and survey was conducted is given in Table 2.

Table 1 Computer Courses Offered by Different Universities in Gujarat

	University/Institutions	C.C.P	B.Sc.	B.E.	DCA	MCA
a)	Gujarat University Ahmedabad	X	-	X	X	X
b)	Gujarat Vidyapith Ahmedabad.	-	-	-	X	-
c)	M.S.University Baroda.	-	-	X	X	X
d)	S.P. University Vallabh Vidyanagar	X	-	X	X	X
e)	South Gujarat University, Surat	-	X	X	X	X
f)	Saurashtra University Rajkot.	X	-	X	X	-

Table 2 List of Courses Offered by Different Institutions/Universities.

Name of Institutions	Courses
Bombay University	DCA, MCA, M.Sc.
SNDT University	DCA, MCA
IIT (Madras & Bombay)	B.Tech./M.Tech., Ph.D.
Rajasthan University	Certi. in Comp. Prog., DCA, MCA
Kerala University	MCA, M.Sc.
IIM, Ahmedabad	Computers & Management Information Systems, Decision Support System etc.
Aligarh Muslim University	MCA, DCA
Bhartiar University	Certificate, MCA, Ph.D.

The above list, of course is not an exhaustive list of institutions that are offering computer courses. In fact there were six national institutes, 17 regional engineering colleges and around 250 university departments and degree colleges offering computer courses in 1990. Thus it can be observed that in two decades growth of professional courses in the area of computers is significant. Over and above the formal courses there are a host of informal courses conducted by private institutions adding to the number of computer professionals.

Today there are a large number of avenues for producing computer professionals. Therefore the issue of numerical requirement of manpower from the existing institutions imparting computer education is satisfactory to some extent but the requisite quality has not been uniformly produced by them. Therefore the government has developed strategies for upgrading manpower in the coming years. These measures include setting-up centres of excellence in the area of software engineering, quality assurance of the courses so that the programmes can be upgraded. The government has also set standards for accredition of courses and degrees offered by private institutions through the accredition board for computer education to ensure quality.

2.1.2 Computer Users' Phase

In order to use computers in the teaching, research and administrative activities effectively, it is necessary to have a good knowledge of computers. This phase calls for "Preparing computer users". This is essential as for an active participation in computer usage, some degree of computer literacy is essential.

In this area, some efforts are being made but these are not enough. The professional courses such as management have given some attention to this aspect. In fact in the Indian Institute of Management, Ahmedabad (IIM), computer courses were introduced in the 1970s as part of curriculum.

Courses such as medicine, law etc, where computer applications are many, students are not provided any computer exposure as a part of the curriculum. In other faculties such as commerce, science etc. the University Grants Commission (UGC) has done pioneering work by providing one to two personal computers to a large number of colleges to provide awareness about computers.

However, there has been no follow up to identify the impact of such an effort. Interviews and discussions with some college teachers and students revealed that in many colleges PCs are kept as show pieces or used only for teaching programming courses.

A top-down strategy of introduction to computers to provide computer literacy/competence will be useful to create a generation of computer users across several faculties/disciplines. Depending on the level of application/use, the courses may be designed. The priority sectors are professional courses, post-graduate courses, other degree courses and the vocational streams. (Jain,1985)

As the obsolescence and development in this area are rapid and continuous, updating is a must. Moreover, life-long learning must become a necessity and reality to update the skills. (Pawar,1992)

2.1.3 Computer as a Tool

Distinction needs to be made between learning about computers and learning with computers. As discussed above, learning about computers has received considerable attention in India. But learning with computers is relatively a neglected area especially in higher education. The concept of learning with computers takes the view that the power and flexibility of computers are gainfully used in the process of instruction.

2.1.3.1 Instructional Computing

Instructional computing has been rapidly expanding over the past few years. Instructional use of computers encompasses a number of ways in which the computer can be made a tool of instruction. For example in Computer Aided Assessment (CAA), Computer Aided Design (CAD), Computer Aided Instruction (CAI), Computer Aided Learning (CAL), Computer Managed Learning (CML), etc., computer is used as a tool.

In CAA the test is conducted with the aid of computer. In CAD, designs can be created and different analysis can be carried out. In CAI, a pre-programmed study plan is developed and the computer is used as a medium. In CAL, teaching and learning in any part of the curriculum are aided by some applications of computers. In CML the use of the computer is made to monitor, analyse and report on student's learning.

The other instructional applications are drill and practice, which attempt to sharpen the already acquired skill, simulation and games, that allow the learner to discover several hidden aspects and solve the problem in an environment that resembles reality. The computer can be successfully used in tutorials and feed-back as it teaches through the process of guided learning. These are some of the ways in which computers can be used in pedagogy.

One finds most of these terminologies in Indian literature too. The recent development in instructional computing is in the area of Intelligent Tutoring Systems (ITS). The ITS attempts to construct systems with human-like tutoring capabilities. In ITS the student has more control and the system guides the learner whenever it is appropriate. This way ITS tends to be more sophisticated than conventional CAI. (Patil et al,1992). Another interesting development is in the use of multi-media for education and training. Multi-media refers to an integrated and interactive storage, retrieval and processing system involving audio, motion video, still images, computer graphics, animation and text. The computer component of multi-media allows the user to create an interactive learning environment.

3. Base-line Survey Results

Gujarat University, Bhartiar University and Aligarh Muslim University received responses from 46, 42, and 8 computer centres of different institutions respectively. These responses cover the details regarding the activities of the computer centres. Over and above, as discussed in earlier chapters, to understand faculty attitude 177, 64 and 97 teachers (responses from research institutes were not considered) from Gujarat, Bhartiar and Aligarh Muslim University responded to the opinion survey regarding the computer use in teaching. The general highlights across all the three universities is summarised in this section.

3.1 Use of Computer in Pedagogy

The central focus is to identify to what extent and how computers are used for instructional purposes. Can computers affect the method of teaching? Do computers affect what is taught ? These are some of the issues which have been examined.

In today's class-room a teacher is able to demonstrate using computers while teaching. This was inconceivable some years ago. For example students can now learn by experimenting simulation of physical processes. One of the ways by which the quality of teaching and motivation for learning can be probably improved is by introducing computers into the classroom : for example, in a math class concept of functions can be taught well by demonstrating the behavior of different functions using different parameters. In physics, computer simulation can be used to visualize physical laws and phenomena. Thus there are a number of creative ways in which computers can be integrated with teaching. This section will sketch the present efforts of computer use in pedagogy that are practiced by institutions of higher education.

The survey was conducted by Gujarat University, Bhartiar University and Aligarh University in the states of Gujarat, Tamil Nadu and Uttar Pradesh respectively to find how computers were used in pedagogy. Most of the computer time as indicated by survey is spent in teaching computer courses. The number of institutions where computers are used as a teaching aid is insignificant. As the institutions are not using computers for pedagogy, the research carried out in the use of computer in pedagogy is also insignificant. The reasons for this low use may be due to lack of technical support to the faculty for developing computer aided material and availability of relevant hardware and software.

However, in some of the institutions serious efforts have been made to use computer for model building, which can be used as a pedagogical tool. One such example is in a design institute, where the computer is used as a tool to design a product, for which different design alternatives are simulated and explored. These simulated models are used in teaching. In a school of architecture, computer aided architectural design and computer aided planning, structural analysis are also explored. In one of the engineering colleges, program modules are developed for simulating circuit design, logic design and micro processors circuits, which are used for teaching purposes. In another engineering college extensive use of computer graphics, is made in video lessons.

The computer centre of Sardar Patel University, Gujarat, has developed a quality question bank management system on a large scale. In this system of question bank, Boolean & Multiple choice questions could also be maintained. One could draw tutorials and quizzes and also conduct drill and practice. Performance and evaluation of students could be captured. This system is very handy for teachers. This system is available on both Unix and DOS platforms. The centre has developed simulation package for data structure and CPU instruction for teaching and experimented computer aided packages for teaching of Geography.

The credit for the above efforts made at different centres may be given to one or two individuals who can be recognised as faculty/product champions. (A champion is an individual who promotes the development of an innovation within an organization).

3.1.1 Classrooms And Computers

It is certainly exciting for the teacher and the student to have the graphs and the charts shown through the computers in the class room. But the consolidated survey results indicated that portability, small size of the screen in the large class rooms without projection system, requirements of air-conditioning, lack of remote control and administrative problems related to transfer of the PCs to the class rooms were the major difficulties in the use of computers in class rooms. All these problems were perceived to be of equal importance by the respondents. So without an appropriate projection system use of computer in classroom is very limited.

3.1.2 Area of Computer Usage

In the survey questionnaire, a question listing several areas where use of computer is emphasised such as programming, problem solving, etc. was posed to the respondents.

Programming and problem solving are the major emphasis areas of computer in pedagogy as can be seen from Table 3. This is true in case of all the three universities indicating that major use of computers is in learning about computers rather than learning with computers.

3.1.3 Constraints in Computer Use

In order to identify what are major and minor constraints on the increased use of computer in pedagogy, a question listing several constraints was posed to Universities/Institutes and colleges (Table 4). Gujarat University and Bhartiar University survey results indicated that cost was the most important constraint followed by availability of computer/terminal, and training of faculty. The minor constraint that emerged was space.

In the case of Aligarh Muslim University, major constraints were identified as non-availability of software, faculty inertia and the need to learn a new discipline. The minor constraints were space and availability of computer terminals.

Table 3 Distribution of the Areas Where Use of Computer is Emphasised

Emphasis of Computer	Gujarat university (n=46)	Bhartiar University (n=42)	Aligrah Muslim University (n=8)
Programming	3 4	3 5	6
Problem Solving	3 0	3 5	6
Access Database & Analysis	1 9	2 1	4
Analysis & Report	1 7	1 6	5
Simulation & Model Building	1 0	1 2	5
Academic Games	0 7	0 9	1
Graphics / Drafting	1 5	1 9	4
Audio Visual Presentation	1 0	0 4	1
Drill & Practice	0 4	0 2	1
Tutorial	1 7	1 5	2
Self Paced Study	1 4	0 8	2
Programme Learning	1 6	1 3	1
Preparation of Instructional Material	1 1	0 8	3
Question Bank	0 9	1 1	2
Conducting Quizzes	0 4	0 7	0

3.1.4 Faculty Attitude

When computer technology is being considered for application in an institution, serious efforts should be made to understand the attitude, needs and expectations of users. This is especially true when computers are used for teaching, where faculty opinions and perceptions, are important criteria in evaluating instructional methods.

In order to identify the perception of teaching community on the role of computers in teaching, a few statements describing the process of computers in teaching were given to different faculty members in Gujarat University, Bhartiar University and Aligarh University (177, 64, 97) asking them to show their agreement/disagreement. The responses from research institutes were not considered as their primary objective is research, not teaching. The percentage favoring the statement is shown in the Table 5.

Table 4 Distribution of Constraints on the Increased Use of Computers in Pedagogy

Constraints	Gujarat University (n=46)		Bhartiar University (n=42)		Aligrah Muslim University (n=8)	
	Major	Minor	Major	Minor	Major	Minor
1. Cost	23	11	24	12	3	3
2. Space	09	16	09	24	1	5
3. Availability of computer terminals	17	10	15	14	1	5
4. Availability of software	09	13	08	21	5	2
5. Compatibility of computer systems	04	13	09	15	2	2
6. Capacity of available time on on mainframe computer	07	06	03	11	-	-
7. Training of faculty	17	10	15	13	1	-
8. Training of students	07	13	02	22	-	1
9. Faculty inertia	09	04	07	12	4	3
10. Difficulty in using hardware or software (The technology isn't transparent)	04	12	05	17	2	3
11. Inadequacy of software for computer-assisted instruction	08	13	11	13	2	3
12. Lack of awareness of such a tool	08	14	09	14	3	-
13. The need to learn a new discipline	15	14	09	12	4	2
14. Lack of time	10	10	09	18	3	4
15. Question of technology effectiveness	06	11	06	15	2	-

Table 5 Statements Favoring Role of Computers on Teaching Percentage of Respondent Showing Agreement

	Statements	Gujarat University (n=177)	Bhartiar University (n=64)	Aligarh University (n=97)
1,	Computer can help increase productivity in the educational process.	88.7	90.6	88.7
2,	Computer can help achieve higher quality of learning.	78.0	90.6	86.6
3,	Computer can help to individualize instruction to the needs of particular students.	65.0	71.9	59.8
4,	Computer motivate students	63.8	73.4	75.3
5,	Computer can help the students of weaker sections by repeated exposure.	53.7	64.1	46.4
6,	Though development of computer based pedagogical modules are very time consuming and costly they are still worth the efforts.	44.1	46.9	43.3
7,	Computer will bring about a revolution in the pedagogy of higher education.	63.3	79.7	80.4
8,	Computer will increase creativity of the teachers, researchers, and students.	73.4	82.8	87.6

As can be observed from the above table, the university teachers showed very high agreement on the potentials of computers as a pedagogical tool. It seems that the teachers understand and value, the role of computers in learning. Though in practice very little has been actually done, the highly positive attitude on the part of the teachers is an indication that if enough facilities are made available to them, they would definitely go for computer aided teaching.

4. Experiences from Case Studies

Case studies of several institutions/universities and interviews with faculty members who are involved in the use of computers in teaching revealed the following :

1. At the SNDT University, computer is used as a teaching aid with emphasis on programming, problem solving and question bank. Research is done in the use of computer as an aid in instruction, the area being the use of artificial intelligence techniques in education and in particular, the design of suitable communication interfaces for effective learning in intelligent tutoring systems.

2. The survey revealed that many of the professors at the Indian Institute of Management (IIM), Ahmedabad used computers as an aid in their

teaching sessions. The class-rooms are well equipped with computers and appropriate projection systems. They have experimented with CAI in the remedial programmes, simulation, management games and graphic based learning packages. They are very positive about the role of technology in teaching.

Ramani K. V. (1991) of IIM discusses the design and development of two graphics based packages, namely INTEGER and BAYES for teaching optimization algorithms. The INTEGER package presents the Branch and Bound algorithm for integer programming problems. The BAYES package presents Bayesian algorithm for decision tree analysis. The key features of the software are the powerful screen management, ability to solve moderately sized problems, user friendly menu and visual display of solution using graphics. The author has used this package in teaching of management graduates students and in training of executive development programs in India as well as in Singapore and he has received encouraging response.

3. The Indian Institute of Technology, Madras is conducting research on computer Assisted Language Learning (CALL) and developing CAI in Indian languages. They have a centre for educational technology where packages best suited for students' temperament, background, style of learning etc. are developed and experimented with.

5 . Computer Use in Pedagogy in Other Centres

In India, there is a lack of empirical studies of computers in the classrooms of higher education. During the recent years, some research studies have been carried out in different disciplines at various centers of national importance such as National Centre for Software Technology (NCST), Tata Institute of Fundamental Research (TIFR) etc. The efforts have been made in teaching languages, computer courses, mathematics and science. The review of literature indicates that there are some experiments done at training institutions of banking industry, engineering colleges and some studies at school level.

5.1 Computers for Testing Purposes

National Centre for Software Technology (NCST), Bombay has a group working on the applications of Artificial Intelligence (AI) in education. This work is primarily focused at two targets: high school students and students learning programming. NCST has developed an on-line Generative Testing System called VEDA. It supports the design and administration of tests, on-line and off-line. VEDA provides tools for test designers to create question generators and maintains complete security. The package provides complete house-keeping regarding candidates' performance and calculates all relevant statistics. The system is developed in C under UNIX. This package is used extensively. VEDA provides an authoring system called KBAS (1,1992).

5.2 Computers for Language Teaching

Computers have the potential to play a major role in language teaching. There are several efforts in India in this area. The initial forays in to Computer Assisted Language Learning (CALL) involved direct application of language teaching methodologies. Many of these systems used grammar based approach to teach language. In this method,student is taught a language by first being taught its grammar.

The Foreign Language Institute at Hyderabad is doing research in language teaching using computer aided instructions and it also offers courses on CALL.

Vidya: A Hindi Language Tutor is another Computer Assisted Language Learning (CALL) on PC. This is developed by NCST. This system uses a situation based approach to a language teaching. Teaching in Vidya covers the presentation of vocabulary, sentence pattern and dialogues relating to a particular situation with the aid of pictures. It attempts to teach Hindi by using concept lessons and situation lessons arranged in a hierarchical structure. At NCST this package is used for teaching Hindi. Attempts are being made to evaluate this package by actual Hindi learners. (Anjaneyulu et al,1992)

5.3 Computers for Teaching Maths and Science

There are successful efforts in designing and experimenting Intelligent Tutoring Systems (ITS) in the area of trigonometry, solutions of simultaneous equations and basics of probability (Patil et al,1992).

At the Tata Institute of Fundamental Research (TIFR) many programs in formal and informal education are carried out for students, teachers and general public. The Homi Bhabha Centre for Science Education program of TIFR has its own computing facilities. The computers are used for instructional purposes. They have developed software for teaching maths and science.

Lalitha and Shailaja (1986) conducted a study on Computer Assisted Instruction (CAI) in relation to traditional teaching and came out with the conclusion that CAI in relation to traditional teaching was more effective with respect to imparting knowledge but not so much as regards developing understanding.

Pamela Wright (1983) conducted a study on CAI for remedials in mathematics at secondary level and found that CAI produced a significantly higher achievement as compared to conventional class-room instruction, in particular class-rooms in two selected schools.

Singh, Ahluwalia and Verma (1991) conducted a study to compare results of computer aided instructions and conventional method of instructions in teaching mathematics in selected topics. The results of the study showed significant differences between mathematics achievement of the students who use computer for specific topics compared to the students who were taught through conventional methods. The students who used the computer scored significantly higher on the post-test than those who did not use the computer.

5.4 Computers for Computer Teaching

In order to write programmes in the LISP language, a novel method of representing the language which is called DRLP (Data Flow Representation Language for LISP) has been developed and implemented at NCST. This is used by novice programmers to create programmes by a graphical representation of the programmes instead of writing actually the code. The control experiments were conducted to study the impact of DRLP. The group using DRLP had a better comprehension of the programmes, had lesser errors and took significantly less iterations to get the problem solved. (Anjaneyulu et al,1992)

The experiences at NCST emphasise the fact that a proper and judicious use of computers in remedial instructions and testing can contribute to learning and teaching greatly, having maximum effect with relatively low cost.

The Computer Consultancy and Services Division of Uptron India Ltd has launched a computer based training (CBT) software developed using hypertext and computer graphics. Designed for technical training in the airlines, shipping industry, power and petroleum plants, the CBT is for dissemination of technology and expertise gained by a select few to others.

A range of self-paced packages (SSP) were recently introduced by Digital Equipment(India) Ltd for technical and non-technical users. Available in formats ranging from text based to computer based instruction, the SSP curriculum includes Unix and C, Computer Systems, Office Automation, software engineering, CASE tools and VAX/VMS. Computer Maintenance Corporation (CMC) offers Computer-based text (CBT) packages for teaching programming languages like BASIC, Pascal and C. The CMC has developed authoring system INSTRUCTS for development of CBTs.

The National Institute of Information Technology (NIIT) has set up a computerised automated learning centre at Bombay for training purposes. This has got a very sophisticated CAI system with projection system, touchscreen monitors etc. The centre provides around 1000 training packages on several topics such as sales, finance, programming etc. (Computer Today,1992)

Thus many private training institutions and computer companies are experimenting with several facets of computer as an instructional technology. These learning packages are gaining momentum as these provide a cost-effective way to train more people as the pace and pitch of instruction can be modified to suit the learners' requirements.

5.5 Computers for Engineering Curriculum

A.Kuppuswamy and R.Natarajan (1986) have described that CAI and CMI are productive and efficient computer based learning systems. They have also recommended for updating of the syllabus and improving the standards. To prepare the students to tackle the problems of future, the curriculum must encompass latest technological advancements relating to Robotics, Computer Aided Design (CAD) and Computer Aided Manufacturing (CAM).

5.6 Banking Training with Computers

Mohanadoss B (1991) describes that human resource planning development is essential for growth of organizations, therefore education and training programme is very vital for the work force. He emphasises the use of computer as a training aid. Education and training can be made faster and effective using Computer Aided Learning (CAL). Use of CAL allows the development of individual training as defined by the personal requirement of the student. It implies that information to be conveyed may be varied not according to the form and content but also according to the intellectual and practical capability of the students. Thus CAL can be on an individual basis, at free will, self-corrective to shortcomings and weaknesses, stimulates alternatives and has an interactive feed-back system.

A. M. Nagarkar (1992) of National Institute of Bank Management has provided a frame work of Computer Aided Learning in Indian banking based on the experiences of a foreign bank. The framework consist of computer-based tutorials, induction programs for new recruits, segment based programs and capsule programs aiming at improving the knowledge in specific tasks of banking. Computers have been installed in zonal/regional offices of most of the Indian banks. The educational software can be installed on the zonal office machines. A mechanism can be evolved to promote learning at zonal offices as well. This will enable zonal offices to play the role of "learning centers" as well as "control centers".

Banarji (1990) has carried out a novel experiment in the State Bank Institute of Information and Communication Management. He has developed a computer based simulation approach for training in Foreign Exchange (FX) dealings. Pc based FEDS (Foreign Exchange Dealing Simulation) is a training tool by the use of which one can make purchase and sell decisions at the most appropriate time observing how the market news alters the currency exchange rates.

5.6 Computers for Blind

Indian Institute of Technology, Delhi and the All India Institute of Medical Sciences (AIIMS) have developed a new system called Universal

Graphical Braille Classroom Communication System for teaching as well as a reading aid for visually handicapped. This system can be used by the blind as a communication aid. This is a major benefit to the handicapped as they find a better avenue for learning (University News, 1992).

5.7 Computers in Adult Education

Thrimurthy P. and his group at Sardar Patel University, Vallabh Vidyanagar have undertaken a project on Technology Transfer on Adult Education. They have designed, developed and released software packages on adult literacy. This package can handle Hindi, Gujarati and Punjabi languages. The purpose of these packages, is to demonstrate the writing methodology of alphabets in each language. Adult literacy could be speeded up in such a way that the participants could write the alphabet in a few days in comparison with the traditional methodology which was taking several months. No computer background is necessary to operate these packages except the "cursor keys understanding". Initial problems of motivating the participants on correct writing skills are minimized as the methodology of writing is demonstrated. Quick repetition of the "process of writing methodology" enhances understanding. Using the packages the time required for adult reading and writing Gujarati alphabets reduced from 40 days to 4 days (University News,1992).

5.8 Multilingual Applications through Computers

India being a multi-lingual country, the penetration of technology will be effective if it is possible to represent the computer data in different Indian languages. In this direction GIST technology provides support for Indian language representation of data. GIST (Graphics Intelligent Script Technology) is the product of sustained research and experimentation in this area which was initiated first in the Indian Institute of Technology, Kanpur on the DoE project, and now being continued on a larger scale at the Centre for Development of Advanced Computing (C-DAC) at Pune. GIST provides a very innovative solution for Indian Language Computing. At the core of technology is the concept of a phonetic key board. This can be used by most major Indian languages like Hindi, Marathi, Gujarati, Tamil, Telegu, Oriya etc. The state of the art GIST technology offers a phonetic key board, use of Indian languages on the DOS, UNIX/XENIX platform, use of all standard application tools like word processing, database and spread-sheet. GIST implements the Indian Standard Code for Information Interchange (ISCII) along with fonts developed as per Indian Standard Font Code (ISFOC) guidelines. With this breakthrough the computer application in Indian languages will take a giant leap forward (Pani,1991).

5.9 Computers in Distance Education

Distance education has paved the way for providing education to the masses, who for some reasons are not able to pursue formal education or participate in class-room learning. The use of computer technology in distance education is marginal in comparison with other technologies such as audio-video etc. However, efforts are now being made to integrate computers as a learning tool in distance education programs.

As the distance education requires self-instruction, individualised, feed back oriented approach, computers have infinite capacity to meet this requirement. Appropriate infrastructure and adequate man-power are pre-requisites for successful use of computers in distance education (Menon,1992).

Prof. Pant (1992) suggested a model for use of information technology in distance education. The model consists of a device called "student/home computers", which has very basic hardware-software and communications facilities. At the next level one envisages a "student booth" where a student can down load the information and take print-outs of learning materials. The means of distribution of information at these student booths would be through a set of CD-ROMS, high density magnetic tapes and floppies. The students can interact with other group members and academic counsellors through 'students centre'. The students' centres would be connected to the main university system and other facilities such as schools, library etc.

Shamim and Ramarao (1992) have provided a conceptual scheme for communication network in distance education. The network is aimed at incorporating and interactive multi-media information service and facilitating computer supported co-operative work (CSCW). The network is planned at local, regional and national levels.

Those who have experimented with computer as a tool to supplement and to complement the conventional teaching show that the technology helps in learning the subjects thoroughly because repetitive revision is possible. Moreover, it enhances imagination, quickens the process of logical thinking and reasoning. By using simulation with suitable animation and graphics, complicated situations can be illustrated for improving understanding. Thus today the computer should be viewed as a tutor, simulator for teaching and learning purposes, and as a quiz master. The use of computer in pedagogy should be accelerated because of the user-friendly environment created by PCs.

However, to achieve successful integration of the computers into the existing curriculum, it is important to be quite critical. Uncritical computer use, of course, may confuse students more than it helps. One must continuously pose the question whether there is a real pedagogical advantage to be gained by using a computer here?

6. Experiences from Training and Experiments at the Computer Lab on the Role of Computers in Teaching

At Gujarat University, as a part of the UGC/CIDA project, a center known as "Computer Training and Applications Laboratory (COMTAL) with the help of the University of Regina and Digital Equipment (DEIL), India was established with the following objectives :

a. To train university and college teachers in computer technology so that they are aware of the different uses and applications of computers in higher education.

b. To develop pedagogical software which will be useful in teaching.

c. To conduct experiments to identify the utility of computer aided packages in teaching of different subjects.

6.1 Training Activities at COMTAL

With the need for computers for higher education having been accepted, one is faced with the problem of training large numbers of teachers both to teach about computers and to teach with the aid of computers. For the purpose, three broad areas of knowledge and associated skills were identified such as computer literacy, teaching about computers and teaching with the aid of computers.

The computer training programmes for college and university teachers acquire importance because well trained teachers can help improve the overall quality of teaching. The training contents cannot be the same for all the teachers. It should consist of two components : General introduction and orientation and subject specific training. At COMTAL, Gujarat University, seven training programs (mathematics, economics, social science, library science, physics, statistics and chemistry) were conducted for college and university teachers.

In the first part, participants were acquainted with the computer system, its components and functioning, which was common to all the programs. In the second part of the training, software useful for different disciplines and subjects was introduced. A number of sessions were devoted to demonstrate the use of software and computer application in imparting knowledge in subjects like Physics, Chemistry, Mathematics, Statistics, etc. All the participants by using the computer software suited for their subject prepared a project at the end of training programme. (For details refer Appendix-B).

'Computer Activities for Calculus' is a package meant for teaching the basic concept of Calculus. This package was demonstrated to the Statistics and Physics teachers in the training program. Each participant spent nearly a two-hour session with the package. At the end of the session a questionnaire evaluating the software was given to all teachers. All twenty two teachers (15-Statistics & 7-Physics) responded that the use of such package supplemented the classroom teaching to a great deal. The graphical display provided by the package will be very helpful in understanding the behavior of several mathematical functions. Teachers were of the opinion that such educational software will supplement the classroom teaching.

6.2 Input from COMTAL

From the training experiences gained at COMTAL it is felt that Computer literacy programs must be made compulsory for all teachers. A center imparting training in different uses of computer in educational system should be made available for orientation as well as for refresher courses. A perspective plan for the coming decade should be worked out. On a continuing educational basis, advanced and more advanced courses must be introduced for interested teachers. Thrust must be to develop discipline/subject specific training programs.

To increase the effective and efficient use of computer in pedagogy, proper faculty training and exposure to different authoring packages and other software such as simulation in different disciplines may prove very helpful.

6.3 Experiments in use of Computers in Teaching

In addition to computer training programme at COMTAL, computer aided instructional software on transportation and linear programming problems were developed.

The transportation package (TP) was developed in Vax C on the Micro Vax system and linear programming (LP) package was developed using TURBO-C. LP is a PC based package. The packages were reviewed by the MBA students of the Gujarat University. The objective of this exercise was to obtain feedback on the package. The MBA class of 32 students was divided into two groups. The first group had already studied LP/TP concepts. The other group did not have any idea about the same. Both groups were given this package to learn the concepts of LP/TP. Blending suggestions and reactions from both the groups helped in improving the package to a great deal. Their views and ideas were collected and modifications were made to the packages to make it more user-friendly.

Once the packages were reviewed and revised, it was experimented on a class of Diploma in Computer Applications (DCA) students who had to learn linear programming and transportation topics in their syllabus.

6.3.1 Methodology

The experiment was carried out in a class of 30 DCA (Diploma in Computer Applications) students and the two specific problems chosen for computer aided instruction were : 1) Linear programming and 2) Transportation. The students in question, all having been chosen through an entrance exam for the DCA course can be considered to have had nearly the same intelligence, educational level and exposure to the problems selected for the experiment was quite the same. The class was then divided into two separate groups of 15 students each and each group was subjected to problems and classroom teaching for the others, thus forming control and experimental groups. Thus, both the groups at the end of the experiment had received instruction for two problems - Linear programming and Transportation, either through computer or through classroom teaching.

Later, a test on these techniques was administered to the whole class and the test scores for each group were used as a parameter to judge how effective computer aided instruction had been vis-a-vis classroom teaching. The two groups exposed to either of the techniques on the computer were also asked to respond to a self-administered questionnaire to find out their assessment of the package as a suitable medium of instruction.

6.3.2 Analysis

Table 6 gives mean scores for the different variables that the subjects rated on a scale (1-4) [1 being poor and 4 - excellent]. Despite certain problems of non response and subjects claiming insufficient knowledge to rate certain variables in the questionnaire mean scores for both the techniques are in the range 2.5 - 3.5 suggesting that the packages have been found to be fairly good as a medium of instruction. In the case of the transportation problem, one finds that flexibility of programme content, mobility within the program and ease of accessibility of on-screen help with provision to return to original point of instruction is low. Such marked cases are absent in the linear programming problem.

When asked to comment freely on their assessment of the programs most of them (12 - TP, 9 - LP) have thought it reasonable to use the computer for such instruction. In the case of the transportation problem around 50% recommended its usage as it is and 33% subject to improvements. However, in the case of the LP problem, 60% recommended its use without any modification and 21% recommended its usage subject only to improvements. Rest were indifferent. There was no significant difference between the mean test scores of the two groups in both the situations. The experiment was carried out providing due consideration to target the group, curriculum content, general and specific objectives of the course, teaching and evaluation methods and amenability of computers as a medium.

Table 6 Mean Score on Variables (DCA GROUP)

	VARIABLES*	TRANSPORTATION Mean Score	n	LINEAR PROG. Mean Score	n
	CONTENT				
1.	Content is accurate.	2.6	(13)	2.7	(14)
2.	Content is appropriate to instructional intent.	2.5	(12)	2.7	(14)
3.	Level is appropriate for intended user.	3.0	(13)	3.2	(14)
	PRESENTATION				
1.	Purpose of program is clearly stated.	2.8	(14)	3.1	(12)
2.	Program fulfill the stated purpose.	3.0	(13)	2.8	(13)
3.	Content organization & presentation are methodologically sound.	3.0	(14)	3.0	(13)
4.	Subject matter is relevant to a variety of textbooks.	3.2	(13)	3.0	(14)
5.	Subject matter is adaptable to a variety of textbooks.	3.4	(13)	2.8	(13)
6.	Questions and expected answer are clear, not ambiguous	2.9	(14)	2.8	(13)
7.	Individual lessons are appropriate.	2.6	(14)	2.5	(13)
	RETENTION OF STUDENT INTEREST				
1.	Amount of information in each screen frame is appropriate.	2.4	(14)	2.8	(14)
2.	Presentation of program is appealing.	2.9	(12)	2.9	(14)
3.	Student has mobility within program.	2.0	(10)	3.1	(13)
4.	Program employs principles of motivation.	2.4	(14)	2.3	(13)
5.	Program stimulates student creativity.	2.5	(12)	2.6	(13)
	COMPUTER TECHNIQUES				
1.	Capability of computer is exploited.	2.4	(14)	2.8	(12)
2.	Use of computer is a suitable medium.	2.6	(12)	2.7	(13)
3.	Student can easily operate program.	3.0	(14)	3.3	(14)
4.	Student can easily go to on screen help from any part and back to the same point of instruction.	1.6	(13)	3.1	(12)
5.	Student can easily bypass on-screen instruction if desired.	1.9	(11)	2.7	(13)
6.	Student can easily save lessons or parts of lessons on print	2.6	(10)	3.0	(12)
7.	Student can easily save lessons or parts of lessons on disk.	2.1	(14)	2.0	(12)
8.	Feedback provides error analysis and correction/explanation.	2.6	(14)	2.2	(13)
9.	Feedback differentiates substantive from mechanical mistakes	2.5	(12)	2.2	(14)
10.	Feedback is adequately timed.	2.6	(13)	2.5	(12)
11.	Feedback frequency is appropriate.	2.5	(14)	2.4	(14)
12.	Presentation of format is appropriate.	2.5	(14)	2.6	(13)
13.	Appropriate use of graphics.	2.3	(13)	3.1	(12)
14.	Upper & lower case differentiation is easy to manipulate.	2.2	(14)	2.5	(14)
15.	Program is technically reliable.	3.0	(13)	2.8	(14)

* Variables are taken from Lisa B. Carnick "Evaluating Foreign Language CAI : A checklist". Die Unterricht Spraxis vol 17, 1984 p 316-318.

In summing up, it can be said that these experiments had a favorable result if not overwhelming. Students were more positive than negative in their attitude towards immediate feed-back and two-third of the class agreed that they would take another class of CAI. The result of this experiment is limited by the facts that this was a small scale investigation and the sample size was also small. To have a wider and deeper utility of computers different computer based drills, practice, and tutorials using authoring systems can be prepared and evaluated at COMTAL.

6.3.3 Directions

More empirical experiments could be conducted on specific control groups for specific type of computer based tutorial materials in specific training programs. On the basis of these experiments, the software developed could be tested, refined and evaluated and a comprehensive policy decision could be taken to make computer aided learning an integral part of training.

The central computing facility of the university may take initiative to develop educational software. One agency should be appointed to look after the common pool of software which any one can access. The agency should know what is developed at which place, in which subjects and a floppy disk is an inexpensive and handy medium to circulate the software. The Government must encourage professional bodies to develop and distribute curriculum based educational software. Some selected teachers from different disciplines can act as consultants in preparation of such courseware.

7. Major Issues

Adoption of any technology presents a great challenge. This is true in the case of computer technology too. The education system faces a host of issues ranging from providing sufficient computing facilities to computer enthusiasts, persuading others to adopt to the minimum level. Thus many problems relating to resource allocation among several disciplines/users, lack of training, attitude of decision makers, resistance of employee, etc., have to be faced and resolved. In India diversity, magnitude of social needs, size and distribution of total population and educational needs of each social strata, with limited resources poses greater challenges to the resolution of problems.

7.1 Software Related Issues

The computer itself is not an automatic source of good teaching. Successful and easy learning of this new technology requires an educational conception of high standard, with quality software and suitable other materials.

In fact, not many commercial educational software suited for accepted curriculum of different disciplines are available. When available, either they are too costly or are not very exciting. As a result they cease to be worth acquiring. The authoring and multi-media packages are also not available in many of the centres. Whenever some attempts of CAI or CMI are made, they have developed their own programs. The portability of such software is difficult. Moreover, it is very difficult to evaluate such programs on a broader platform. Apart from time-consuming efforts, development of software requires skilled, qualified inter-disciplinary team efforts, which is also a major bottleneck in usage of educational software.

7.2 Computer Literacy Issues

In today's world of education computer literacy is of immense importance. In order to use computers in teaching, the teacher must be convinced that computer can enhance the teaching and learning of any subject. Lack of technical skill and ignorance of potential use of computers in pedagogy are the major bottlenecks. Efforts must be concentrated on developing discipline specific training modules.

Linked to this is the essential need to have a computer literate generation. Government had begun with CLASS programme in some of the selected schools. Similar efforts are being continued in Navodaya schools. However, a much more concentrated attempt is needed if any impact is to be made. At the university level (graduate & post-graduate) there is a need to upgrade the contents of our degree programs. At undergraduate level a course on introduction to computers must be introduced. This must be done across all the faculties irrespective of the subject. More specific computer application papers can be introduced depending upon the specific discipline. For example, it is desirable to introduce theoretical concepts relating to computerised audit and computer application in accounting for the commerce stream. At the post-graduate level more emphasis on PC packages must be provided so that students are comfortable in carrying out their project work. The courses relating to the computers needs constant revision and updating as this technology is growing very fast.

7.3 Language Related Issues

India being a multilingual country and with hardly 3% of population knowing English language, computerization in higher education can be successful only if software are developed in different regional languages (Vittal N.,1992). This is required as in many of institutions of higher education the medium of instruction is the regional language. GIST technology will prove to be a boon to computer application in different Indian languages.

7.4 Hardware Related Issues

Adequate availability of hardware is a major problem in most of the universities who are offering computer courses. With obsolete and poorly maintained systems, teaching of computer courses is not very effective. The student-computer ratio or terminal time required for the courses must be an important consideration while designing computer courses for professionals as well as end-users. In college and university departments, the pedagogical experiments cannot be successfully conducted with just one or two PCs where the class size ranges from 50 to 100 students. It is necessary to have atleast a PC Lab. having 15 to 20 PCs.

7.5 Lack of Funds

The greatest problem faced by universities which decide to computerize is the limited resources. The acquisition and infrastructure for computer system, maintenance cost, operational cost, etc. pose several problems due to the lack of funds.

7.6 Lack of Management Support

Management awareness of computer technology and support is considered to be one of the most important factors contributing to the successful implementation of computer systems. Many decision makers in several universities are not aware of the vital role that computers can play in the University system. They are often afraid of the technology and are resistant to its introduction.

Luke warm response shown by the decision makers of the university is another major obstacles in the successful implementation of computer technology. The inherent fear that the computer will ultimately replace some administrative staff and computers might vest undue power in the hands of few computer personnel are the major contributing factors for the resistance.

7.7 Low Infrastructure

Lack of pertinent infrastructure like steady electricity supply, temperature control, presence of dust are some of the reason for successful use of computers in institutes of higher education.

7.8 Lack of Inter-disciplinary Approach

Most universities in India are very rigid in their policies pertaining to curriculum. Computer education is inter-disciplinary in nature. Many universities in India do not have inter-disciplinary approach in higher education.

8. Role of computers in Instruction: A SWOT Analysis

8.1 Strengths

a. Flexibility and interaction in teaching.

b. Variation in competence levels of instructors can be reduced.

c. Variation in pace of learning can be achieved.

d. Wide range of subjects ranging from alphabets to advance level courses such as Astro-physics can be taught from a single source.

e. Training can be made more interesting using simulation,drill etc.

f. Complex mathematical and mechanical operations can be better taught and appreciated with the aid of the computer.

g. Increase in productivity of Instructors.

h. Can be a very useful tool in speeding up research process and thus in the long run strengthen the R & D base of the country as a whole.

i. Computer is a patient, untiring and consistent instructor which may be of immense value to slow learners.

j. The pedagogical use of the computer brings innovation and provides challenges to any curriculum.

k. Advances in computer technology such as multi media advent and the GIST technology have the potential of making education interesting as never before and possible in vernacular languages.

8.2 Weaknesses

a. The traditional teacher-pupil interaction process may be affected. Odd, diverse and different mindsets can not be answered.

b. The class-room touch and emotion attached with the instructor may be missing. This may lead to indifferent and unsatisfied attitude. Dehumanization of learning may cause a problem.

c. Monitoring of performance and other qualitative variables of a student may be difficult.

d. It assumes certain level of literacy on the part of the leaner/teachers.

e. It cannot be offered to entire mass because of high capital cost, operational cost and infrastructural requirements.

8.3 Opportunities

a. Vast population of illiterates can be offered packages to educate them.

b. Enormous amount of knowledge data can be transmitted, shared among communities wide apart.

c. Satellite- link up can make computer aided instruction to play a vital role in distance education.

8.4 Threats

a. Inadequate infrastructural facilities may not allow computer to be successfully operating at the grass root level.

b. Without proper planning, the entire system of computer aided instruction may have unpleasant consequences.

c. High capital cost and operating cost for acquisition and operation of hardware, software and infrastructure may dampen the system.

d. Resistance to technology in general and its acceptability as an instructor may pose a serious problem.

e. Computer literacy may prevent further spread of computer as a tool of instruction.

9. Summary and Conclusions

On the basis of the findings the following conclusions emerge:

a. In the institutions of higher learning, use of computers is not very encouraging. Although in some institutions of higher education in India introduced computers two decade ago, the impact of computer technology seems to be still limited to a few prestigious institutions.

b. In the universities and colleges computers still occupy a minor role in most of the classrooms other than that of computer courses. At present computers are mainly used for quantitative topics.

c. Use of computers have made contributions, in management/engineering/ architect/design studies by making business games/structure design/ simulation more realistic and easy to understand and use.

d. The use of computers in teaching is hampered by the following reasons :

(i) Lack of quality of the software in educational terms.

(ii) Lack of relevance of the software to formal curriculum.

(iii) Difficulties experienced by the teachers in learning software features and in evaluating software in relation to their classroom practices.

(iv) Practical difficulties of organising effective student use of the software/hardware.

(v) Hardware related problems: Chief among the hardware problems are

(i) Those of numbers

(ii) non-availability of high resolution terminals to transmit graphic displays

(iii) non-availability of versatile and inexpensive terminals which are a must for increased use of computers in teaching

e. Computer as a supplement to traditional instruction as a remedial vehicle has been found useful. Though it has been demonstrated that use of computers in teaching is useful, there is no conclusive evidence that use of computers can achieve certain types of behavioral objectives more economically, more efficiently, or more effectively than the other teaching approaches.

f. Availability of funds was another important factor which contributed to the success story of computerization in several national institutions. The accessibility of computers to the students in some of the elite institutions is as high as one is to four. In case of colleges and universities, this ratio is meaning less.

g. Computer usage can be improved by paying more attention on details like students/computer ratio, availability of appropriate software, teacher training.

h. The national level institutes and several other central universities have adopted and integrated computers successfully in to their system. In many other universities where "product champions" are making constant and continuous efforts, the impact of computer technology is felt. In the rest of the universities computer technology penetration is only peripheral.

- Contributed by Sarla Achuthan

References

Anjaneyulu KSR, S.Ramani,KN Prakash and P Srinivas "Educational Technology Activities at National Centre for Software Technology",National Centre for Software Technology: Bombay,1992

Banarji A.K. & M.A. Sathyavasu, "FEDS - A Computer Aided Learning Approach for Training Foriegn Exchange Dealing", Bala Guruswamy E. and Shushila B. (ed.), Computer Systems and Application - Recent Trends : Proceedings of the Indian Computing Congress, New Delhi: Tata McGraw-Hill Publishing Co. Ltd., 1990, 490-495.

Bhatnagar S.C.(ed.), Information Technology Manpower: Key Issues For Developing Countries,New Delhi: Tata McGraw-Hill Publishing Company Limited,1992.

Campus News, University News, Monday April 13,1992.

Carnick B.Lisa, "Evaluating Foreign Language CAI :A checklist", Die Unterricht Spraxis, vol 17, 1984, 316-318.

Computer Today, January-August, 1992.

Evans E. Woherem, "Information Technology Manpower Development Strategy at the Organisational Level", Bhatnagar S.C.(ed.), Information Technology Manpower: Key Issues For Developing Countries, New Delhi: Tata McGraw-Hill Publishing Company Limited, 1992, 147-160.

Goyal M. L. (ed.), Information Technology in Everyday Life, Proceedings of XXVI Annual Convention of Computer Society of India, New Delhi: Tata McGraw-Hill Publishing Co. Ltd., 1991.

Kuppuswamy G. & R. Natrajan, "Emerging Role of computers in engineering Education", New Technologies in Higher Education, New Delhi: Association of Indian Universities, 1986, 39-48.

Lalitha, M. S. and Shailaja, H.G. Computer Assisted Instruction in Relation to Traditional Teaching, A Research Study, University of Mysore, Mysore, 1986.

Mohanadoss B. "IT For Human Resource Development", Goyal M. L. (ed.), Information Technology in Everyday Life, Proceedings of XXVI AnnualConvention of Computer Society of India, New Delhi: Tata McGraw-Hill Publishing Co. Ltd., 1991, 81-92.

Menon M.B., "Computer Based Learning in Distance Education" presented at IGNOU-UGC sponsored workshop on Distance Learning and New Communication Technologies, Aug. 1992, 25-26.

Nagarkar A.M., "Computer Aided Learning in Indian Bank", Bhatnagar S.C.(ed.), Information Technology Manpower: Key Issues For Developing Countries, New Delhi: Tata McGraw-Hill Publishing Company Limited, 1992, 182-189.

Pani S., "Strategy for Computerization of Land Records", Goyal M. L. (ed.), Information Technology in Everyday Life, Proceedings of XXVI Annual Convention of Computer Society of India, New Delhi: Tata McGraw-Hill Publishing Co. Ltd., 1991, 56-74.

Pawar, Rajendra S.,"IT Manpower in India: The Burning Issue", Bhatnagar S.C.(ed.), Information Technology Manpower: Key Issues For Developing Countries, New Delhi: Tata McGraw-Hill Publishing Company Limited, 1992, 7-19.

Pant M.M., "IT Strategies, The Developing Scenario" Presented at IGNOU-UGC sponsored workshop on Distance Learning and New Communication Technologies, Aug.25-26, 1992.

Ramani K.V., "Graphics Based Instructional Software For Decision Tree Analysis Using Bayesian Methodology"; Computers Education vol 00, No. 0, 1992, 1-7.

Ramani K.V., "Graphics Software For Teaching Optimization Algorithms", Proceedings Optimization Workshop, Singapore, 1991, 257-263.

Rajan P. & Patil P., Anjaneyulu KSR., Srinivas P. ,"The Trigonometry Tutor"; National Centre for Software Technology (NCST),Bombay, 1992.

Jain R. & Raghuram G., "Strategy for promoting Computer Literacy", Presented at Workshop on Computers in Education, Indian Institute Of Management, Ahmedabad, December 7-8, 1985.

Shamim A.A. & Rama Rao V., "Architecture of an Interactive Communication Network for Distance Education, A Conceptual Scheme"; Presented at IGNOU-UGC sponsored workshop on 'Distance Learning and New Communication Technologies' Aug.25-26, 1992.

Singh R.D., Ahluwalia S.P. & Verma S.K., "Teaching of Mathematics : Effectiveness of Computer-Assisted Instruction (CAI) and Conventional Method (CM) of Instruction",Indian Educational Review, October 1991, 15-33.

Suresh Kumar V, Srinivas P & Anjaneyulu KSR "A Review of Techniques in Intelligent Language Tutoring Systems"; Proceedings of the "East-West Conference on Emerging Computer Technologies in Education", Moscow, April 6-9 ,1992.

Tata Institute of Fundamental Research, Annual Report, (1990-91).

Thrimurthy P. "Harnessing Information Technology for Total Literacy" University News, Monday, June 8, 1992, 9-9.

Vishnu P.S. & Bhasker C. (ed.), Computer Education and Role of Computer Professionals, Proceedings of the Workshop, Computer Society of India, Hyderabad Chapter, Sept. 20, 1992.

Vittal N., "CSI Annual Conventional Address", Srinivasan (ed.), Information Technology and Management, Proceedings of 27th Annual Conventional of Computer Society of India, Allied Publisher Ltd., iii - xii.

Wright Pamela, "A Study of CAI for Remediation in Mathematics on the Secondary level", D.A.I., 15 p. 1063-A, 1983, 15,p. 1063-A.

CHAPTER 6

COMPUTERS IN RESEARCH

1. Introduction

Since independence, efforts are being made to develop infrastructure for education, research and industry in India. The Science Policy (1958), the Technology Policy (1983), the National Policy on Education (1986) and the Industrial Policy Resolutions, from time to time, have all helped in achieving the present level of development in these areas.

In terms of scientific expertise, India is well recognised. The level of scientific activity and the quality of results are rated highly. About 1% of the GNP was devoted to research and development activities in the country during 1990-91 through 189 universities and 1084 specialised labs and institutions dealing with different scientific areas (GOI,1991). There are also over 1163 in-house research and development (R & D) units set up by private and public sector undertakings largely to meet their own needs. An important recent development is the rapid growth of consultancy organizations providing engineering, design, construction and advisory services and acting as interface agencies between research and development institutions and industries (GOI,1991).

Research is carried out in a large number of institutions in India : (1) Establishments working as part of traditional academic institutions such as the universities; (2) Autonomous organizations like the national laboratories; (3) Government departments set up for specific types of research (for example, various defense research establishments), and (4) Laboratories or research bureaus maintained by the private sector.

Teaching and research are the two main functions of a university. If a university has to realize its objectives, the pursuit of research and teaching is essential. In fact, these two functions are complementary to each other. Today no university can function at its best unless its research activities are integrated with teaching. Moreover, teaching staff in higher education play a vital role in preparing better trained manpower. The University Grants Commission (UGC) has been making all efforts to keep the standard of teaching staff up-to-date in knowledge, technical know-how and skill, by providing requisite facilities and incentives through faculty improvement programs and other related schemes (GOI,1991). Modernization and introduction of technology, such as computers in institutions of higher education is one such step to achieve this objective.

2. Current State of Art

The first computer in India was introduced in the Indian Statistical Institute, Calcutta in 1956 for conducting research in the area of statistics.

Later, in the sixties, many of the scientific laboratories acquired computers for research purposes. In the seventies a few of the Indian universities also acquired computer systems. Because of the availability of micro-processor-based computers made within the country, use of computers has been further faciliated.

Use of computers has made an invaluable contribution in various fields of science and technology. In recent years, computer applications have centered around Office Automation, Information and Management System, Automated Control and Instrumentation, Signal Processing and Communication Applications, Remotely Sensed Data Processing, etc.

In order to sketch the picture of the current status of computer technology and its use in research institutions and universities, a survey was conducted by Gujarat University, Bhartiar University and Aligarh Muslim university in Gujarat, Tamil Nadu and Uttar Pradesh, respectively. Case studies of some research institutions of national importance and selected universities were carried out to understand the usage of computers, its area of application, and the nature of application in research.

2.1 Base-line Survey

Gujarat University, Bhartiar University and Aligarh Muslim University received responses from 46, 42 and 8 computer centers of different institutions respectively. The highlights of the survey from all the three universities can be summarized as follows :

2.1.1 Computer Use In Research

(a) Institutions of national importance use computers widely. These institutions have large computers, mini-computers and a large number of PCs for research purposes. In some of these institutions distributed computing is available to foster sharing of research data-bases and software. These institutions have E-mail and network facilities. The faculty and researchers are conversant with the use of computers in research and on an average 70 to 80 per cent of the computer time is used for research-related activities. The computer centers of these institutions provide continuous assistance to researchers to keep pace with the technology.

(b) The survey also indicated that research use of computers in universities comes next to computer science education in importance. On an average 20 to 30 percent of central computer time is utilized for research activity. Some departments use the central computer facility of the university for research purposes. For research projects undertaken by the university departments, funding agencies provide funds for hiring computer time or even to buy computers. Prominent use of computers in research work is in subjects like Physics, Statistics, Social Science, etc. At the Linguistic Department of South Gujarat University, computers are used for linguistic research in areas of Phonology, Morphology, Syntax and Lexicography.

(c) The survey data of all the three universities revealed that undergraduate colleges are not involved in any significant research activity and, therefore, computers are not generally used in colleges for research related activities. However, some teachers of undergraduate colleges do carry out their research work in university departments where they pursue research for M.Phil and Ph.D. degrees.

2.1.2 Nature of Computer Use in Research

In order to further understand the use of computers in research, certain areas such as literature survey, model building, data analysis, report generation, computer science and research, number crunching, etc. were identified. The responses from the institutions/universities are as follows :

Table 1 Distribution of Institutions, by Areas of Computer Use in Research

AREA	Gujarat University (n=46)	Bhartiar University (n=42)	Aligarh Muslim University (n=8)	Total (n=96)	Rank
Literature survey	7	1	1	9	6
Model Building	15	12	4	31	2
Data Analysis	29	20	5	54	1
Report Generation	14	9	6	29	3
Computer Science and Research	10	12	4	26	4
Number Crunching	9	8	3	17	5

From Table 1 it is evident that data analysis, model building, and report generation are major uses of computers in the area of research. As many libraries are still in the process of computerisation, the use of computers in literature survey is limited at the moment.

2.1.3 Software Usage in Research

As indicated in the survey, for most of the data analysis, statistical and numerical packages are used. Researchers normally develop their own programs for model building and simulation depending upon the problems. For report generation PC-based word processing packages are very popular. As can be seen from Table 2 the most popular microcomputer software is word-processing. However, some of the institutions are using Desk Top Publishing (DTP) systems for their publishing work.

Table 2 Distribution of Institutions by Software Usage

Software	Gujarat University (n= 46)	Bhartiar University (n = 42)	Aligarh Muslim University (n=8)
Word processing	42	38	7
Data-base	39	38	7
Spread-sheet	28	32	7
Statistical package	17	13	6
Operation research package	05	04	1
Report writer	14	07	3
Graphic packages	18	22	3
Desk top publishing	05	01	2
Course Authoring	03	00	0
Computer Aided instructions	05	10	1

In short, the major uses of computer in research are for data analysis, model building and report generation. Word processing software is the most widely used package.

2.2 Experiences from Case Studies

As the survey was directed towards quantitative data regarding computer use in research, some specific case studies were carried out of some institutions such as Indian Institute of Management, Ahmedabad, Indian Institutes of Technologies ,etc., to find out the exact nature of computer application in research. The following is a brief summary of the findings :

2.2.1 Nature of Computer Application

(a) Anna University at Madras has been exerting a major thrust in establishing industry-institution collaboration through consultancy and sponsored research. The computer center at the University has a Vax 11/780 and Magnum - II computer systems and a number of micro computers with an ETHERNET LAN and MODEM facilities. The university is also involved in remote sensing related work. The Remote Sensing unit of Anna University has a Multispectral Interactive Data Analysis System (MIDAS). This is specially designed for the analysis and interpretation of satellite data and is capable of displaying, analysing, classifying and generating maps. The university is carrying out considerable research/extension work in water resources, environmental studies, bio-technology, etc. The university has adequate computer facility which contributes substantially to the quality of research.

(b) At the Bhartiar University, many researchers are working on expert systems. Some faculty members are doing research in software engineering, database management systems, and multilingual script processing.

(c) At the Gujarat Institute of Area Planning (GIAP), Ahmedabad, infrastructure for using computer facilities for research has been built up during the last five years and now all academic staff members use computers for data analysis and reporting.

(d) At the Indian Institute of Management,(IIM) Ahmedabad, computer applications in the field of research include building of mathematical models, designing decision support systems and other Computer Aided Management(CAM) projects. Many faculty members at the Institute are involved in developing computer models for operational decisions such as vehicle scheduling, crew scheduling, trip design, depot assignment, and for developing simulation models for building large irrigation and power projects. The faculty has pioneered the use of graphics to achieve better man-machine co-operation in decision making activities.

(e) At the Indian Institute of Technology, (IIT) Bombay the major thrust areas of research include CAD/CAM, remote sensing, robotics, process control, etc. For this purpose, a separate CAD center with its own minicomputers and work stations supplemented by additional computing facilities has been developed. The IIT, Bombay has also access to international network such as UNET, BITNET and INFONET. They also have powerful computers such as CYBER.

(f) At the Indian Institute of Technology, (IIT) Madras, research constitutes the major proportion of computer usage. The activities of the center span over a broad range as a national resource in computing, and as campus resource for education, training and software development for new computing environments. There is a separate department for industrial consultancy services and research. Here,industrial research is undertaken both for the purpose of Ph.D. programmes in the fields of Civil, Mechanical, Chemical and Electrical Engineering and also for other industrial purposes. Different computerised techniques like CAD, computational fluid flow, finite element analysis, etc., are used in research.

(g) In the Indian Institute of Science, Banglore, significant work has been done in areas like numerical techniques, computational algorithms, algorithms for VLSI design, computer networking and communication, artificial intelligence including natural Indian language processing, computational linguistics, hardware implementation of multiprocessor architecture and computer performance evaluation. They are also planning to install CDC 992 and CDC 4360 machines to aid the research work.

2.3 General Research Applications

There are many other institutions in India, where extensive use of computers is made; but could not be covered under the baseline survey/case study. Therefore, to gain an understanding of the research use of computers in such institutions, secondary data such as their annual reports/published papers were relied upon.

(a) Applications in Scientific Institutions

The Physical Research Laboratory at Ahmedabad has a versatile DEC-1091 computer system, a work station DN-3500 and an HCL BusyBee AT. The center operates in two shifts on all days including Sundays. At present 48 terminals are connected. Four of them have graphic capabilities. The time sharing TOPS-10 operating system supports the full configuration. The main activities of the center are development of software, support research work in computer related areas of Numerical Methods, Statistics, Operations Research, Neural Network, etc., and providing training to the user on an ongoing basis. The center develops and maintains a good library of various software packages such as Mathematica and several other subroutines for general use to help scientists in carrying out research in Astronomy, Astrophysics etc. (PRL,1991)

The activities of the Tata Institute of Fundamental Research (TIFR) span a wide spectrum of pure and applied sciences. Research is pursued in several branches of Mathematics, Physics, Astronomy, Molecular Biology, Computer Sciences and Material Sciences. TIFR has CYBER 170/730 and VAX 11/780 computer systems to support the research work in the above areas. At present, around 100 terminal connections have been provided on CYBER and 50 connections on VAX. The institute has provided the facility of electronic mail and BITNET links to exchange and share data communication among the researchers within and outside the institute.

The TIFR has a basic dental research unit also. The unit is currently pursuing research in the prevention of oral cancer. A research project for estimating tobacco attributable mortality has been initiated. In this project, TIFR has used a novel method of data collection. Instead of using a printed questionnaire, data are being collected into hand held computers. The questionnaire has been imputed in the form of a computer programme. This method provides many advantages like on the spot automatic checking of inputted information, better record keeping and direct transfer from one computer to another computer. (TIFR,1991)

(b) Applications in Technology

The Indian Institute of Technology, Kanpur has installed an ETA 10 computer. This computer has the facility to solve large problems because of its high speed scalar and vector processors, large memories, broad band widths and extensive input output capabilities. A large number of work stations are connected to this machine. The application areas include Computer Aided Engineering, Robotics, water resources engineering, large scale simulation, optimization, VLSI and electronics design, condensed matter physics, quantum and molecular chemistry, metal alloys analysis, expert systems, etc.

At the University of Hyderabad, considerable research is carried out on Object Oriented Data Base Management Systems (OODBMS). The various applications of object oriented DBMS are reported in the areas of CAD/CAM, VLSI CAD, Robot programming, Graphics, AI, Office Information System (OIS), Image Databases, Pattern Recognition, Software Engineering, Music Composition, Natural Language Processing, Vision and Speech Recognition and Synthesis.

(c) Application in Phonetic Studies

Research activities at the Indian Statistical Institute at Calcutta center around acoustic phonetic studies of speech of some major Indian languages, automatic speech recognition, speech synthesis, problem of speech perception, acoustic, recognition and synthesis studies of Indian classical music. This kind of research will help the disabled a great deal. (Majumder,1991)

(d) Application in Weather Forecasting

Another interesting and significant area of computer use in research and operational work is done in the National Weather Services. Kulshrestha

S.M.(1991) describes that the National Weather Services are indeed the prime users of computer technology (computer plus communication : C+C) . The weather services generate, exchange and analyse weather related data in large volume. The India Meteorological Department (IMD) has a super computer (CRAY XMP - 1/54) for weather forecast. This center also makes use of other modern technologies, such as satellites and Radars for generating weather related information.

(e) Application in Drug Formulation

Ramani K.V. et al (1992) has designed, developed, and implemented a computer-based expert system for Cadila Laboratories to aid pharmaceutical experts in drug preformulations. Drugs such as tablets contain many chemicals (called excipients) in addition to the main active drug. A preformulation study identifies compatible excipients and their relative proportion in the final formulation. The expert system has saved about 35 per cent of the total R and D time besides providing substantial savings in manufacturing cost.

(f) Application in Rural Management

The Computerised Rural Information Systems Project (CRISP) is a Government initiative to promote decentralised management of the Integrated Rural Development Programme (IRDP) in India. The basic objective was to develop micro based information system to improve the local level decision making. A large number of action oriented research projects are being done using the database created. One of the problems encountered with the CRISP was lack of adequately trained manpower. Language created another problem. (Madan S.,1992)

The examples cited above, even though not exhaustive, illustrate the impact of computers in different research problems.

Many of the above institutions such as TIFR, PRL, IITs, etc., are centers of excellence in their respective areas. Quality research is carried out in these institutions. They are the pace-setters in the computing technologies and their achievements are at par with those of similar institutions in advanced countries.

3. Role of Network and Databases in Research

India being a large country,the need for an efficient and low cost data communication system was felt since long. It was in the early eighties that the development in network activities began.

The opportunities offered by the Information Technology are tapped to improve and accelerate the planning process. Several networks are available today, to share databases and exchange data/text. E-mail based on dial-up, leased lines and Unix to Unix Communication Protocol (UUCP) have been established with links to world wide academics and research network and presently cover more than fifty institutions in India. INDONET was established using terrestrial links to hook up metropolitan cities.

3.1 NICNET and Related Activities

National Informatics Center (NIC) had set up a Nation-wide Satellite based Computer-Communication Network (NICNET) in close co-operation with State Governments as well as District Administrations. NICNET is planned to facilitate development of district database on sectors of importance and also to standardize and rationalize the information exchange between the District and the States and then to the center. As a result, Governments, both at the Center as well as at the State, will be in a position to have interactive information-based infrastructure for decision support at all levels.

An indigenously developed electronic mail system, namely NICMAIL, is used on NICNET. NICMAIL is an attempt to achieve the following objectives:

(a) To facilitate efficient information exchange among the government offices at the central, state and districts levels.

(b) To promote wider exchange of ideas and information supporting analysis and decision making.

The General Information Services Terminal-National Informatics Center (GISTNIC) is designed with an objective to make available general information to public about India, important national and international information, infrastructural and recreational facilities and other static and near static information through a query system.

NEWB is a special purpose electronic bulletin board service for NICNET users. NEWB is designed to run on a powerful node namely NEC-S1000 system.

The National Informatics Center (NIC) has developed a district Information System program (DISNIC). With the active cooperation of State Governments through their support to numerous pilot projects, the NIC has developed DISNIC data base for 26 sectors. Using NICNET, a distributed Geographic Information System has also been developed. These databases offer wide scope for researchers interested in planning and management processes of government.

In fact, there have been attempts to develop suitable on-line analysis packages for planners. The package, such as ANALYST, the generic on-line analysis package, completely menu driven and user friendly are developed and tested to support better decision making. The packages have the capability of carrying out a number of statistical techniques and modelling.

3.2 ERNET and its Activities

The Government has set up an Education and Research Network (ERNET) to connect education and research institutions all over the country. ERNET promotes information exchange among these research institutions. The ERNET connects more than 3000 people and 100 institutions all over the country. Universities may be encouraged to use ERNET facility to have larger interaction with other universities. A vital role could be played by these networks in research and distributed systems. Using networks Indian Institutes of Technology (IITs) and Indian Institutes of Management (IIMs) located at different places are carrying out common research projects sharing and exchanging data and results. Many national institutions are using a gateway to talk and interact to a wide area network of institutions within the country and abroad. Thus in recent years one can see an upswing in the importance of convenient integration of systems into networks.

4. Research in R and D organizations, Research Laboratories, University Departments and Colleges

The experiences gathered from survey and case studies clearly indicate that the research facilities provided in the national level institutes in comparison with the other institutions of higher education such as universities and colleges are far superior.

4.1 Research in R and D Organizations

According to Research and Development Statistics (GOI,1991), 77.4% of the total R & D expenditure of the major scientific agencies was consumed by five agencies : Defense Research and Development Organization (DRDO), Department of Space (DOS), Indian Council of Agricultural Research (ICAR), Department of Atomic Energy (DAE) and Council of Scientific and Industrial Research (CSIR) in that order with DRDO accounting for 27.5% . The priority areas of research are defense, space, scientific and industrial research. Under the R and D group of institutions, private and government, the situation is such that computers are being used for scientific and technical applications extensively, whatever be the thrust area of the respective organizations. If specific needs of the institution's scientific/technical work requires, super computers or equivalent computing, solutions are by and large found within the available resources. Thus computing requirements generally do not become a bottleneck for scientific and technical applications at national level institutes.

4.2 Research in University and Colleges

Only a small portion of the total research funding comes to universities. As a result, high quality research generally takes place outside the university environment. However, there are efforts being made by several funding agencies such as Council of Scientific and Industrial Research (CSIR) and Indian Council of Social Science Research (ICSSR) which provide funds to teachers in Indian Universities to carry out research projects.

The UGC has encouraged faculty members in the universities/colleges to take up well defined, time bound research projects in pure and applied sciences, engineering/technology areas related to national research and development efforts or in new fields and inter-disciplinary areas of importance. The basic objective has been to promote the culture of research in the university system and to enable the faculty to keep themselves abreast of the latest developments in their subject areas. During 1991, 170 such major projects in science and technology were supported by the UGC. As Ph.D. research is an indicator of the quantity and the direction of research in Indian universities, an analysis of data of Ph.D. degrees was undertaken during 1989-90. It reveals that 51.3% of them were from Science & Technology (S&T) faculties. Pure science alone accounted for 36.5% of the total Ph.D. degrees awarded during 1989-90 (GOI,1991). The major research is in science and technology with special reference to pure science. The climate in Indian universities also started changing with regard to career prospects of the university teachers and promotions became linked with the research output of teachers. As a result, during the last two decades, a lot of attention has been paid to research in universities. Today most university departments have some research projects and individual teachers do devote attention to research work. In case of colleges where teaching is mainly focused on undergraduates the research output is not significant. However, the teachers of colleges are joining M.Phil and Ph.D programmes for their career advancement.

5. Major Issues

The major portion of investment in research in India is made in professional and scientific research institutions. Therefore, research carried out in many of the universities may not be comparable with that of prestigious national level institutions in quantity and quality. This is perhaps the root cause of the present state of research in universities. Additionally, organizational and administrative constraints also adversely affect the psychology of the researcher in many universities.

Manpower resource development requires a good educational system. In order to achieve excellence in higher education, quality research is very important. To do quality research it is essential to have a general academic ambience, supported by modern technological aids besides interaction with industry. However, many of the universities lack this ambience and the required support.

5.1 University-Industry Interaction

Professional institutions and national laboratories and a very few universities such as Anna University, Hyderabad University, etc., have been giving a major thrust in establishing industry-collaboration through research. Besides promoting research and disseminating knowledge gained therefrom, it fosters co-operation between academic and industrial communities. However, these linkages are restricted to a handful of universities. In the rest of the universities this kind of interaction is lacking. Interaction within the university and among the universities is also not very common. The linkage between industries and university will promote research work that is relevant to industries. This will have a larger impact. The faculty from the universities may be encouraged to work on problems which are relevant to industry in particular and society at large. The Anna university case can be considered as a good model to emulate.

The Swaminadhan Model (1992) of university-industry interaction is worth implementing for all the universities to optimally use resources. A synergetic effect of resources such as men, material and finance can be achieved by pooling and sharing these resources. This way teaching and research activities in universities may get enriched.

5.2 Technology Related Issues

As seen from the case studies, computing facilities provide a great impetus to research. In several universities, the computers are not used much. In order to identify the reasons, certain questions were posed to teachers of Gujarat University, Bhartiar University and Aligarh Muslim University. As observed from the survey and the case studies the computer penetration was deeper in national level institutions, therefore, the responses to the non-use of computers were deleted and only responses from the colleges and universities have been analysed.

As can be seen from Table 3, the survey indicates that the two major hurdles are : (i) lack of technical skills and (ii) ignorance about potential use of computers. The results indicate that the proportion of teachers lacking technical skill and knowledge about potential use of computers are more or less same in three different regions. Moreover a significant proportion indicated the same reasons. ($P>.5$)

Table 3 Percentage Indicating Reasons for Non/Inadequate Computer Use

University	n	Lack of technical skill	Ignorance about potential use
Gujarat	159	90.6	76.1
Bhartiar	59	88.1	66.1
Aligarh	92	79.4	73.9

The above factors perhaps may become constraint in carrying out quality research by university teachers. Intensive training programs of different disciplines at various levels may be a possible solution to overcome these problems.

Though there are several training programmes offered by many organizations, most emphasize basics of computer hardware and software. The training programmes should have relevance in the areas of interest and work of teachers. Conduct of specific discipline-oriented training emphasizing software related to research and refresher courses from time to time in educating teachers will go a long way in providing help to them.

5.3 Lack of Infrastructural Facilities

Poor infrastructure facilities such as inadequate computer facilities at times become a hindrance in carrying out research activities in several universities. Paucity of funds to acquire and maintain computers is also a major problem. To have access to any of the national networks and E-mail facilities requires better tele-communication facilities in the university environment. At present several university departments have inadequate communication facilities. So the access to network and E-mail facilities may not be available in the near future to most of the university teachers. However a decentralised computing facilities to researchers having access to a large system may provide an appropriate environment for promoting research.

6. Changing Nature of Research

Technological impact on any activity is very common. Research activity has been changing its nature from time to time with the technology. High technologies and computer integrated models can be inducted effectively only if there is a streamlined mechanism to co-ordinate research and development efforts, material, man-power, resources and funding among institutions which are separated geographically. The computer technology has provided solutions to issues concerning sharing of resources and in dissemination of knowledge. The computer technology has made its impact on every stage of research.

6.1 Data Capturing and Recording

The use of computers in research now permits new sets of data types such as images, photographs, voice, etc. So far research data was limited to numerals and characters. The method of data capturing is also more flexible. Instead of having filled questionnaires, data could be directly fed into computer or images/voices could be received from remote places .

6.2 Changes in Approaches/Methodologies

With the introduction of computers in research, research tends to be more quantitative in approach even in disciplines like the social sciences. The number of alternative models a researcher can evaluate before finding the exact relationship is now increasing with the help of computers. More sophisticated research techniques are now being used. The quantity of research papers has considerably increased with the use of computers. The accuracy level of prediction has also increased. Moreover scientists can now simulate experiments especially in situations where experiment- time is high, is unsafe and equipment used is costly. Researchers can now supplement experiments using computer simulation. Complex research problems having astronomical alternatives and enormous calculations can be handled easily with computers. Research now seems to be more application oriented and has become more inter-disciplinary in nature. Parallel computing will open broader and newer areas of applications in research.

6.3 Sharing of Resources

Sharing of resources such as disk space, data, sophisticated equipment etc., are the greatest advantages of the technology.

Secondary data base created for research is also available for different researchers dealing with the topic. The research data and results can be shared with the larger community due to the availability of database and LAN/WAN facilities. Networking of libraries permit sharing of journals/books. Large multi-media data bases can be easily handled.

6.4 Research Documentation

With the help of computers, documentation and presentation of research have improved considerably. The researchers feel that paper writing has now become easy with the availability of word processors. However some others feel that documents undergo several revisions which at times becomes a waste of resources. With the advent of multi-media documents one can now integrate graphics, text, images etc., in the document. With the help of this technology, the time required for printing research reports has decreased substantially. Most journals accept research papers on floppies.

6.5 Dissemination and Communication

Computer technology has made it possible for researchers, who are geographically apart, to work closely using E-mail facilities. The researchers can now easily exchange software, text, data, etc. across the ocean within a short period and interact with the counterparts. By the use of this technology an efficient way of information delivery system is possible. For example a useful software developed at an industry can be exchanged among several universities and modification can be easily made to suit one's needs. If a university develops a new product/design through research it can be distributed to a number of organizations for implementation. This can be done through a software. In other words, the concept of Electronic Data Interchange (EDI) could be very useful in industry-university interaction and in dissemination of information.

The several applications cited in the chapter indicate that availability of powerful machines has provided a proper environment for conducting innovative research. The accessibility and increased use of powerful PCs has provided greater impetus to research.

Computerization has, thus helped improved the quality of research output in terms of speed, accuracy, reliability, flexibility, dissemination and style of reporting. With this technology networking among the universities, their departments and computer centers may be made for sharing research information. Development of common data bases on sharing basis among different institutions will be useful. This kind of facility will provide a greater thrust to research and may result in achieving the desired excellence in the university sector.

7. Summary and Conclusion

(a) The national research efforts are concentrated in a few national institutions. In fact large resources are being expended on research outside universities. Computers are used very widely by these institutions for research. Innovative and creative work is done exploiting the versatility of computers.

(b) The recent trend in the national institutes is to integrate computer systems into networks. There is a shift from central mainframe to decentralised work stations.

(c) The paucity of financial support and lack of research facilities such as inadequate computing facilities are the major bottle-necks in universities for carrying out research.

(d) Writing the research paper has become an easier task with computers. Many researchers view computers as a personal productivity tool that can help them to produce attractive documents faster.

(e) With the introduction of computers, researchers are doing a lot of experimental work. This is particularly helpful under several circumstances such as when equipment is not easily available, is very expensive, experiments are not very safe or time consuming etc. With this technology scientists have an option of simulating experiments using computers.

(f) Lack of technical skill and knowledge of potential uses are the major reasons for the non/inadequate use of computers in research among university teachers as indicated in the survey.

(g) Word Processing software is the most widely used package.

(h) The major uses of computers in research are data analysis, model building and report generation.

(i) A large number of institutions have given researchers individual PCs which are connected to a centralised system. It has been observed that wherever the hardware and the training facilities are appropriate the use of computers is much higher and its impact on research is significant.

- Contributed by Sarla Achuthan

References

Association of Indian Universities, Universities and Research Delhi:, 1980.

BalaGuru Swamy E. & B. Sushila, Computer Systems and Application Recent Trends, Proceedings of the Indian Computing Congress, New Delhi : Tata McGrow-Hill Publishing Co.Ltd., 1990.

Bhatnagar R.P., "Organizational and Administrative Constraints of Quality Research in Education", University News, Monday, June 15, 1992.

Govt. of India (GOI) Research and Development Statistics (1990-91), Delhi Department of Science & Technology, 1992.

Kulshrestha S.M., "National Weather Services as prime users of Information Technology" Goyal M.L. (ed.), Information Technology in Everyday Life, Proceeding of the XXVI Annual Convention of the Computer Society of India, New Delhi : Tata McGraw-Hill Publishing Company Limited, 1991, 42-47.

Madan S., "The Computerised Rural Information Systems Project (CRISP): Manpower and Training Needs", Bhatnagar S.C. (ed.), Information Technology Manpower, Key Issues for Developing Countries, New Delhi : Tata McGraw-Hill Publishing Company Limited, 1991, 171-179.

Majumder D.D., "Man-Computer Interaction by Speech & Vision", Goyal M.L. (ed.), Information Technology in Everyday Life, Proceeding of the XXVI Annual Convention of the Computer Society of India, New Delhi : Tata McGraw-Hill Publishing Company Limited, 1991, 3-21.

Ramani K.V., Patel M.R., Patel S.K., "An expert System for Drug Prefomulation in a Pharmaceutical Company", Interface 22.2, March-April 1992, 101-108.

Physical Research Laboratory (PRL), Annual Report, 1990-91.

Swaminadhan D., "Imperative of University-Industry - R & D Organization Interaction for National Development", University News, Monday, May-18,1992.

Tata Institute of Fundamental Research (TIFR), Annual Report, 1990-91.

CHAPTER 7
ADMINISTRATIVE USES OF COMPUTERS

Computers are being used increasingly by the managements in business and industrial organizations for office automation, transaction processing, management information system and decision support system. These are also being used by the managements for manufacturing and process control environments in the industries. Likewise possible uses of computers in the instructional process, similar to their uses in manufacturing process, have been examined in the earlier chapter. In this chapter, an attempt will be made to assess the availability and use of computer in the management functions of colleges, universities, and research institutions.

1.. Current Use in Administrative Functions

1.1 Survey Results-Administrative Aspects

The installation of computers in universities, colleges and research institutes initially was for educational and research purposes. But gradually the management realized the potentiality of the computers and started using this equipment in the area of administration, namely examination, admissions, accounting etc. But not all such institutes having computers are using the equipment for administration. In the base line survey conducted by Gujarat University (GU), Bharatiar University (BU) and Aligarh Muslim University (AMU) in their respective regions, the use made by the respondent units in the area of administration is summarized in the table below :

Table 1 Use of Computer in Administration

Type of Institution	GU		BU		AMU	
	Total Respondents	Use in Administration	Total Respondents	Use in Administration	Total Respondents	Use in Administration
Undergraduate College	08	01	17	06	01	—
Undergraduate & Postgraduate College	21	16	17	11	01	—
P.G. Department	03	03	02	02	01	01
Research Institute	04	03	05	05	01	01
Other	10	05	01	—	04	03
Total	46	28	42	24	08	05

As can be seen from the table, 28 out of 46 institutions in Gujarat region, 24 out of 42 in Tamilnadu and 5 out of 8 in Uttarpradesh used computers in the area of administration. This means that around 60% of the respondent sites use computer for administrative function. But looking to type of institution, the use is very low in undergraduate colleges. The use in other undergraduate and postgraduate colleges, postgraduate departments, research institutions and universities, vary from 50% to 100%. This fact must attract the attention of the planners who, in the process of prioritization, often overlook the fact that a streamlined and efficient administration can better support research activities. And to bring the administration to the level where it can satisfy the needs of researchers and put them on the accelerated path of exploration, the use of computers today undoubtedly have to be made in all appropriate areas of the administration.

The following table gives the break-up by the type of application in the institutions.

Table 2 Use in Administration by Type of Application

Activities	Computerised		
	GU (n=46)	BU (n=42)	AMU (n=8)
Students Registration & Record	17	08	03
Students Admission	16	11	04
Students Examination & Evaluation	17	10	04
Accounting	16	06	03
Payroll	30	23	04
Inventory Record (Material/Stores)	07	02	01
Cost analysis	03	01	—
Personnel	14	07	05
Scheduling	08	07	01
Integrated Information System	05	01	01
Office Automation	17	13	04
Library Cataloging	11	11	03
Library Requisition/Circulation	04	07	01

The payroll is the single application which has found its place in almost 65% institutions in Gujarat, 55% in Tamilnadu and 50% in Uttarpradesh where sample size is, however, small. The payroll is merely a routine application which has no direct bearing on the services being offered to the students and researchers in the institutions. It of course, helps the management in the accounting process and speedy disbursement of salaries as well as certificates. The other application areas which, if computerized, can substantially improve the functioning of the institutions and provide better services to students are students' registration, admissions, examinations and evaluation. The survey results show that at most 37% institutes in Gujarat and 26% institutes in Tamilnadu have computerized these functions. Class scheduling and library automation have not been considered seriously for various reasons. Delays in providing services have been observed due to this fact during the process of admissions, processing of results and in fixing the problems of scheduling for lectures and practicals.

Financial accounting is the area through which better control can be exercised in the management of funds and particularly the system of payment can be effectively controlled to generate confidence amongst the suppliers of external services and goods. It can be observed that the present situation of poor financial management is perhaps due to non- implementation of the accounting function on the computer.

With the increased sophistication of the hardware and the higher level of service demand from the management, it is becoming difficult to procure application specific software usefull for administrative functions in the institutes of higher education. Due to this, most of the respondents seem to be developing software in-house. This fact comes out in the following table which shows various softwares whether supplied by the vendor or developed in-house.

Table 3 Software for Administration

	Activities	GU			BU			AMU		
		**{ 1	2	3	1	2	3	1	2	3 }
1.	Students registration & record	03	01	12	03	01	04 *	—	—	03
2.	Students admission	02	01	13	04	01	06	—	—	04
3.	Students examination & evaluation	02	01	12	01	—	09	01	—	03
4.	Accounting	04	—	11	03	—	03	—	—	02
5.	Payroll	03	01	23	04	02	13	—	—	04
6.	Inventory record (material/stores)	01	—	05	01	—	—	—	—	01
7.	Cost analysis	—	—	02	—	—	01	—	—	—
8.	Personnel	01	—	10	04	01	02	—	—	04
9.	Scheduling (time table, room allocation...etc)	01	—	07	02	01	03	—	—	—
10.	Integrated information system	—	—	04	01	—	—	—	—	01
11.	Office automation use (use of word processor)	08	02	03	08	02	03	03	—	01
12.	Library cataloging	01	—	09	02	02	06	—	—	02
13.	Library requisition/circulation	01	—	03	02	02	03	—	—	01

* Total of these figures may not be same as in the previous table due to non-response.

** 1 = Used vendor supplied software, 2 = Modified vendor supplied software, 3 = Developed in-house software.

Library management is an area through which the thirst of students, researchers and faculty members for study, references and exploration can be satisfied. The library system is an integral part of the institution of higher education. As can be made out from the following table, only 7 institutions from Gujarat and Tamilnadu each have attempted library automation in their organizations. This constitutes only 15% of the total number of respondents. Surprising is the fact that only one university has attempted to computerize its library system. The INFLIBNET programme of U.G.C. has plans to link the libraries of the institutions of higher education through network in the country. Yet some ground work needs to be done in this area to develop awareness and enthusiasm in the staff of the libraries so that when the technology comes to them, they would whole heartedly accept the same and participate profitably in the process of automation.

Table 4 Computer Use in Libraries

Type of Institution	Library System Computerized		
	GU (n=46)	BU (n=42)	AMU (n=8)
Undergraduate College	01	01	—
Undergraduate & Postgraduate College	01	04	—
P.G. Department	01	01	01
Research Institute	03	01	01
Universities	01	—	01
Total	07	07	03

With the growing enrollment in the universities and colleges, the management task is becoming more and more difficult. The immediate requirement, therefore, is to use computers in all the service areas within the campus. With today's hardware providing time-shared and on-line facilities as well as distributed computing through LAN, work stations, PCs and terminals, the approach of deploying more and more technical staff for day to day processing is out of question. The existing administrative staff has to be given orientation in the use of the hardware and application software for day to day processing of the applications for which they are responsible. Developing an atmosphere of end-user computing only will permit a healthy growth of computerisation in the organization. As there will be direct participation by the staff, they will continue to feel an integral part of the whole system and might not develop any sense of dissatisfaction. The results of the survey (Table 5) very clearly show that it is the lack of user training which is responsible for the low use of computers in the area of administration.

Table 5 Reasons for Low Use of Computers by Administrative Staff

Reasons	GU (n=46)	BU (n=42)	AMU (n=8)
Lack of Training	17	16	02
Not Interested	04	03	01
Too much of Time Investment so not worth	03	04	—
Complicated Technology	—	05	—
Does not provide extra allowances	—	05	01

The current status in making use of network and electronic mail for communication purpose is shown below :

Table 6 Network and Electronic Mail

University	N	Network		Electronic Mailing	
		Yes	Plan to get	Yes	Plan to get
GU	46	03	06	02	08
BU	42	—	03	03	02
AMU	8	—	—	01	01

Only two institutions of Gujarat, three institutions of Tamilnadu and one of Uttarpradesh have access to electronic mail facility through network like ERNET. The others do not have any kind of network even within their location. The future decisions for installation of hardware, whether by the funding agencies or the recipient organization, will have to look seriously to the aspect of networking of computers especially in the universities and research institutions.

1.2 Experiences from the Case Studies

The case studies of computerisation in selected universities and institutions of the country have been included in a separate report under the title "Computer Scenario of Higher Education in India - Selected Case Studies".

The equipment installed in each of the institutions covered under case studies, (refer Table 4 of Chapter 8) can easily permit computerisation of internal administrative functions. Yet only Anna University, SNDT University, Bajaj Institute, IIT Bombay and IIT Madras have computerized all the functions like payroll, financial accounting, admission, examination processing and library systems. Bharthiar University as well as Bombay University have computerized examination processing as well as payroll function. Casual or insignificant use is being made in the area of administration by University of Rajasthan, Kerala University and VJTI, Bombay. It is significant to note that IIT Bombay as well as Indian Institute of Science, Banglore have established a network connecting all computers on the campus. Terminals have been given to various locations on the campus. The E-mail facility is available at IIT Bombay, IIT Madras and IISc Banglore (a deemed university). One must remember that these institutions are national institutions and therefore obtain their funds from the Central Government relatively easily as compared to the state universities and colleges.

1.3 Experiences of Use of Computer in Examination and Admission at Gujarat University

As pointed out earlier, the major applications which have a direct impact on the students are examinations and admissions. As a representative case, the experiences of Gujarat University will be discussed here. The Gujarat University has an enrollment of about 1,40,000 students in the annual examinations conducted during April and 40,000 in the supplementary examination conducted during October every year. All the major examinations where the registration is more than 300 have been fully computerized right from the stage of the preparation of lists of candidates, to declaration of results, preparation of registers, marksheets and several other reports. The processing of the examinations which have low registration is handled manually; however, the registers, marksheets etc. are prepared on the computer. In terms of registration, almost in excess of 95% of the candidates are covered and their results are processed directly by the computers. It is interesting to note that the highest registration in a single major examination is about 22,000 candidates.

Ever since the computerisation process was started in the year 1962 it has been observed that :

1. The whole process of the conduct of examinations and declaration of results becomes manageable.

2. It is cost effective and time saving.

3. Confidentiality can be maintained to a greater extent.

4. The system of fictitious numbers can be implemented.

5. Other processes related to examinations can be handled easily on the computer since the same database is to be used.

6. The data for qualitative analysis and improvement are made available.

Although no RDBMS is being used due to high cost of procurement and license, the system developed in COBOL runs satisfactorily on the in-house VAX 11/730 system. The admission process of B.Ed. course being offered by about 15 colleges has been computerized since 1982, where against a total number of 2000 seats, approximately 20,000 applications are received every year. Similarly admissions to other competitive courses like M.B.A., M.C.A., D.C.A., P.G. Medical have been computerized. Experiments have been made to give admissions to undergraduate courses in Arts, Science and Commerce in the affiliated colleges of Ahmedabad city a few years ago. The L. D. Engineering College affiliated to Gujarat University handles computer based centralized admissions to engineering colleges of the state. Similarly admissions to medical colleges of the state have also been computerized several years ago. A brief history of computerization at Gujarat University is given in Appendix-C.

Needless to mention that a computer based centralized system offers great relief to the students and parents since they have to fill-in only one form. This saves their time and also helps them to work out their own alternative career choices since the admissions are decided through the computerised system.

Today the availability of cheaper hardware should make it possible for all organizations in higher education to transfer these administrative functions to the computer. The only question is, who will develop the relevant software for the specific requirements ? As regards the Universities where staff is provided by the U.G.C, this can be developed in-house, though they may take longer time to implement. The problem is serious for the affiliated colleges. They need easy availability of specific software for various administrative functions.

1.4 Organizational status of Computer Centre in the Universities and Colleges

The Computer Centres in the universities are established with the financial assistance of the University Grants Commission. Though, there are no specific guidelines as to the size of the university and the system to be granted to the university at present, the U.G.C. scrutinizes proposals in so far as the current use and expected use of the computer in the organization is concerned. More emphasis is given to the research use of computer followed by educational use. The staffing pattern of the computer centres as recommended by U.G.C. is given in the Appendix-D.

The Computer Centres are considered by the U.G.C. to be a central facility on the campus. The system must be accessible to all the faculty members and researchers first and then to students of Computer Science as well as non Computer Science branches. The administration may make use of the central facility. Though the administrative use is not emphasized, it may be limited to 30% of the total time. The typical position of Computer Centres in the universities is given below :

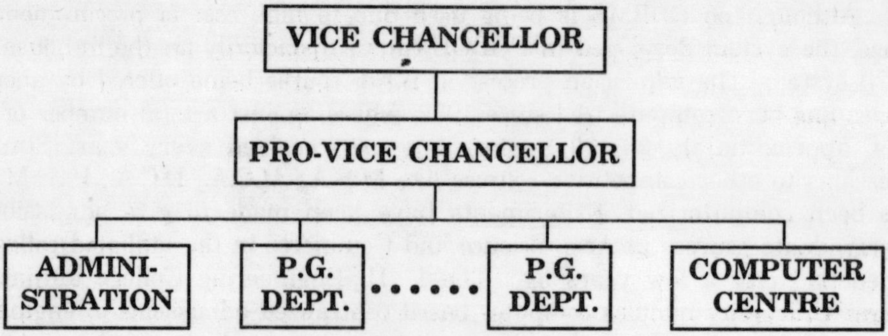

The affiliated colleges, unless they are on the campus of a residential university, can install computers either from the funds from U.G.C. or through internal financing. Almost all such respondent colleges in Arts, Science and Commerce stream except Engineering colleges of Gujarat have created a small computer room in the building with installation of two or more personal computers. At present no staff is being provided by U.G.C. to colleges. However, in the colleges affiliated to Gujarat University, a Programmer and a lecturer can be appointed with funds from the State Government if the college opts to offer Computer Science as an optional subject to the students. Additional fee of Rs. 300 per term is charged from students to provide for incidental expenses for the maintenance of computers. It would be much desirable, however, to provide one Programmer in each college for creation and effective use of computing centre facilities by the faculty and students. If the funds cannot be given to the colleges, atleast they may be encouraged to raise their own funds for installation of computers. Necessary guidelines and incentives may be framed by the authorities in this regard.

1.5 Existing Guidelines of UGC & DOE

The University Grants Commission is the main funding agency in respect of development of central computing facilities in the universities. The Department of Electronics (DOE) formulates plans for development of manpower in the area of computer science and applications and supports the expenditure for purchasing hardware/software specially for conduct of courses like M.C.A. and D.C.A. The DOE also supports cross-migration training programs to meet the shortage of teachers in Computer Science. Recurring expenditure for the staff engaged by the university in conduct of M.C.A. and D.C.A. courses is borne by the U.G.C. for the first five years. The colleges and institutions, not coming under the purview of U.G.C. are funded directly by DOE and Ministry of Human Resources Development (MHRD) for the conduct of M.C.A. and D.C.A. courses, purchase of hardware and software as well as recurring grant for the staff.

The U.G.C. had initially categorised the computer system as type A, type B and type C equivalent to IBM 1620, IBM 1130 and IBM 360 systems or configurationwise equivalent systems. The classification has been changed in 1990 on the basis of the value of hardware installed. The aggregate value for type A is up to Rs. 10 lacs, for type B between Rs.10 to 50 lacs and for type C above Rs.50 lacs.

The Computer Development Committee of U.G.C. advises the Commission in respect of releasing funds to individual universities depending on the size of the university, level of research activities, student use of computer as well as non-computer courses, administrative work load, etc. It has been decided by the U.G.C. to provide atleast one computer in each University/Institution of higher learning. The Appendix-D shows the details of policies for granting type A, type B and type C computers as well as the recurring grant for each category. It also gives the details about the staff sanctioned under each of the types A, B and C. As part of the funds, about 10 to 20% additional amount is provided for creation of infrastructural facilities like site preparation, air-conditioning, electrical installation, etc.

2. Major Issues

2.1 Planning and Prioritisation of Computer Related Activities

As can be seen from the case studies and survey results the applications attempted by the universities are :

1. Payroll
2. Examinations
3. Financial accounting
4. Admissions
5. Inventory management
6. Personnel information system
7. Library system.

Each university has its own priority and sequential use of computers for different administrative functions. Some use this technology for research, some for examinations, and some others for Financial Accounting in the beginning. Hence the approach for prioritization of the application is best decided by the Institution itself. This may depend on various issues like volume of processing, need for better accuracy, difficulty in manual processing, requirement of speedy results, and so on. However, if we consider service areas resulting into direct impact on the user community, namely students and the researchers, then the high priority applications are :

1. Admissions
2. Examinations
3. Library Systems

Needless to say that in Indian situation, with an ever increasing number of students against a limited number of colleges and institutions, the admissions to various courses must be computerized. Similarly, examination processing is another application that will bring accuracy and will remove the common snags like processing delays, illegible hand written marksheets, skipping the printing of question papers for some subjects, etc. As pointed out earlier the library system quickly benefits the researchers and faculty members for exploration of new information for teaching as well as research.

While the examination processing has been attempted by most of the universities, the computerized admission seems to have been given a relatively low importance due to the very fact that there is no mechanism for enforcement of the admission rules. This being the situation, it has been observed that the principals or heads of departments usually do not show interest in computerizing the admission process. The computerisation of library information system needs special funds for installation of hardware and software. Hitherto it was not possible to computerize library functions due to lack of funds for computer facilities. Now the INFLIBNET has taken up the task of computerizing the libraries. It is expected that good progress will be made in computerisation of the libraries during the next five years.

The other computer applications which can be added after covering the high priority areas, are :

1. Financial accounting
2. Payroll accounting
3. Personnel information system
4. Inventory management system

These applications will bring in efficiency of operations leading to a better control by the management over the entire functioning of the organization. The financial accounting system can be tailored to suit the specific requirement of the organization, so that it can provide timely information to reduce excess expenditures as well as obtain replenishment grant from the funding agencies. A separate accounts payable system can be implemented for regulating the payments to the suppliers of services and goods in the situation of having insufficient funds for disbursement.

While there can be several other activities within universities which can be computerized, the above are the major activities to be concentrated upon for efficient running of the universities. The recent trend in industries is to create and operate on central database of the entire organization. This has became possible for the industry since the availability of DBMS packages and 4GL tools in the Indian market. The cost, however, of putting the organization on the database is very high and also requires restructuring of responsibilities at various levels. Looking to the educational sector, it has been observed that no organization has totally gone the database way so far, because there is less flexibility of restructuring the responsibilities of the staff as well as high cost of procuring the hardware, software and its implementation. It would be desirable if some attempt is made to promote the use of database packages for implementation of an integrated information system. If necessary, the U.G.C. may specifically give one additional computer on the pattern of Delhi University and Jawaharlal Nehru University to be linked with the main computer for development of such integrated information system (Rammurthy 1989). Ideally the additional machine may be housed in the central computing centre with terminals available to the administrative staff.

2.2 Requirement of Hardware for Administrative Uses

Besides major activities described above, the areas which will need to be computerized by the management of the university are :

1. Estate and Maintenance management
2. Stores and purchase management

While selecting appropriate hardware one would need to consider the total size of the database, the response time requirement and number of service locations. Typically for a large affiliating university, this machine would be having about 15 terminals and storage of about 1000 MB. This configuration can be scaled down for a medium university to 8 terminals with 500 MB of storage. Each of the machine will require a good line printer. The smaller universities may be able to handle the task with PC/XT or AT in different locations. Connecting this machine with the main machine in the central computing facility will provide the advantage of load sharing, back up and optimum utilisation of the equipment.

The other major requirement on the campus of the universities which will come up as a result of computerization process is data communication. The departments will need data to be off loaded on to their work stations for local processing and analysis. The campuses of IISc and IIT Bombay are getting networked for distributed processing, remote access and data communication. The universities, it is expected, will also have to move in this direction in the near future.

The affiliated colleges have the major computing requirement in the area of admissions and examinations. Only for a large college, other areas which can be computerized gainfully are finance and payroll. These requirements can easily be met with by using the local PC machines being provided by the

U.G.C. However, there is a lot of document exchanges taking place between university and colleges. Communication links through telephone exchange may be difficult and in many places impossible at present, since several of the colleges are located in rural areas. Until efficient dialing system in the rural areas become available, the exchanges of important documents like examination results, list of students, list of staff, financial statement, etc. can be exchanged using floppies.

The hardware industry has grown considerably in the last 15 years. As a result, the quality of maintenance services offered by the vendor has also improved.. This is true for the mini computers supplied by the vendors. As regards micros and personal computers, several agencies are offering third party maintenance services. While in-house maintenance in the universities may not be feasible at this time due to limited hardware installed on the campus, this possibility may have to be explored when the number of micros and terminals grows within the campus. It has also been observed that for limited hardware, vendor maintenance is the best option. In the case of more but multivendor equipments, a third party maintenance will be a more useful arrangement. The in-house maintenance option should be explored in case where large number of micros, terminals and other hardware are to be maintained for continuous availability.

2.3 Software Requirement

In India, though a wide variety of hardware is available, its use in the educational sector, particularly in the universities has not reached a level where the management can think of replacing the existing software by appropriate packages implemented on RDBMS. However, considering the current trend, the administration of universities must go online on databases as soon as possible. The option available here is to procure the software through contract programming since no such packages are available off the shelf in the market which can be used by the universities directly. Alternatively such software can be developed in-house but that would be difficult with the limited number of technical staff and varieties of applications to be integrated. It would be desirable to procure such software through contract programming and entrusting the operational as well as maintenance task to the technical staff. The INFLIBNET too is considering this alternative to procure the software through contract programming. Similarly the colleges may have to think of getting software requirements satisfied through contract programming, since very few generalized packages are available in the market and which may not suit the specific requirements of the colleges.

To speed-up the process of computerization in the higher education sector in the country, the authorities may think of designating a large university in each state as responsible for development of the software using its own resources. This software would be readily usable by the universities and colleges in that state since there will be less variation in the mode of functioning of the university and the colleges within the state. This would also accelerate computerization process in that big university of the state which may become a model centre having computerized its administration.

2.4 Infrastructure Facilities

We have observed above that either the central facilities have to be used or the additional equipment for administrative computing should be linked with the central facility. The central computing centre, in turn, will be responsible not only for research and educational computing but also for the administrative support. The computing centres, therefore, should have adequate space so that different classes of users can use the facility comfortably and continuing education programs can be offered for the benefit of the administrative and academic community. The following is a suggested model for the space requirement under Type 'A' :

Table 7 Central Computer Centre Under Level 'A'

	Description	Total area in Square Feet
1	C P U Room	150
2	Terminal Room	250
3	Storage area	150
4	Work area for users, students and visitors	200
5	Technical Staff	300
6	Maintenance area	100
7	Administrative office	150
8	Lecture room (One)	400
9	Library	300
	Total : -	2000 Square Feet

The Computer centre must have its own library for use of the technical staff, users and faculty members. Similarly for offering training programmes to internal as well as external users, it would need provision for a lecture room. The space requirement for Level 'B' and Level 'C' can be increased proportionately considering the sitting arrangement for the total staff, enough work area for the users, number of terminals to be installed, the requirement for CPU room etc. For Level 'C', the minimum requirement of total space would be around 5000 square feet.

Option of window/split airconditioning, wherever necessary, may be considered in lieu of central airconditioning, since the latter requires continuous attention of maintenance staff which is not feasible in the university environment. While providing airconditioning, the CPU room, terminal room and the work area must be covered so as to have minimum temperature of around 75 degrees Fahrenheit when the equipment is up and running.

2.5 Training

The difficulty in creating the environment of end-user computing is mainly because of lack of training in the area of administrative computing. National Institute of Educational Planning and Administration (NIEPA) had recommended to the U.G.C. to conduct special courses for the principals of the colleges and administrative staff. It recommended about 80 courses to be conducted during 5 years plan period. The Association of Indian Universities (AIU) conducts courses for the administrative staff of the universities. The administrative staff college of India (ASCI) offers several courses on computer application for educational administrators.

Occasionally other institutions as well as universities have been offering courses on computer orientation to the administrative staff of universities. These courses are not of regular nature nor they are function–oriented. There is, therefore, a real requirement of initiating application specific courses for the administrators at few chosen locations. These locations can also be designated by the U.G.C. for conducting the courses for principals and administrative staff of the colleges. The NIEPA (NIEPA 1989) has recommended an outline for orientation programmes for principals and administrative staff. The application specific software required for the training, may either be developed in-house, transferred from their own Computer Centre or can be procured from external agencies.

The training of the principals and administrative staff of universities as well as colleges must be given high priority. Although, the recommendations have been made by NIEPA during 1989, such programmes could not be initiated by the U.G.C. till 1992. It is time now that the training locations be identified and the training programme started as early as possible which only will spread awareness amongst the principals and administrative staff leading to optimal use of computers in the universities and colleges. The Computer Training and Application Laboratory set up under this collaborative project has all the infrastructural facility and can take-up the task of training administrators in addition to the subject specific teachers training programmes.

2.6 Confidentiality and Security

With the computers acquiring ubiquitous status, the probability of computer crimes has increased many fold. This is also true for the educational institutions which handle the sensitive data of examinations and evaluation as well as of admissions on the computer. Though there is no definite reference available on computer crimes in India, a few cases have been reported in different institutions. It would, therefore, be proper to build up adequate safeguards against accidental data loss, intentional data manipulation and data misuse.

The computing centres must have built-in procedure for computer security as well as data recovery. Steps like periodical backups and preservation of multiple copies of important data files at different locations should be implemented with better control. Full insurance of the equipment must be taken out as a precautionary measure for planning of replacement/ repair in the event of an unexpected disaster. In India commercial services are not available for backup and storage of data in different locations. However, an arrangement can be worked out with another institution to store the backup. This would speed-up recovery process in the event of a disaster.

Of more concern to the educational institution is the possibility of computer crime. The computer crime in general involves fraudulent addition or manipulation of records or unauthorised access to important data files for the purpose of obtaining some benefit or financial gain. The better checks for possible computer crimes are audit trails, access controls and procedural controls. The heads of the computer centres and user departments must implement and monitor these controls.

3. Conclusion and Summary

A summary of the observations made in this chapter is given below :

1. Less use is being made in the area of administration by universities and colleges despite availability of the computers.
2. The payroll is the single application which has found its place in many institutions followed by admissions, examinations and accounting.
3. Very few universities and colleges have computerized their libraries. However, the INFLIBNET has taken up the task of implementing library systems and connection of libraries through a network.
4. The low use of computers in the area of administration is due to the fact that administrative staff has not been given proper training.
5. It is highly desirable to develop end-user computer environment in the universities and colleges. This would be possible only through proper function–oriented training programmes.
6. The better-off institutions like IIT and IISc have established campus networks and obtained connection on BITNET.
7. Considering the present industry trend, the administration of the universities must go online on databases.
8. The computing centres in the universities must be established as central facility under the direct control of Vice Chancellor/Pro Vice Chancellor as in the case of other departments.

9. The colleges must be encouraged to raise their own resources for installation of computers.

10. While providing assistance under the three types, the U.G.C. should encourage and provide some support for networking on the campus.

11. For larger universities, the U.G.C. may think of providing additional computer for development of integrated information system.

12. Data exchanges between universities and colleges should be attempted on floppies.

13. A large university in each State may be designated as responsible for development of software for the State universities and colleges.

14. The central computing facility should have minimum 2000 Sq.ft. area for type 'A' and around 5000 Sq. ft. for type 'C'.

15. The computing centre should be entrusted with the task of offering training to the principals, heads and administrative staff of universities as well as colleges.

16. The computer training and applications laboratory established under this project can be given the responsibility for conducting training programs for principals, heads and administrative staff in the initial stage.

Contributed by R. P. Soni

References

Gujarat University

Computer Scenario of Higher Education in India - Selected Case Studies. April 1992, Gujarat University.

INFLIBNET

Development and Establishment of Information and Library Network in 8th Five Year Plan. September 1991, INFLIBNET Programme, Ahmedabad.

Mehta J. M., Soni R. P.

"Use of Mechanical Aids in Examinations of Gujarat University", University News, April 1972, 16-18.

Mehta J. M., Soni R. P.

"Use of Mechanical Aids in Examinations", Management of Examinations. Association of Indian Universities, 1977.

NIEPA

Management of Computers in Colleges. Report of Meeting 25-27 May 1989, 6-10.

NISSAT

A Report on the feasibility study on automation and networking of science and technology libraries at Calcutta. 1989, NISSAT, New Delhi.

Parker, Dorn B.

Computer Security Management. Reston Publishing Co, 1981.

QED Information Sciences.

Critical Issues in Information Processing Management and Technology. 1989 QED Information Sciences Inc.

Rammurithy V.

"Computers in Financial Management- Experiences of Delhi University", University News, May 8, 1989, 12-16.

UGC

Computer Facilities and Human Resource Development at Universities/ Colleges - Status Report. March 1990, University Grants Commission.

.—. Status Reports presented at National Symposium on Computer in Educational Management. 20th January 1991, Vallabh Vidyanagar.

.—. Computer Centre facilities - IIT Kanpur Internal Report.June 1991.

CHAPTER 8

TECHNOLOGY STATUS AND PROCESS OF COMPUTERIZATION

In the preceding three decades, the computer technology has moved from single user batch processing to multiprogramming, and from mere multiuser timesharing to on-line interactive systems. The new architecture, known as Client/Server computing, which combines the power of all the computing resources, i.e., the powerful desktop micros, minis as well as mainframes in an organization leading to enterprise-wide computing, is on the horizon. It will dramatically affect the application development methods and end-user interfaces (Datapro 1992). Looking to the educational sector, the universities which opted for computerization in the seventies, have slowly moved from batch processing to multiuser timesharing. The colleges have gradually started acquiring some micros for the benefit of faculty and students. We will examine in this chapter, the type of hardware and software available in these organizations as well as in the country. Also the current technological developments will be reviewed and a model for computerization process will be presented at the end.

1. Present Status of Technology

1.1 Base Line Survey - Present Trend

Tables 1 and 2 present the scenario of equipments installed in universities and institutions in Gujarat state. All the six respondent universities have installed mini computers with number of terminals ranging from 4 to 23. At the time when survey was being conducted, Bhavnagar University was planning to establish a central computing facility. The North Gujarat University, which was established in 1988, still did not have a central computing facility; however, one of the constituent colleges did have computing equipment and the same was accessible to North Gujarat University. The Ayurved University, Jamnagar did have computing facility in the departments. Similarly, major institutes also have installed mini and mainframe systems. Out of such multiuser systems, five systems are from DEC and the rest either Intel 80386 or MC 68020 based systems. The others have installed work stations and PC range of equipment. It is clear that all the universities have installed multiuser mini computer systems. The equipment in the research institutes is more needbased than general computing machines. Whenever they need more computing power, the choice is towards higher end mini computers or large main frames.

Table 1 Type of Computer Installed in Universities of Gujarat

Name of University	Major Equipment Installed	CPU	No of Terminals	OS	Year of Install-ation
Gujarat University	VAX 11/730	VAX/730	8	VMS	1983
M.S. University	NELCO FORCE-20	68020	16	UNIX	1989
S.P. University	WIPRO 386	80386	23	UNIX	1988
South Gujarat University	HCL	68020	8	UNIX	1987
Saurashtra University	WIPRO 386	80386	8	UNIX	1988
Gujarat Vidyapith	NELCO FORCE-20	68020	4	UNIX	1987

The institutes, listed in Table 2, have teaching and/or research facilities in different disciplines like Management, Physical Sciences, Engineering and Technology, Pollution and Health, Space Science and Social Sciences. The computing equipment acquired by them is mainly used for education and research studies in the related subject areas.

Table 2 Type of Computer Installed in Major Institutes of Gujarat

Name of Institute	Major Equipment Installed	No. of Terminals	Year of Installation
Indian Institute of Management	Vax-11/750	12	1986
Physical Research Laboratory	DEC-10/91	44	1983
Indian Space Research Organization	Vax-11/780	35	1981
Institute of Plasma Research	Vax-8810	3	1989
Gujarat Institute of Area Planning	PC/AT,XT,PC	8	1987
Gandhi Labour Institute	PC/XT	2	1987
Centre for Environment Planning & Technology	WIPRO,APOLLO	6	1985
S.P. Institute of Economic Research	PC/AT,XT,PC	6	1986
National Institute of Occupational Health	PC/XT	1	1986
National Institute of Design	Macintosh	7	1988

The major software available on these systems is given in Table 3 below. The operating systems being used are VMS, UNIX, TOPS-10, MS DOS & APPLE DOS. The trend in software acquisition is to procure directly usable packages for problem solutions, application development and information systems development. There is more emphasis on such higher level software and 4GL tools than on conventional method of application development and problem solution through programme writing. Though no sophistication and integration of administrative systems implemented on RDBMS are visible in these organizations, they have attempted to satisfy internal needs through whatever software tools and techniques are at their disposal. It would be worthwhile to examine the trend of hardware, software acquisition and application refinement in these organizations in the years to come.

Table 3 Software Availability in Gujarat

Sr.No.	Software Components	Name/Brand
1	Operating System	MSDOS,UNIX,VMS, TOPS-10, APPLE DOS
2	Language Compilers	Fortran,Cobol,Basic,Pascal,C
3	Statistical Packages	SSP,SPSS,IMSL,Mathematica
4	DBMS	UNIFY,ORACLE,INGRES,Dbase, RDBMS
5	Graphics Packages	GKS,CAD,PCB design,IGL,AUTOCAD PLOT-10,GMR
6	Other Specialized Packages	Library Automation

1.2 Present Trend - Colleges

As many as 41 out of 77 (53.25%) respondent colleges in Tamilnadu, 3 out of 19 (15.78%) respondent colleges in Uttarpradesh and 43 out of 144 (29.86%) respondent colleges in Gujarat have installed computers. The majority of the Arts, Science and Commerce colleges of Gujarat which have computers, have installed PC range of equipment only. For them, it is a beginning in the area of learning as well as teaching computer science and computer use. Hence the usage is limited to the computer science teachers and the few students offering computer science as an optional subject. For other students as well as faculty members, this equipment is merely a demonstration equipment. This can be attributed to several factors, as brought out earlier, like insufficient number of machines, lack of awareness, lack of training, and so on. The Engineering colleges, however, have multiuser system and graphics equipment. The main reason for installation of such higher level equipment is that they offer B. E. programmes in Electronics, Computers, Instrumentation, Communication, etc. Out of about 4700 eligible colleges only 790 colleges were given two PC/XTs until March 1990, and by the end of VIII plan this figure is expected to be around 2400. But even by the end of VIII plan the scenario may remain the same in most of the colleges in terms of usage by faculty and staff unless firm plans for imparting training to faculty and administrative staff are implemented by the UGC in the coming years.

1.3 Case Studies - Present Trend

Table 4 lists major equipment available in the selected universities and institutions of India covered under case studies. The IITs and IISc are the institutions which have a heavy computing load for research as well as education and hence they need large main frame machines as campus computing facility. The other smaller institutions like VJTI and Bajaj Institute have smaller 68000 series machines. As regards universities, the scenario is the same as that of the universities of Gujarat except that the Anna University, Madras does have a variety of machines like IBM 360/44, PRIME 240, VAX 11/780 and other 80386 as well as 68000 series mini computers. An important observation from the case studies is that some of the premier institutes are developing networks on the campus and installing the facility of access to BITNET for the national as well as international academic communication. It can be stated with some degree of confidence that these premier research institutes are more dynamic in acquiring needbased hardware and software as well as implementing research and educational applications. The expected change in the case of universities will not be as fast as can be seen for the premier institutions.

Table 4 Major Equipments Installed by Institutions Covered under the Case Studies

Sr.No.	Name of the Institution	Major Equipment/Facility
1	Anna University, Madras	IBM 360/44, PRIME 240, VAX 11/780, MAGNUM II, WIPRO
2	Bharthiar University, Coimbatore	HCL 68020
3	Bombay University	ECIL 68020, TDC-316
4	University of Rajasthan, Jaipur	HCL 68020
5	Kerala University, Trivendrum	WIPRO
6	SNDT University, Bombay	NELCO, HP
7	Jamnalal Bajaj Insti., Bombay	MC 68000
8	I I T, Bombay	CDC CYBER 180, WIPRO, CAMPUS NETWORK, BITNET
9	I I T, Madras	SIEMENS 7584, 500 PCs, BITNET facility
10	Indian Institute of Science, Banglore	VAX 8810, CYBER 991, CAMPUS NETWORK BITNET facility
11	VJTI, Bombay	ESPL 68020, OASIS 80386, MAGNUM 68030

2. Impact of Technology on Educational Organizations

The institutions of higher education can be compared with other business organizations as relates to the management structure, internal operation and end-product to be delivered to the market. The business organizations have improved their operations in the changing competitive market conditions and have been able to maintain their existence with a better impact on the consumers mainly due to the use of information technology in all possible functional areas of the organization. Needless to say that there has been a significant impact of use of the computer technology on the business organizations, their products, their customers and the business and industrial society at large. The massive computerisation programmes of airlines and railways (DOE June 1992) have not only improved the passenger services but also have provided a greater degree of convenience to the agents and travelers in designing travel plans. The weather forecasting systems and remote sensing applications are helping to a great extent the rural farmers in their farming operations. Virtually every major area in Government where computerisation has been accepted has not only improved its functioning but has made indelible impression on its clientele.

The impact of computer technology on students, however, has not been significant. This is due to the inability of the educational organizations to cover all the students under computer science training programmes. This inability is generally due to the lack of financial resources. Nevertheless, wherever the students have been imparted computer skills, the feed back has been positive. It is generally observed that when the students come in contact with computers, they gradually realize the greater and unmatchable power the machine possesses. This brings in an improvement in discipline and changes the outlook of the students.

The computer technology has now become available to the teachers in the class room which can prove to be a very powerful media for imparting instruction. Use of multi media technology like video, audio, computer, LCD plates and large screen projectors is increasing in the instructional process in many countries. The authors have observed at Regina University that the classes in computer science are mostly conducted using computers with LCD plates and projector being used by the teacher in the class room. Though there is some controversy in the use of this technology in the class rooms of regular undergraduate and postgraduate courses, it is certain that use of this technology does produce better results and helps the teacher in imparting effective education (Stahl 1990, Chambers 1980, Balkovich 1985).

There is an implicit force in using computers in the area of research activities, as the research areas are being explored by all universities and institutions in the world, and maintaining a lead and clear distinction during the period of research is very important to every researcher and his organization. This is possible only if computer technology is used for information retrieval, speedy data analysis and high speed computing for number crunching problems. This technology, therefore, is unavoidable for all researchers and research organizations.

An observation was made in the earlier chapter that a streamlined and efficient management can act as a catalyst in the process of research activities. Management information systems through use of computers in transaction processing areas, office automation implementation and use of decision support tools can improve the administration manifold which in turn can encourage the faculty and students in using this technology in teaching, research and learning process. The key to improve the administration with increasing complexity is in the use of computer technology in high priority areas of administrative functions. The organizations in the near future will be under enormous pressure to handle information efficiently and effectively. And those that do not manage this transition may have to suffer extinction.

Straub and Wetherbe (1989) report in their study that :

> "Organizations in the 90s will be transformed by computers with user friendly interfaces which demonstrate high level intelligence. Among the scenarios to be carefully considered by technology investigating units is an office that processes, stores and searches personal, departmental and organizational level information by several orders of magnitude over the present. This information will result in knowledge workers exploring far beyond present information boundaries as a result of ease of use. This social change will be accompanied by vastly expanded communication links made possible by the networking technologies . . .
>
> The office of late 90s will have its staff surrounded by intelligent devices that speak, listen or interact with them to determine what is to be accomplished and how it is to be done. Contacts with other departments, other divisions, customers, vendors, and other organizations are made with little effort and without human intervention. Behind the scenes systems are being developed by system developers equipped with versatile and highly integrated software . . .
>
> In sum, where management understands the potential of these high return information technologies and takes steps to implement them, they will be able to respond more proactively to the expected turbulence and functional fragmentation of the 1990s."

As regards the future impact of computer technology on higher education, Jhon Sculley (1989), Apple's Chairman of the Board, comments in his report:

> "They (three core technologies -hypermedia, simulation and artificial intelligence) will allow us to set loose an avalanche of personal creativity and achievement. Once we have thousands of ideas to harvest, we may have chance once again to create a second Renaissance, perhaps every bit as important as the first, in the early part of the next century. It would represent a rebirth and revival of learning and culture unleashed by new technologies. It would bridge the gaps between the arts and sciences. And it would signify the emergence of an integrated environment for instruction and research.

It is an exhilarating time to live. I cannot think of any other time in history in which such profound change has gripped each decade. It is destined to be an eventful journey to the 21st Century. And there is no place that journey will be more exciting than the higher education. "

3. Technology Trend

The activity in the area of Electronic Computer Development started in 1954 at Tata Institute of Fundamental Research (TIFR) which resulted into a pilot model known as TIFRAC. This machine was commissioned in 1960. This pioneering project helped to spread computer consciousness amongst research workers in India. However, the technology of TIFRAC became obsolete by the time it was completed. Another project was taken up jointly by Indian Statistical Institute and the Jadavpur University, Calcutta. The machine which they developed was known as ISIJU-1 and became operational in 1966. It was again the R & D efforts of Atomic Energy Establishment which developed technology for a machine which was later on commercially manufactured by Electronics Corporation of India Limited (ECIL) at Hyderabad commencing early 1970. This initial tempo of indigenous development of computers got receded due to nonavailability of components and peripherals.

The use of computers by business and industry started around 1961. An IBM 1401 was installed at Esso Petroleum Company in 1961, an event that marked the beginning of use of computers in India. By 1970, India had around 120 computers installed in various organizations. During the 60s punch card oriented computers were installed in several educational and research institutions. Prominent amongst them were CDC 3600 at TIFR and IBM 7044 at IIT Kanpur. At the same time, several IBM 1620 machines too were installed in the country. Notable locations where these machines were installed, are Physical Research Laboratory, Ahmedabad, DRDL Hyderabad, University of Delhi, and Jamnalal Bajaj Institute, Bombay.

While the scientific computers had found acceptance amongst the scientific research and educational institutions, the business computer systems were considered to be primarily useful for labour saving applications and therefore did not find easy acceptance in the Indian environment. By the early 70s, computer applications in India had given impetus to R & D activities covering a wide range of fields such as structural engineering, power systems analysis, ballistics, nuclear physics, cryptography, demographic research, agricultural statistics and so on. However, the use of computers in the universities and technological institutions accounted for only 10% of the meagre computer population.

In the early 70s IBM started manufacturing unit record equipment in India and exported the range of card punch machines to international market. IBM also started marketing of refurbished 1401 machines from 1966 onwards. IBM supplied 360 series machines to various organizations which were imported from other countries. Another company operating in India at that time was International Computers and Tabulators Limited which later came to be known as ICL. This company too supplied refurbished machines in the Indian market. It was around 1970 when Electronics Corporation of India Limited (ECIL) decided to manufacture computers based on the design of Bhabha Atomic Research Centre, Trombay that indigenous manufacturing of computers started in India. The initial product was known as TDC 12 (Trombay Digital Computer), which was a 12 bit machine based on unibus architecture. ECIL later on produced 16 bit and 32 bit machines known as TDC 316 and TDC 332. The operations of multinationals such as IBM and ICL in India could not provide opportunities to other entrepreneurs, and as a result no significant technological developments took place in India during the span of their presence. In 1977, the Government announced new guidelines for participation in the equity by the foreign companies. IBM did not accept the new guidelines and therefore decided to withdraw its operations from India effective June 1978. The ICL accepted the guidelines and came to be known as International Computers India Manufacturing Limited (ICIM). Due to the encouraging guidelines, several companies were set up as subsidiary units by large industrial houses. The independent companies established were Computer Maintenance Corporation (CMC) whose charter was to provide continued maintenance services to the imported equipment, Hindustan Computers Limited (HCL) whose goal was to manufacture floppy based data entry and micro computers. Others were DCM Data Products, Operations Research Group (ORG), NELCO, UPTRON, PSI, etc. The initial systems rolled out by these companies were based on either Z-80 or Intel 8080 or their variants. All of them were 8 bit machines. The manufacturing of 16 bit machines based on micro processor chips started around 1981-82. By the end of 1980 the total installed base of computers in India consisted of around 500 systems (Banerjee 1987).

The new computer policy of November 19, 1984 aimed to encourage and promote appropriate use of computers in various industries and to fulfill the needs of the users to obtain computers either from indigenous sources or from abroad. Minimum configuration prescribed for import was 32 bit CPU, 1 MB main memory and disk capacity exceeding 300 MB. The import policy, however, has been revised from time to time in terms of minimum configuration and applicable duties. During the period 1985-1990, the total number of computers allowed to be imported by DOE is given in the following Table (Tripathi 1992).

Table 5 Import of Computers During 1985-90

Value of System	1985	1986	1987	1988	1989	1990
Above Rs. 200 Lakhs (Very large/ Super)	11	20	06	14	09	04
Between Rs. 200 and 30 Lakhs(Midi/Large)	48	57	20	82	10	07
Between Rs. 3 and 30 Lakhs (Minis)	126	157	147	196	162	65
Below Rs. 3 Lakhs (Micros)	40	190	95	160	75	07

The figures show a declining trend in imports largely due to indigenous availability of midi/large system from ECIL, ICIM and PSI; and also due to a wide availability base established for a range of micros, minis, workstations, DTP system, etc. apart from peripherals. The import of computers by the educational/R & D organizations constituted only 13% (by value) of total imports permitted during 1985-90 (Tripathi 1992). Through a notification in October 1992, the government has lowered the minimum limit for import of computers including PCs from Rs. 6 Lacs to 1.5 Lac. It is expected that this change will provide a benefit of choice to the end-users, but they will have to pay higher import duty at 146%.

The initial entry of PC was restricted due to its high cost which was at that time in the range of Rs. 1.50 to 2 lacs. After the changeover of Government in 1984, an encouraging computer policy emerged which provided a much needed impetus to the industry and several companies were established for manufacturing of PC range of equipment in India. The following table shows the computer population during the period 1981 to 1991 :

Table 6 Computer Population in India

Year	Large Systems	Percentage Growth	Minis/Micros	Percentage Growth
1981	56		486	
1982	100	78.57	520	7.00
1983	131	31.00	1717	230.00
1984	65	-50.38	3060	78.22
1985	148	127.69	7516	145.62
1986	261	76.35	29614	294.01
1987	116	-55.56	45872	54.90
1988	73	-37.07	60354	31.57
1989	98	34.25	91987	52.41
1990	265	170.41	95635	3.97
1991	206	-22.26	74500	-22.10

(Minis/Micros include Personal Computers)

Source : Computers Today, March 1992

The estimated total installation of micro computers is around 4 lacs. The growth rate has been significant during 1985-86 but declined in 1990 generally due to slump in the demand and increased cost of manufacturing. However, the estimated production for the year 1992-93 will be around 3,20,000 as indicated by DOE in its report of VIII five year plan. This may not be realistic considering the actual production of 1991, yet it can be definitely said now that in the changed economic situation, the production of micros may exceed 1,50,000 machines.

3.1 Micros & Local Area Networking

Indian companies supplied single user micros based on Intel or equivalent chips from NEC, such as 8088, 80286, 80386, 80386 SX and 80486. These are DOS machines and fully compatible for PC range of software available in India as well as in international market. The use of Windows has started only recently as it requires higher end 80386 or 486 platforms. LAN is a convenient method of resource sharing and suitable in office automation environment. NOVELL is the standard operating system used in LAN environment. Though Macintosh machines are available but the use is largely restricted to DTP applications.

3.2 Mini Computers

Multi processor systems from WIPRO, ORG and HCL have found wide acceptance in the market. Both kinds of architectures i.e. tightly coupled and loosely coupled processors are available in the market. These machines are based on 80386-486 or 68030. The machines come with EISA (Extended Industry Standard Architecture). Other super minis available are from Digital Equipment India Limited which supplies the MicroVAX 3300, 3400 and VAX 4000 series machines. Obviously, the operating systems on these machines are UNIX and VMS. These machines are capable of supporting around 50 terminals. As the machines use standard operating systems, a wide range of software is available from the vendors as well as third party dealers for varieties of applications.

3.3 RISC Machines

RISC machines entered India only about a year back. Such machines are available from HCL-HP which offers 9000 series based on HPRISC Chip, Tata Elxi based on RISC chip R3000, DRS/6000 using Sparc chip from ICIM, DEIL 5100 which uses R3000 chip and SUN micro system from WIPRO containing Sparc chip. As RISC technology has just entered the market, the prices are very high for entry level machines. It is expected that in the coming years this technology will be used as a good platform for implementation of RDBMS applications and the cost will come down with increased production of machines.

3.4 Large Systems

Other than the large RISC machine suppliers, Electronics Corporation of India (ECIL) located at Hyderabad manufactures mainframe computers known as Medha 900 series machines. Around twenty five such machines have been delivered by ECIL within the country to segments like defense, railways, banks and R & D organizations involved in transaction and seismic processing, large database management and simulation studies. The ICIM supplied S-39/ M-29 series machines and the PSI sold DPS 7000 mainframe class machines.

3.5 Work Stations

Work stations are mainly used for CAD/CAM applications. The Apollo and HP 9000 work station of HP, Sun work station from WIPRO, Decstation of DEIL, IRIS 4D from OMC and Roltastation from Rolta are main products available amongst other special engineering design machines.

3.6 Super Computers

All the super computers today being used in research and Government organizations have been imported from U.S.A. and Japan. These machines are mainly from Cray Research Corporation. The indigenous development of super computer was assigned to C-DAC which has now come out with a 256 node PARAM parallel super computer having peak computing power exceeding one Gflops/7500 Mips. It uses parallel disc array of over 20 Gbytes. The machine uses Inmos T800/T805 transputers. The machine is considered to be ideal for applications like image processing, computational fluid dynamics, oil reservoir modelling, seismic data processing, power system analysis, computational physics etc. The technology is being transferred to the industry by C-DAC and the machine is likely to be available in the Indian market shortly.

3.7 Computer Networks

During the last five years, several computer networks have come up in the country. The first network was established by Computer Maintenance Corporation for the purpose of offering computer communication and data transfer services to the business houses. Today this network known as INDONET consists of IBM 4361 located at Madras, Bombay and Calcutta. Remote terminal facilities are provided to various other cities in the country. The dedicated data link has transfer rate of 4800 BPS. The network provides specialized application software useful for mathematicians and engineers in the area of simulation and mathematical analysis applications.

Another network was established by National Informatics Centre (NIC) whose headquarter is at Delhi with three other main computer facilities located at Pune, Bhuvaneshwar and Hyderabad. This network provides terminals at State capitals and District head quarters. The communication is through a micro earth station using the geostationary satellite. An amount of Rs. 160 crores has been invested on equipment and staff so far. The NICNET provides services to the Government departments of finance, agriculture, water, human resources, industry, commerce etc.

The project titled "Education and Research in Computer Networking" (ERNET) has been taken up by DOE along with 7 other academic/research institutions. The ERNET envisages setting up of local networks in the institute campuses and interconnecting them through a satellite link to form a wide area network. This academic network is connected to several networks worldwide like BITNET, ARPANET, CSNET etc. The participating institutions are developing software for a reliable networking environment. More than 70 institutions are now connected to ERNET for access to each other as well as to international academic and research networks. The range of services provided is being extended to file transfer, remote log-in, directory services and database access apart from electronic mail which is available to all users. A significant work done by the participating institutions is development of OSINET software which is an implementation of ISO's Open Systems Interconnect (OSI) model for LAN environment.

Apart from the above networks, several other networks have also been established such as OILNET, BANKNET, SIRNET (Scientific and Industrial Research Network) besides airlines network, which was installed in 1980. Another network is the PRESSNET where newspapers are connecting their head quarters with regional offices. The I-NET, established by Department of Telecommunication, provides fast data transfer services between several cities at the rate of 9600 BPS.

3.8 INFLIBNET

U.G.C. has promoted INFLIBNET programme initially with an outlay of Rs. 150 crores for establishing a full fledged library network covering universities, R & D laboratories, colleges and resource centres. It is expected to support 500 libraries and information centres. This will be done with the help of a computer communication network making use of both satellite as well as terrestrial means of communication. Due to resource crunch a revised plan has been prepared which now envisages an outlay of 91.5 crores and a reduction of satellite nodes from 400 to 220. The project will be implemented during 1992 to 1997. The INFLIBNET will have one national centre, 2 regional centres, 170 university libraries, 3 UGC information centres, 65 document resource centres and 160 R & D/sectoral centres interconnected through computer networks. The INFLIBNET will provide the following services:

1. Cataloging
2. Bibliographic data base service
3. Document supply service
4. E Mail services
5. Automation of local library functions
6. Inter library service etc.

The headquarter of INFLIBNET is currently located in Ahmedabad and will implement the project in two phases. During the first phase of three years it will identify the locations, acquire hardware, communication links and implement automation in national as well as regional centres linking about 150 universities, 15 sectoral centres and 15 document resource centres. If implemented successfully, the capability of the network will be enhanced to cover the entire country in the 9th plan period (1997-2002).

3.9 Technology Development

The Department of Electronics is implementing timebound projects through separate institutions like Centre for Development of Advance Computing (C-DAC), IITs and IISc. Significant developments are recorded in parallel computing, artificial intelligence and expert system application and computer networking.

The C-DAC has developed the PARAM parallel machine in the class of super computers. The technology is being transferred to commercial organizations and very soon the machine should be available in the Indian market.

The C-DAC has also developed Graphics based Intelligent Script Technology (GIST) card for use on the DOS machines. It uses an indigenously designed special purpose VLSI chip called GIST-9000. This technology provides the capability of input and display in all Indian languages, on PCs and the other computers. The GIST technology also provides facilities for word processing, DTP, TV subtitling, Multi-lingual telex, Teleprinters and hardcopy printouts in Indian languages (Kutty 1991). Through the use of this card, the user can easily use Indian scripts on the computer for word processing and data base operation. Most of the EMRC centres are now using this GIST technology in video production as well as data presentation in Indian languages.

Under Knowledge Base Computer Systems programmes (KBCS) several expert systems like Tanker scheduling, Diagnostic systems for multi computer systems, Intelligent Medical case history and family health guide system, Speech recognition system, Optical character reader for Devnagari script have been developed. Work is in progress using KBCS technology in the area of scheduling applications in transport sector, diagnostic system for telephone exchanges, ITS for industrial and specialized training, vision system for industrial inspection, etc.

Another programme initiated by DOE for technology development in Indian languages has the objectives of developing technology tools to facilitate information processing in Indian languages and multi lingual knowledge systems. Tools for human machine interface systems, machine translation system, language learning system and natural language processing systems will be developed. Specific emphasis has been given to the study of Sanskrit and its relevance to computers. The Bureau of Indian Standards has already brought out the Indian Script Code for Information Interchange (ISCII) to ensure uniformity and transportability of various products being developed in India.

4. Export of Hardware and Software

The Department of Electronics has established software technology parks with all infrastructural facilities at various locations in the country. The technology parks at Pune, Banglore and Bhuvaneshwar are already in operation. Companies like PSI Data Systems, Motorola, CEGELEC, Verifone, Eurolink, Transtek and Hughes Software are participating in the software export activities. The following table gives export figures for data processing systems and computer software during the period 1981 to 1990.

Table 7 Export of Computer Hardware and Software (In Million Rupees)

Year	Data Processing Equipment	Computer Software
1981	16.53	59.06
1982	16.09	129.10
1983	220.23	186.48
1984	466.02	291.74
1985	345.00	340.05
1986	376.00	490.00
1987	406.89	705.00
1988	1378.00	1010.00
1989	2430.00	1569.68
1990	2074.61	2000.05

Source : Guide to Electronics Industry in India - 1992
Department of Electronics

Though there is a great potential in the field of computer software export, the contribution of India was only 3500 million rupees out of a total global market of $ 175 billion. According to Electronics and Computer Software Export Promotion Council, the world market is expected to cross $ 300 billion by the year 2000. The software technology parks are expected to perform very well due to the expanding global software market. The major winning factors for the anticipated better performance in software export are low labour cost, technical competence, Government incentives and acceptance of English in software development (Computers Today September 1992).

5. Impact of Government Policy Decisions

With the economic liberalization programme launched by the Government many foreign companies have decided to come to India and set up joint holding companies for manufacturing of hardware and export of hardware and software to other countries. Notable amongst them is the IBM Company which is now setting up its manufacturing operation at Banglore in collaboration with Tatas. The new company known as Tata Information System will be manufacturing PS/2 range of equipment and later RS 6000 RISC based machines mainly for the export market. HP has also joined hands with HCL and started marketing RISC based machines. The strategic alliances between Apple Computers with DEIL for manufacturing of Macintosh range, Compaq with Microland Electronics, Dell with PCL for manufacturing and distribution of high end PCs, are the results of a changed economic situation in the country. The presence of these companies together with the plans of HCL-HP and DEIL to manufacture Vectra and DECPC respectively will, surely, help the end-user to acquire quality products from the indigenous market. It is expected that the use of computers will increase due to these policies of the Government and computer industry's growth will turn out to be very impressive in the coming years.

6. VIII Plan Projections

The estimated production of computers during VIII plan, i.e. up to 1995, which was worked out before Gulf crisis and economic liberalization, is given in the following table :

Table 8 Production Estimates of Computers : (Quantity in nos.)

Computers	1991-92	1992-93	1993-94	1994-95
SUPER	2	2	4	5
LARGE	90	115	150	220
MINI	1215	1660	2140	2800
MICROS	2,40,000	3,20,000	4,00,000	5,00,000

Source: Working Group, Department of Electronics

The ET&T had come out with low cost PCs during 1989-90. It is now enlarging its range by adding PC/AT 286, 386, 386 SX, 486 and 486 SX. With more and more companies offering products at slashed down prices, the installed base of micros will increase significantly and provide boost to the software industry as well as software export programme.

In the educational sector the UGC plans to distribute computers to universities and colleges as under :

Table 9 Addition of Computers in Universities & Colleges

	Status	Universities	Colleges
1	Already received computer from UGC	104	790
2	Will receive computers during 8th plan	38	1600
3	Balance without computers after 8th Plan (Approxly.)	37	3600

Even through best efforts from UGC, a few universities and several colleges will remain without computers by the end of 8th plan. The serious consideration which is required by the planners is to mobilize resources for bringing this technology to the colleges and universities of the country and upgrade this technology in pace with the developments in the industry so that the faculty and students of the institutions of higher education can get maximum benefit of the current technology.

7. Role of Technology in Distance Education

The Indira Gandhi National Open University (IGNOU) and few State Open Universities are actively engaged in distance education. IGNOU offers various courses in Management, Library Science and Computers as well as undergraduate bachelor programmes. There are study centres established in various states which are controlled by the regional centres. The communication with the students is through postal services.

The UGC broadcasts educational programmes for the benefit of undergraduate students studying in different colleges of the country. This is known as country-wide class room programme. The programmes are telecast on the national channel. Taking advantages of this infrastructure, IGNOU also telecasts educational video programmes for the benefit of its students spread all over the country (IGNOU Newsletter May 1992).

Experiments were conducted recently in one way video and two way audio telecast known as video conference. Apart from this, no use is being made at present of the computer technology in distance education. This is due to several factors such as lack of infrastructural facility for communication like ISDN, unaffordable cost of micros, high cost of installation of computer networks and so on. However, the multi-media approach, which integrates newer information technologies including computers into existing education practices are being experimented by several sites engaged in distance education elsewhere around the world. They are trying to bring education and training opportunities into the environment of home or the workplace for delivering instruction and to support the learning processes (Bacsich 1986).

8. Manpower Development Efforts

With an increasing population of computers in the country, the need of the industry, government and other sectors for skilled manpower trained in computer technology has also increased. The estimated requirement of the manpower and the output from present institutions during VIII plan period, is given in the following table:

Table 10 Manpower Requirement and Supply

	Level	Requirement		Supply from Formal
		Domestic	Software Export (*)	Institutes.
A.	Formal Courses			
	Ph.D.	250	-	240
	M.Tech.	14,500	4,000	2,500
	B.Tech.	24,000	12,000	7,000
	MCA	40,000	20,000	18,000
	DCA	99,000	60,000	80,000
	DCE	18,500	4,000	7,000
	Total	1,96,250	1,00,000	1,14,740
B.	Vocational Courses	6,70,000		
C.	Short-term Courses	16,40,000		

* The manpower requirement for software export is estimated on the basis of the assumption that the software export will touch Rs. 2,000 crore mark by the end of 8th plan.

Source: (1) Report of 8th Plan Study Team on Manpower Development, Department of Electronics.

(2) Report of Working Group, Department of Electronics.

The DOE plans to reduce the shortfall at the lower level including vocational courses by covering more Polytechnics and Industrial Training Institutes and charging them with the responsibility to initiate the training programs for data entry operators, computer operators, data processing assistants, computer maintenance technicians, programmer assistants, etc. The combined output is expected to be about 20,000. However, the requirement at this level can at best be met by retraining the existing employees. A large number of private institutions are providing training at this level. At higher level, it is the responsibility of the formal education sector, to reduce the gap between demand and supply. But this sector may not be able to do so in near future, since it is dependent largely on the government for additional financial resources. The output from this sector will increase only marginally, as only few new centres for MCA (10) and B.E./B.Tech (1) programs were permitted during 1990-91. Therefore, DOE has implemented a scheme known as DOE Accreditation scheme, under which, private training institutions having approved level of infrastructure are given accreditation for conducting 'O' level, 'A' level, 'B' level and 'C' level courses as per the syllabus and teaching standards laid down by the department. The examinations for 'O' and 'A' level courses are being conducted by Computer Society of India. The examinations for 'B' and 'C' level will be conducted by the Institution of Electronics and Telecommunication Engineers. These courses are considered equivalent to Certificate, Diploma, Graduate and Masters level in computer science respectively. More than 200 private institutions in the country have been given accreditation for conducting 'O' level courses.

The 8th plan study team of DOE recommends a multi-pronged strategy for manpower development. According to its recommendations, the strategy should specifically be targeted at:

(a) Improving the infrastructure and quality of output of the existing institutions.

(b) Expansion of teachers training programs (in computer science) to reduce the shortage of teachers. The teachers of other disciplines, too need to be trained as computers are invading all the other disciplines.

(c) Expansion of education and training base to reduce the gap between demand and supply.

The higher education institutions, therefore, have the special responsibility to improve the skill base of training by upgrading the existing hardware or by employing the state of the art hardware and software technology, and address the manpower needs of local industry as well as software export market. In addition, they should offer continuing training programs for teachers of all the disciplines, so that they become equipped to use this potential technology profitably in education, research and administration.

9. A Model for Computerization Process

We found from our studies that no specific guidelines exist for computerisation in the educational institutions at present. The funding agencies were making only general recommendations and the other decisions were left to the institutions themselves. The recommendations were only in terms of creating infrastructural facilities but not for the operational and service aspects. An attempt is being made here to prepare a model containing observable guidelines and strategic issues to help the intending university going in for computerisation.

9.1 Define Strategic Issues

The institutions of higher education are experiencing an unprecedented level of stress during the last few years. The high rate of inflation, uncertain and insufficient Government support, and continuous increase of student population have challenged functioning of many colleges and universities.

The survival or success of an organization depends in a large measure on the extent to which it looks to the future, identifies the opportunities in the turbulent world around, and adopts its special competencies to those opportunities. The strategy, therefore, is fundamental means for an organization to achieve a match with its environment. The educational organizations therefore, should set up their goals and define desired outcomes. This should be followed by specification of resources which can be deployed for realization of the goals (Arns and Curran).

The educational institutes can consider applying the computer technology in the following areas ·

1. Research computing
2. Educational computing
3. Instructional computing
4. Administrative computing

The Institution, after looking to its position amongst broader set of similar institutions, must define the priorities for the end-use and develop its strategy for acquisition, installation and operationalisation of computing facility. After prioritisation, the issues involved in each of the areas should be identified. Such issues could be like volume of application, complexity of application, extreme dependency on external agencies, improved services to the students community, support facilities to the student of Computer Science, need for imparting training to high level as well as low level staff, desire of bringing innovations in the educational process, level of communication facilities to be established and so on. The objective should be to gain competitive advantage in the educational area.

9.2 Pool Resources Together

It would not be appropriate to depend only on the funding agencies for the requirements of computing facilities. Various resources in the form of funds or support services available for computerisation of administration, research grants, and special fees charged from students for use of computing facility should be pooled together so that the same can be used for acquisition and maintenance of the computing facility.

The trend of bifurcating the central computing facility into academic computing facility and administrative computing facility has started reversing in the recent years. This can be observed from the history of computing at the University of Regina. Such single facility on the campus not only ensures continuous availability but also becomes a nucleus to which everyone can look for help and service whenever required. Ample use of micros can be made through distributed networks, whereas the central facility can be looked upon as a platform for voluminous and compute intensive research and administrative task. The central facility will act as a repository of all the databases and these would provide a better control and easy maintenance. The Director of the computing services, by whichever designation he is called, should be directly responsible to the Vice Chancellor or Pro Vice Chancellor as the case may be.

9.3 Plan Layout Carefully

The physical layout for the computing services should be so planned as to provide ample scope for expansion of facilities and growth of services. The location should be easily accessible by all the users i.e. students, faculty and administrative staff. The design must consider risk factors like water logging in heavy monsoon, vulnerability in case of student unrest, etc. The physical design must account for all the general requirements like space for staff, administration, good library, besides special requirements like a conference hall and class rooms.

The System Manager and visitors should get a full view of the user area including the equipment installed. An efficient building design may reduce the total requirement of airconditioning for the user area.

9.4 Select Current Technology

In planning for acquisition of hardware, the important issues to be considered are Reliability, Maintainability and Expandability. The capacity planning can be worked out by estimating the current as well as projected computing requirements. But the choice should be towards current and state of the art technology. High rate of obsolescence may increase the cost of operations or impose over heads in maintenance in the future. Any innovative product, until it settles down in the market, should be avoided as the risk involved may be very high. This has happened with many educational institutions where the equipment could not be used because they were the victims of the newly designed product pushed by the vendors. The institutions can not think of replacing the hardware after a short cycle of just 3 to 4 years. It is necessary, therefore, to check for the availability of maintenance services as well as components and spares for the planned period of use. It should also be possible to upgrade the computer system as and when more financial allocation is made or when acute shortage of computer power is realized.

9.5 Consider Distributed Computing

For a very wide campus housing different departments at distant locations, the option of distributed computing may be considered seriously. This of course, would depend on the quantum of local computing requirements at each of these locations. The distributed computing is easily accessible by the users at the respective locations but the cost of the operation and maintenance is likely to be very high. Therefore, this option will need more financial resources for capital expenditure as well as for recurring expenditure.

Alternatively, such sites may be provided with few micros hooked up to the main computing facility, which would be useful for local processing as well as remote log-in.

9.6 Define Application Priorities

After installation of computer hardware, the authorities are likely to face enormous demands from different user groups. The initial phase normally witnesses acute shortage of manhours, since this is the time when applications have to be designed and implemented. The same amount of manhours may not be necessary once the applications settle down. In order to have systematic and planned growth, the strategy of prioritisation of applications must be adopted.

In deciding the priority the applications which are likely to have a greater impact on the functioning of the organization should be taken up immediately and routine data processing application should be considered last. The approach however, must be to integrate all administrative applications and to provide easy access to versatile packages for research and educational computing. The other approach, would be to concentrate on strategic systems rather than operational or financial systems. The strategic system may be described as the ones which provide a new thrust to the organization and its advantage can be best realized through the use of information technology (Buckland 1989).

9.7 Buying Software Against Development of Software

For specialized common applications like library information system, students admission, an option of buying software packages should be given priority over development of such software. Development of software is a very very lengthy process and results into enormous delays and possible additional expenditure. It would also be strange to redevelop whatever has already been developed and readily available in the market. Therefore, wherever possible, standard application software should be procured and utilized.

Another option available is to entrust the task for software development to an experienced external agency. It would be worth while in the initial stage to get the application software developed by an external agency under a time bound programme. This software will be more specific and will greatly satisfy the immediate needs of the organization. As there is full possibility of source code being available, further modifications and maintenance can be easily carried out in-house.

9.8 Initiate User Training Programmes

User training is a very important task which directly affects the usage level of the technology. The technical staff will have to be given the orientation on the features and technical aspects of the equipment being acquired. The faculty, similarly, will have to be oriented towards the computational use of the facility. The administrative staff should get orientation to important application packages and data base access. For each set of users separate documentation should be generated and initial training programmes should be arranged, if necessary, with the help of the supplier or the designated agencies.

Attempts should be made to organize general appreciation programmes for the high level staff so that they can understand new computing environment, its complexities as well as profitable uses.

9.9 Service Oriented V/s Control Oriented Approach

It is very important that users access the facility without any impediment or restrictions nor there should be delays in satisfying their requirements. Prompt attention to their needs will encourage all classes of users to make best use of the available facility and thus will improve the environment on the campus. Continuous efforts must be made to allocate various resources like staff, computer time, consumables as well as consultations even during the extended shifts. Efforts must also be made to run the central facility 24 hours a day.

9.10 Set up an Advisory Committee

An Advisory Committee should be formed for setting up guidelines in respect of development of campus computing plan, acquisition of hardware and software as well as for upgradation strategies. The Committee can also recommend service improvement plans. The role of this committee should be only of advisory in nature and not of controlling the operations of the computing facility.

9.11 Develop End-User Computing Environment

In contrast to past computing practices, the information processing today is once again becoming the responsibility of local operating department. A wide range of hardware as well as software tools is available which can be connected on the network and used directly by the end-users. The role of end-user is to directly use the available facility with very little assistance from the technical personnel. The concept of end-user computing attained prominence after IBM Canada's experiment with Information Centre (Wetherbe 1985).

Use of 4GL tools and the relational databases greatly facilitated bringing in the environment of end-user computing. With little training, the user can himself put queries to the database, produce reports from the database or manage/update the database as per his own requirement. Similarly researchers can easily use an interactive application package where only parameters have to be passed and data files have to be supplied. However, full support in terms of initial training or help in critical situation must be extended to keep all the users well satisfied. It must be emphasized that the task of the users must be accomplished by themselves. With limited staff at central facility, the expectation of supporting development, modification and continuous processing by this staff is no longer valid and neither practical. Hence, the traditional support cannot be extended. Further, all developmental activities must become user centered. "If the users can not do it themselves, then it cannot be done", implies that all sort of changes in the user interface must be carried out to make it more userfriendly (James E. B.).

9.12 Networking is Next Step

With growing computing requirement, the institutions are likely to set up departmental facilities and install micros for local processing. The software licensing policy usually allows only one CPU where it can be installed. The other users who need to access such proprietary software will find difficulties as they will have to move to the location where it is available. There will be further difficulties in transfer of data files from one machine to another.

Networking of campus computers basically addresses these problems. In addition, networks provide remote log-in facility to any computer from any locations on the campus. While the central system should become the backbone system, the others connected to it can also function as alternate sites in case of increasing computing load or malfunctioning of any of the systems. The faculty and students will find it immensely useful. This will open up communication possibilities not only within the campus but with international academic communities as well. Serious consideration, therefore, should be given to connect computers to establish campuswide network facilities for electronic mail, file transfer, remote log-in and operating the bulletin boards.

9.13 Electronic Data Interchange (EDI) with Colleges

In the affiliating universities, all colleges can not expect to install minis or powerful machines and get connected to the network, due to severe restriction of finance. This being so, a beginning must be made atleast in the area of document exchanges between university and colleges which have installed micros. The current procedure of using postal services for paper borne documents should be discontinued, instead, documents must be exchanged through media like floppies, accompanied by, if necessary the print-outs. This will save time as reentering the contents for further processing and analyses will not be necessary. After some experience is gained in using this method, attempt should be made to electronically transfer the data files using STD facilities on telephone line. The colleges may be asked to install modems along with computers for this purpose. The experience gained by colleges will help them in using the INFLIBNET communication facility effectively.

9.14 Continue Training Programmes

The central computing facilities of the universities have a direct responsibility to generate computer consciousness amongst the faculty, staff and students on the campus as well as of the colleges. While it may not be possible to offer training programmes to the students on a regular basis, it must run specialized training programmes for the faculty members and the administrative staff. This activity must continue until it is found that no further training is necessary and all the members of staff have been covered. Arrangements can be worked out for financial support to these activities in consultation with colleges, university or funding agencies. Without such training programmes, the spread and use of the computer technology will remain very slow which in turn will affect the end-product i.e. the students coming out of these institutions.

9.15 Computing Must Become Cost Conscious

All the users must become aware of all the costs associated with computer use. Given our situation with scarce resources, this would be all the more necessary. Computing centre must educate the users about the increasing cost of operations. The users must know about hardware cost, software cost and the maintenance cost. The user will definitely appreciate this and will become cost conscious while using the resources, especially the consumables and communication facility. With decreasing hardware prices, high computing cost should invite a serious analysis of the efficiency of the computer use.

9.16 Mobilise Resources

The computing centres must plan for future upgradation and acquisition of specialized software. It would become difficult for the funding agencies to support such activities on a continuous basis. Therefore, it is imperative that the computing centres start planning for mobilising additional resources. The opportunities available to the computing centres of educational institutions in generating resources by selling computer time have diminished. However, new opportunities are available today in the area of offering specialized training programmes to the staff of business and industrial houses. This task seems to be massive one and good opportunities are available for computing centres. The other sources available are, development of special softwares for external organizations, offering technical consultation services and preparation of feasibility reports. The computing centres can also help industry in setting up local computing facilities. These all available opportunities must be seized to plan for future expansion of the computing activities on the campus.

- Contributed by R. P. Soni

References

Arns R. G and Curran F. A.
"Information System Requirements for Strategic Planning and Strategy Implementation" University of Vermont.

Avashia, Dhiren
Distance Education through Satellite-Canadian Experience, 1992, University of Regina.

Bacsich P., Kaye A. & Lefrere P.
"New Information Technologies for Education and Training - A Brief Survey" Oxford Surveys in Information Technology Vol.3, 271-318, Oxford University Press, 1986.

Balkovich Edward, Lerman Steven and Parmelee.
"Computing in Higher Education: The Athena Experience" Communication of ACM, November 1985, 1214-1224.

Banerjee U.K.
Computer Management and Planning, Tata McGraw-Hill, New Delhi, 1987.

Bhatkar, Vijay P.
Advanced Computing, Tata McGraw-Hill, New Delhi, 1991.

Blackmun, Hunter and Parker.
User Support for Evolving Technologies in Higher Education, University of North Carolina, December 1987.

Bowonder B. and Monish Singh.
"Information Technology: State of the Art", Electronics Information and Planning, May 1992, 397-428.

Buckland, John A.
"Strategic Information System", Critical Issues in Information Processing Management and Technology, Vol. I, QED Information Sciences, 1989, 2-68.

Chambers, Jack A. and Sprecher, Jerry W.
"Computer Assisted Instruction: Current Trends and Critical Issues", Communication of ACM, June 1980, 332-342.

Cotterman W.W and Kuldeep Kumar.
"User Cube: A Taxonomy of End Users", Communication of ACM, November 1989, 1313-1319.

Datapro
"All about Client/Server Architecture", Computers Today, December 1992, 59-65.

DOE
Guide to Electronic Industry in India 1992, Department of Electronics, Government of India.

DOE
Annual Report 1991-92. Department of Electronics, Government of India.

DOE
Report of the Working Group. Eighth Five Year Plan 1990-95 Electronics Industry, Department of Electronics, Government of India.

DOE
"Role of Electronics in Tackling National Priorities" Electronics Information and Planning, Department of Electronics, June 1992, 451-467.

Friedman E. A.
"The Wired University", IEEE Spectrum, November 1984, 115-120.

Gujarat University
Computer Scenario of Higher Education in India - Selected Case Studies, April 1992, Gujarat University.

Heeks, Richard
"Past and Future Conditions for Exports of Software from India", Electronics Information and Planning, February 1992, 240-246.

INFLIBNET
Development and Establishment of Information and Library Network in 8th Five Year Plan, September 1991, INFLIBNET, Ahmedabad.

James E. B.
"Small is Beautiful: The Next Ten Years in University Computing", SIGUCCS Newsletter XVI/3.

Joshi S. R.
Satellite for Higher Education : An Evaluative Study of UGC Talkback Experiment, 1992, DECU, ISRO Ahmedabad.

Kutty, Krishan K.K
"Computers and the Indian Languages", Electronics Information and Planning, December 1991, 123-129.

Rao PVS and Sadanandan P.
Modern Trends in Information Technology, Tata McGraw-Hill, New Delhi, 1988.

Sculley, Jhon
"The Relationship between Business and Higher Education: A Perspective on the 21st Century", Communication of ACM, September 1989, 1056-1061.

Stahl W.
Evaluating the Electronic Blackboard, University of Regina, 1990.

Straub D. W. and Wetherbe J. C.
"Information Technologies for the 1990s: An Organisational Impact Perspective", Communication of ACM, November 1989, 1328-1339.

Tripathi R.C.
"Import of Computers in India - An Overview", Electronics Information and Planning, March 1992, 325-332.

UGC
Computer Facilities and Human Resource Development at Universities/ Colleges, Status Report, University Grants Commission, March 1990.

Wetherbe J.C. and Leitheiser R.L.
"Information Centres: A Survey of Services, Decision, Problems, and Successes", Journal of Information Systems Management, Vol. 2, No.3, 1985, 3-10.

Yaseen P.A. Mohd.
"I-NET and Beyond", Telematics India, March 1992, 24-26.

APPENDIX-A

Part-I Questionnaire For University

APPLICATIONS AND SOCIAL IMPACT OF COMPUTER TECHNOLOGY IN HIGHER EDUCATION

(A DESIGN MODEL FOR A COMPUTERIZING UNIVERSITY)

Guidelines for Filling the Questionnaire

1. There are two parts to this questionnaire. You are requested to fill in both the parts.
2. There are several questions against which the possible response categories are given in the questionnaire. Please circle one or more appropriate code(s) indicating your response. For some other questions you may have to write the relevant information in the space provided.
3. Wherever your opinion is sought please write a few lines clearly and legibly.
4. Please skip whatever is not applicable.

Name of the respondent ______________________

Postal Address ______________________

____

____

Telephone No. (office) ____________

Designation ____________

Sex ____________ Age ____________

Educational Qualifications ____________

Faculty/School ____________ Subject ____________

QUESTIONNAIRE

NOTE : This questionnaire is in two parts. Part - I of the questionnaire is to be filled in by the Registrar of the University or any other official designated by him/her. Part - II of the questionnaire is to be filled in by the head of the computer centre in the university. The university which does not have any computer facility of its own, part - II of the questionnaire will be "not applicable" and hence "blank".

PART - I.

(To be filled by the Registrar of the University)

1. **Name of the University** ____________________

2. **Year of establishment** ____________________

3. **Statutory status of the University**

1.	State Government
2.	Central Government
3.	Any other (specify)

4. **Type of University**

1.	Unitary
2.	Affiliatory
3.	Unitary and affiliatory
4.	Deemed university

5. **Total no. of University departments** ____________________

6. **Total no. of affiliated colleges** ____________________

7. **Total no. of recognised institutes** ____________________

8. **Total no. of approved institutes** ____________________

9. Please indicate by placing tick marks in the appropriate cells in the following table the regular courses offered by the University in its affiliated colleges, recognized/approved institutes or University departments. (Please do not write anything in the cells which are not applicable.)

Level / Faculty/School	Certificate	Diploma	Undergraduate	Postgraduate	M.phil.	Doctorate
1. Science						
2. Commerce						
3. Arts						
4. Computer Science						
5. Home Science						
6. Library Science						
7. Engineering						
8. Management						
9. Agriculturc						
10. Medicine (alp.)						
11. Ayurveda						
12. Pharmacy						
13. Nursing						
14. Architecture						
15. Planning						
16. Fine Arts						
17. Design						
18. Education						
19. Law						
20. Naturopathy						
21. Others (specify)						

10. Please mention the total number of students enrolled in the various examinations conducted by the University during the last academic year (1988-89).
(We need information separately for males and females but if this information is not readily available, give the total figures.)

Level	Full time			Part time			External		
	M	F	Total	M	F	Total	M	F	Total
Certificate									
Diploma									
Undergraduate									
Postgraduate									
M.phil.									
Doctorate									

11. Please indicate by placing tick marks the levels and the faculties/school for which University has a centralised admission system .

Level / Faculty/School	Certificate	Diploma	Under-graduate	Post-graduate	M.phil.	Doctorate
1. Science						
2. Commerce						
3. Arts						
4. Computer Science						
5. Home Science						
6. Library Science						
7. Engineering						
8. Management						
9. Agriculture						
10. Medicine (alp.)						
11. Homoeopathy						
12. Ayurveda						
13. Pharmacy						
14. Nursing						
15. Architecture						
16. Planning						
17. Fine Arts						
18. Design						
19. Education						
20. Law						
21. Naturopathy						
22. Others (specify)						

12. State briefly how the centralised admission procedure is organized. (If it is computerised please give details.)

____

____

____

____

13. State briefly how the admission procedure operates where there is no centralised system of admission ?

____

____

____

____

____

14. Please describe the procedure the University follows in deciding the final examination schedule. How long before the final examination is the schedule available ?
(If it is computerised please give details)

____

____

____

____

____

15. Please indicate the total number of faculty members in the university departments.
(Please write equivalent grade of your university)

Grade	Lecturer	Reader	Professor
Sex			
Male			
Female			
Total			

16. Total annual budget of the University for 1988-89 : ____________

17. If your University has an Academic Staff College, please give the following details regarding the number of training programmes organized by the Academic Staff College so far and the number of participants in such programmes.

a. Orientation programmes for teachers

i. Total no. of programmes ____________

ii. Total no. of participants ____________

Males ____________

Females ____________

Total ____________

b. Teaching programmes in the major subjects assigned by UGC.

i. Subject : ____________

ii. Total no. of programmes ____________

iii. Total no. of participants

Males ____________

Females ____________

Total ____________

18. If the University offers any separate paper on computer science and/or its application give the following details about each one of them at the Undergraduate, Post graduate and M.Phil.levels.

<table>
<tr><td colspan="2">Name of course</td><td></td><td></td><td></td></tr>
<tr><td colspan="2">Faculty</td><td></td><td></td><td></td></tr>
<tr><td colspan="2">Year in which the course is offered (I,II etc. of degree)</td><td></td><td></td><td></td></tr>
<tr><td colspan="2">Compulsory or Optional</td><td></td><td></td><td></td></tr>
<tr><td rowspan="3">Enrolment in the last year 1988-89</td><td>Male</td><td></td><td></td><td></td></tr>
<tr><td>Female</td><td></td><td></td><td></td></tr>
<tr><td>Total</td><td></td><td></td><td></td></tr>
</table>

19. If the University offers any certificate/diploma in computer science and/ or applications, give the following details.

Certificate Level

Name of course				
Year of starting				
Duration				
Part Time or Full Time				
Enrolment in the last year	Male			
	Female			
	Total			
No. of students who have successfully completed in the last year	Male			
	Female			
	Total			
Source of funds for conducting these courses (fees,govt. grants,trust,own resources etc...				
Authority giving recognition				

D i p l o m a   L e v e l

Name of course				
Year of starting				
Duration				
Part Time or Full Time				
Enrolment in the last year	Male			
	Female			
	Total			
No. of students who have successfully completed in the last year	Male			
	Female			
	Total			
Source of funds for conducting these courses (fees,govt. grants,trust,own resources etc...				
Authority giving recognition				

20. What steps are being taken to ensure that quality of education improves in the university ?

____

____

21. Will introduction of computer improve the quality of learning, productivity of faculty and improvement in the administration of university ? Please comment.

____

____

22. What policies and programmes if any, exist to provide faculty/students with computer resources ? (Hardware & Software)

____

____

____

____

23. What policies, if any exist to provide faculty with instruction in the use of computer and common software as well as continuing support ?

____

____

____

____

24. Do you have any computer facility of your own ?

No( )/Yes( )

If your response is 'No' please answer the questions nos. 25 to 31.
If response is 'Yes' we request that part II of the questionnaire be filled in by the head of your computer centre.

25. How does the university meet its computing requirements ?

1.	Does not use computing facilities
2.	Gives jobs to outside agencies
3.	Hires computer time

26. Does the university plan to install a computer system in the near future?

No( )/Yes( )/Not decided( )

27. If yes, give a brief description about your plan.

a. Type of hardware planned to be installed. (PC, PC/XT, PC/AT, Micro, Supermicro, Mini, Mainframe) ____________

b. Amount available ____________

c. Sources of funds ____________

d. Time period within which you plan to implement ____________

28. Given the opportunities for use of computers, indicate in which areas will the university be using computers. Rank the areas in the order of priority.

Sr.no.	Activities	Rank
1.	For university administration & accounting	
2.	For admission and examination	
3.	Introduce.computer courses & use computers for teaching	
4.	For research	
5.	As a teaching aid	
6.	Not sure of the areas	

29. Has there been any demand made by faculty /students to introduce computer courses in the university ?

No( )/Yes( )

30. If the university plans to install computer in which of the following areas it would like to have assistance/consultation ?

1.	In selection of hardware
2.	In selection of software
3.	In development of software relating to accounting, examination & administration
4.	In development of educational software
5.	Any other (specify) ....

31. Other comments if any.

____

____

____

____

____

____

Part-I Questionnaire For Institution

APPLICATIONS AND SOCIAL IMPACT OF COMPUTER TECHNOLOGY IN HIGHER EDUCATION

(A DESIGN MODEL FOR A COMPUTERIZING UNIVERSITY)

Guidelines for Filling the Questionnaire

1. There are two parts to this questionnaire. You are requested to fill in both the parts.
2. There are several questions against which the possible response categories are given in the questionnaire. Please circle one or more appropriate code(s) indicating your response. For some other questions you may have to write the relevant information in the space provided.
3. Wherever your opinion is sought please write a few lines clearly and legibly.
4. Please skip whatever is not applicable.

Name of the respondent ____________________

Postal Address ____________________

____

____

Telephone No. (office) __________

Designation __________

Sex __________ Age __________

Educational Qualifications __________

Faculty/School __________ Subject __________

QUESTIONNAIRE

NOTE : This questionnaire is in two parts. Part - I of the questionnaire is to be filled in by the Head of the Institute or any other official designated by him/her. Part - II of the questionnaire is to be filled in by the Head of the Computer Centre in the Institute. The Institute which does not have any computer facility of its own, part - II of the questionnaire will be "not applicable" and hence"blank".

PART - I.
(To be filled by the Head of the Institute)

1. Name of the institute ____________________
2. Year of establishment ____________________
3. University by which it is recognised or approved ?

____

4. Who manages your institute ?

1	Autonomous
2	State Government
3	Central Government
4	Any other (specify)

5. Major activities of the institute.
   1. Teaching regular Certificate/Diploma/Degree courses
   2. Research
   3. Consultancy
   4. Occasional training programmes

6. Major areas of specialization in research.

____

____

7. Major areas of specialization in training.

____

____

8. Please give the details about any certificate/diploma/degree courses offered by the institute recognized by university

Name of the course	Subject	University or Any other authority
1. ________	________	________
2. ________	________	________
3. ________	________	________

9. If the institute offers any training programmes on computer science and/ or its applications give the details.

10. Please indicate the total number of faculty members in your institute.(Please write equivalent grade of your institute)

Grade / Sex	Lecturer	Reader	Professor
Male			
Female			
Total			

11. Total annual budget of your institute for 1988-89 : ______

12. State briefly how the admission procedure is organized in your institute for training. (If it is computerised please give details.)

13. What steps you are taking to ensure that quality of training/research is improved in your institute ?

14. What is the role of computer in research in your institute ? Elaborate.

15. What is the role of computer in the area of training in your institute ? Elaborate.

16. What policies and programmes, if any, exist to provide faculty/students with computer resources ? (Hardware & Software)

17. What policies, if any, exist to provide faculty with instruction in the use of computer and common software as well as continuing support ?

18. Do you have any computer facility of your own ?

No( )/Yes( )

19. If the institute offers any certificate/diploma in computer science and/or applications, give the following details.

C e r t i f i c a t e   L e v e l

Name of course				
Year of starting				
Duration				
Part Time or				
Full Time				
Enrolment in the last year 1988-89	Male			
	Female			
	Total			
No. of Students who have successfully completed in the last year	Male			
	Female			
	Total			
Source of funds for conducting these courses (fees,govt. grants,trust,own resources etc...				
Authority giving recognition				

Diploma Level

Name of course				
Year of starting				
Duration				
Part Time or				
Full Time				
Enrolment in the last year 1988-89	Male			
	Female			
	Total			
No. of Students who have successfully completed in the last year	Male			
	Female			
	Total			
Source of funds for conducting these courses (fees,govt. grants,trust,own resources etc...				
Authority giving recognition				

If your response to question no. 18 is 'No', please answer the questions nos. 20 to 25.

If response is 'Yes' we request that part - II of the questionnaire be filled in by the head of your computer centre.

20. How does the institute meet its computing requirements ?

1.	Does not use computing facilities
2.	Gives jobs to outside agencies
3.	Hires computer time

21. Does the institute plan to install a computer system in the near future?

No( )/Yes( )/Not decided( )

If yes, give a brief description about your plan.

a. Type of hardware planned to be installed (PC, PC/XT, PC/AT, Micro, Supermicro, Mini, Mainframe) ______________________ ______________________

b. Amount available ______________________

c. Sources of funds ______________________

d. Time period within which you plan to implement ______________________

22. Given the opportunities for use of computers, indicate in which areas will the institute be using computers. Rank the areas in the order of priority.

Sr.no.	Activities	Rank
1.	For institute administration & accounting	
2.	For admission and examination	
3.	Introduce computer courses & use computer for teaching	
4.	For research	
5.	As a teaching aid	
6.	Not sure of the areas	

23. Has there been any demand made by faculty /students to introduce computer courses in your institute ?

No( )/Yes( )

24. If the institute plans to install computer, in which of the following areas it would like to have assistance/consultation ?

1.	In selection of hardware
2.	In selection of software
3.	In development of software relating to accounting & administration
4.	In development of educational software
5.	Any other (specify)

25. Other comments if any.

____

____

____

Part-I Questionnaire For College

APPLICATIONS AND SOCIAL IMPACT OF COMPUTER TECHNOLOGY IN HIGHER EDUCATION

(A DESIGN MODEL FOR A COMPUTERIZING UNIVERSITY)

Guidelines for Filling the Questionnaire

1. There are two parts to this questionnaire. You are requested to fill in both the parts.
2. There are several questions against which the possible response categories are given in the questionnaire. Please circle one or more appropriate code(s) indicating your response. for some other questions you may have to write the relevant information in the space provided.
3. Wherever your opinion is sought please write a few lines clearly and legibly.
4. Please skip whatever is not applicable.

Name of the respondent ______________________

Postal Address ______________________

Telephone No. (office) ______________________

Designation ______________________

Sex ____________ Age ____________

Educational Qualifications ______________________

Faculty/School ____________ Subject ____________

QUESTIONNAIRE

NOTE : This questionnaire is in two parts. Part - I of the questionnaire is to be filled in by the Principal of the College or any other official designated by him/her. Part - II of the questionnaire is to be filled in by the Head of the Computer Centre in the College. The College which does not have any computer facility of its own, part - II of the questionnaire will be "not applicable" and hence "blank".

PART - I.
(To be filled by Principal of the college)

1. Name of the college ____________________
2. Year of establishment ____________________
3. University to which it is affiliated to ? ____________________
4. Who manages your college ? ____________________

1	Public trust
2	Public body
3	Religious trust
4	State Government
5	Central Government
6	Autonomous body
7	Any other (specify)

5. Please indicate regular courses leading to Certificate/Diploma/Degree of your university offered by your college in the current academic year (1989-90).

Level / Faculty	Certi-ficate	Diploma	Under graduate	Post graduate	Doctorate
1.					
2.					
3.					
4.					
5.					

6. Do you offer any other Certificate/Diploma courses recognised by some authority other than your university ?

No( )/Yes( )

If Yes, give details.

Certificate level

Sr. no.	Name of the course	Year of starting	Duration	Part Time /Full Time (PT / FT)	Name of recognizing authority
1					
2					
3					

Diploma level

Sr. no.	Name of the course	Year of starting	Duration	Part Time /Full Time (PT / FT)	Name of recognizing authority
1					
2					
3					

7. Please mention the total number of students of your college enrolled in the various examinations conducted by the University during the last academic year (1988-89).
(We need information separately for males and females but if this information is not readily available, give the total figures. If a course is spread over more than one years please include figures for all years, viz., for the first year, second year and third year examinations together in the row for the undergraduate level.)

	Full time			Part time			External		
Level	M	F	Total	M	F	Total	M	F	Total
Certificate									
Diploma									
Undergraduate									
Postgraduate									
M.phil.									
Doctorate									

8. Please indicate the total number of faculty members in your college.(Please write against equivalent grade of your college)

Grade	Lecturer	Reader	Professor
Sex			
Male			
Female			
Total			

9. Total annual budget of your college for 1988-89 : ___________

10. State briefly how the admission procedure is organized in your college. (If it is computerised please give details.)

____

____

____

____

11. How long before the beginning of the term is the class schedule and academic calendar available ?

____

____

____

____

12. Are the students education records and documents kept with your college on a permanent basis ?

No( )/Yes( )

If yes, indicate what kind of information is recorded on a permanent basis ? (If computer is used give details)

____

____

____

____

13. What steps are you taking to ensure that quality of education is improved in your college ?

____

____

____

14. Do you think that introduction of computer will increase quality of learning, productivity of faculty and improvement in the administration of college ? Please comment.

____

____

____

____

15. What policies and programmes, if any, exist to provide faculty/students with computer resources ? (Hardware & Software)

____

____

____

____

16. What policies,if any, exist to provide faculty with instruction in the use of computer and common software as well as continuing support ?

____

____

____

____

17. Do you have any computer facility of your own ?

No( )/Yes( )

18. If the college offers any separate paper on computer science and/or its application give the following details about each one of them at the Undergraduate, Post graduate and M.Phil.levels.

Name of course				
Faculty				
Year in which the course is offered (I,II etc. of degree)				
Compulsory or Optional				
Enrolment in the last year 1988-89	Male			
	Female			
	Total			

19. If the college offers any certificate/diploma in computer science and/or applications, give the following details.

Certificate Level

<table>
<tr><td colspan="2">Name of course</td><td></td><td></td><td></td></tr>
<tr><td colspan="2">Year of starting</td><td></td><td></td><td></td></tr>
<tr><td colspan="2">Duration</td><td></td><td></td><td></td></tr>
<tr><td colspan="2">Part Time or
Full Time</td><td></td><td></td><td></td></tr>
<tr><td rowspan="3">Enrolment in the last year</td><td>Male</td><td></td><td></td><td></td></tr>
<tr><td>Female</td><td></td><td></td><td></td></tr>
<tr><td>Total</td><td></td><td></td><td></td></tr>
<tr><td rowspan="3">No. of students who have success-fully completed in the last year</td><td>Male</td><td></td><td></td><td></td></tr>
<tr><td>Female</td><td></td><td></td><td></td></tr>
<tr><td>Total</td><td></td><td></td><td></td></tr>
<tr><td colspan="2">Source of funds for conducting these courses (fees,govt. grants,trust,own resources etc...</td><td></td><td></td><td></td></tr>
<tr><td colspan="2">Authority giving recognition</td><td></td><td></td><td></td></tr>
</table>

Diploma Level

Name of course				
Year of starting				
Duration				
Part Time or Full Time				
Enrolment in the last year	Male			
	Female			
	Total			
No. of students who have successfully completed in the last year	Male			
	Female			
	Total			
Source of funds for conducting these courses (fees,govt. grants,trust,own resources etc...				
Authority giving recognition				

If your response to the question no. 17 is 'No' please answer the questions nos. 20 to 25.
If response is 'Yes' we request that part II of the questionnaire be filled in by the head of your computer centre.

20. How does the college meet its computing requirements ?

1.	Does not use computing facilities
2.	Gives jobs to outside agencies
3.	Hires computer time

21. Does the college plan to install a computer system in the near future ?

No( )/Yes( )/Not decided ( )

If yes, give a brief description about your plan.

a. Type of hardware planned to be installed. (PC; PC/XT, PC/AT, Micro, Supermicro, Mini, Mainframe) ______________

b. Amount available ______________

c. Sources of funds ______________

d. Time period within which you plan to implement ______________

22. Given the opportunities for use of computers, indicate in which areas will the university be using computers. Rank the areas in the order of priority.

Sr.no.	Activities	Rank
1.	For college administration & accounting	
2.	For admission and examination	
3.	Introduce computer courses & use computers for teaching	
4.	For research	
5.	As a teaching aid	
6.	Not sure of the areas	

23. Has there been any demand made by faculty /students to introduce computer courses in your college ?

No( )/Yes( )

24. If your college plans to install computer, in which of the following areas you would like to have assistance/consultation ?

1.	In selection of hardware
2.	In selection of software
3.	In development of software relating to accounting, examination & administration
4.	In development of educational software
5.	Any other (specify) ....

25. Other comments if any.

____

____

____

Part-II Questionnaire

(To be filled by the Head of the Computer Centre of the Institution)

Guidelines for Filling the Questionnaire

1. There are two parts to this questionnaire. You are requested to fill in both the parts.
2. There are several questions against which the possible response categories are given in the questionnaire. Please circle one or more appropriate code(s) indicating your response. For some other questions you may have to write the relevant information in the space provided.
3. Wherever your opinion is sought please write a few lines clearly and legibly.
4. Please skip whatever is not applicable.

Name of the respondent ______________________

Postal Address ______________________

____

____

Telephone No. (office) ____________

Designation ____________

Sex ____________ Age ____________

Educational Qualifications ____________

Faculty/School ____________ Subject ____________

QUESTIONNAIRE

1. When was the first computer installed/used ?

   a. Installed ____________________

   b. Started use ____________________

2. If the answer to question 1 is 'a' indicate the sources of fund for purchase of computer system by circling the appropriate code(s) in the first column .

1.	UGC
2.	Own funds
3.	Donation/Aid
4.	State government/Central government
5.	Foreign Agency/Foundation
6.	Any other (specify) ———

3. Indicate whether the computer facilities in your campus are :

1.	Centralised
2.	Department-wise
3.	Individualised/ Personalized

4. If the response to the above question is 2 and/or 3,indicate the total number of departments and/or individuals who have their own computer facilities. Please give the names of such departments and the details regarding the number of such departments and the hardware they have.

____

____

____

____

____

____

5. Give a brief history of the computer/s installed in your unit, since inception.

Year	Equipment installed (make/model)	Staff strength

6. Give particulars of existing personal computer/single user micro in your unit.

a.

Systems	Make	No. of units	No. of Printers
PC			
PC/XT			
PC/AT			
Micro			

b. List the major software packages developed in-house on the above installation.

c. Please give the following details about your above installation

1. User group (e.g. students,staff..etc) __________
2. Major use (e.g. research,teaching..etc) __________
3. Number of users __________

7. Give the details about the other computer system if you have on the following dimensions.

(a) Hardware

Systems	Main frame	Mini	Multi user micro	Graphic work station
No.of units				
Vendor name				
CPU type				
Core size				
Tape drives (specify number & capacity)				
FDD (floppy) (specify number & capacity)				
HDD (Winchester) (specify number & capacity)				
RDD (Removable) (specify number & capacity)				
Dotmatrix Printer (specify number & Speed)				
Daisy wheel Printer (specify number & speed)				
Line printer (specify number & speed)				
Laser printer (specify number & speed)				
Colour terminal (Number)				
Monochrome terminal (Number)				
Mouse/Tablets (Number)				
Digitizers (Number)				
Plotter (Number)				

(b) Software

Systems	Main	Mini frame	Multi user micro	Graphic work station
Operating system				
Major language compilers				
Business application software				
Scientific application software				
Data base packages				
Graphic software				
Any other important software				

(c) Usage

Systems	Main	Mini frame	Multi user micro	Graphic work station
No.of users				
User group (eg. students, staff, faculty..etc)				
Major use (eg. research, library, teaching... etc)				

8. What are the future expansion plans in the computing facilities ? Describe briefly

____

____

____

____

9. Have you ever acquired the services of any outside consultant for operating the system or for developing packages ?

No( )/Yes( )

10. Considering total number of application software packages you are using at present, what percentage of software packages have been developed in-house ?

____

11. What percentage of software is acquired from vendors ?

____

12. Does your staff use any of the following softwares ?

1.	Word processing
2.	Data base
3.	Spread sheet
4.	Statistical package
5.	Operation Research package
6.	Report writer
7.	Graphics packages
8.	Desk Top Publishing (DTP)
9.	Course authoring
10.	Computer Aided Instruction & Computer Aided learning packages
11.	Any other (specify)

13. Do you have access to any international or national network such as BITNET ?

No( )/Yes( )/Planning to get access( )

14. Do you use electronic mailing ?

No( )/Yes( )/Planning to get access( )

15. What is the present size of staff in the computer department ?

		Current	Vacant
a.	Data Entry Operator	______	______
b.	Computer Operator	______	______
c.	Technical Assistant /Programming Assistant	______	______
d.	Programmer	______	______
e.	System Analysts/Engineer	______	______
f.	System Manager	______	______
g.	Lecturer in Computer Science	______	______
h.	Reader in Computer Science	______	______
i.	Professor in Computer Science/ Director Computer Centre	______	______

16. Has the faculty being given orientation in the use of computer in teaching/ research ?

No( )/Yes( )

17. What are the areas in which computer is being used in your unit ?

1.	Teaching
2.	Training
3.	Research
4.	Administration

18. Is computer being used as a teaching aid ?

No( )/Yes( )

If yes, please indicate in which of the areas use of computer is emphasized ?

Emphasis of Computer	(Pl. tick)
Programming	
Problem solving	
Access database & analysis	
Analysis & report	
Simulations & Model building	
Academic games	
Graphics/ Drafting	
Audio visual presentation	
Drill & practice	
Tutorials	
Self paced study	
Programmed learning	
Preparation of instructional material	
Question bank	
Conducting quizzes	

19. Does the unit provide technical support or other service to aid faculty in computer assisted preparation of materials ?

No( )/Yes( )

If yes, give details.

____

____

20. Is any one in your unit carrying out research in the use of computer as an aid in instruction ?

No( )/Yes( )

If yes, please list the names and one line description of the areas of research

____

____

____

21. Generally the following are constraints in use of computer in class room teaching. Rank them (Give rank 1 to most significant constraints and 7 to least significant constraints in your opinion)

Constraints		Rank order
a.	Portability	
b.	Air condition equipment required	
c.	Very small screen	
d.	No remote control operation	
e.	Very large class room	
f.	Administration problem (not allowed to transfer to class)	
g.	Non availability of computer for class	

22. What constraints do you see on increased use of computer in pedagogy ? (Tick mark in the appropriate box)

		Major	Minor	None	Don't know
1.	Cost				
2.	Space				
3.	Availability of computer or terminals				
4.	Availability of software				
5.	Compatibility of computer or of computer systems				
6.	Capacity of available time on mainframe computer				
7.	Training of faculty				
8.	Training of students				
9.	Faculty inertia				
10.	Difficulty using hardware or software (The technology isn't transparent)				
11.	Inadequacy of software for computer-assisted instruction				
12.	Lack of awareness of such a tool				
13.	The need to learn a new discipline				
14.	Lack of time				
15.	Question of technology effectiveness				
16.	Any others (specify)				

23. Has the use of computer improved the quality of education in your unit ?

No( )/Yes( )/No opinion( )

24. State the quantum of computer usage in research.

1	No use
2.	Casual use
3.	Limited use
4.	Substantial use

25. Does your unit provide any assistance/training to research scholars ?

No( )/Yes( )

26. What is the role of computer in research ?

1.	Literature search
2.	Model building
3.	Data analysis
4.	Report generation
5.	Computer science research
6.	Number crunching
7.	Any others (specify)

27. Which of the activities of your unit are computerised?

	Activities	Computerised No/Yes	Hardware used (Mini,PC..etc)	
			Hardware	Year
1.	Students registration & record			
2.	Students admission			
3.	Students examination & evaluation			
4.	Accounting			
5.	Payroll			
6.	Inventory record (Material/Stores)			
7.	Cost analysis			
8.	Personnel			
9.	Scheduling (Time table,Room allocation..etc)			
10.	Integrated information system			
11.	Office automation (use of WP)			
12.	Library cataloging			
13.	Library requisition/circulation			
14.	Any other (specify)			

28. Indicate the type of software used in the computerization of the following activities.

	Activities	Used vendor supplied software	Modified vendor supplied software	Developed in-house software
1.	Students registration & record			
2.	Students admission			
3.	Students examination & evaluation			
4.	Accounting			
5.	Payroll			
6.	Inventory record (material/stores)			
7.	Cost analysis			
8.	Personnel			
9.	Scheduling (time table,room allocation...etc)			
10.	Integrated information system			
11.	Office automation (use of word processor)			
12.	Library cataloging			
13.	Library requisition/circulation			
14.	Any other (specify)			

29. Does your unit provide computer facilities to outside users ?

No( )/Yes( )

If yes, give details

1.	Academic use
2.	Commercial use
3.	Consultancy service
4.	Any other (specify)

30. If you provide consultancy service, indicate the areas in which the same is provided.

1.	Developing specification of hardware/software
2.	Assisting in purchase of hardware/software
3.	Development of software
4.	Any others (specify) ———

31. Are the heads of various departments familiar with the use of computer facilities ?

No( )/Yes( )

If 'NO' state the reasons for any or all of them not getting interested in computer.

1.	Lack of training
2.	Not interested
3.	Too much of time investment so not worth
4.	Any other (specify) ....

32. Have you provided any training in computer use to your administrative staff ?

No( )/Yes( )

33. Is your administrative staff using computer facility themselves for their work ?

No( )/Yes( )

If 'NO', state the reasons for not using

1.	Lack of training
2.	Not interested
3.	Too much of time investment so not worth
4.	Complicated technology
5.	Does not provide extra allowance
6.	Any other (specify) ———

34. Which areas will have predominant use of computer in your unit/ organization ?

35. What is the approximate number of faculty/students/support staff using the computer system in your unit ?

	Faculty	Students	Support staff
Male			
Female			

36. Indicate average percentage of usage on the following activities. (on an annual basis)

	Activities	Approx. time (percentage)
a.	Administration	________
b.	Accounting	________
c.	Examination	________
d.	Instruction of computer related courses	________
e.	Use of computer in pedagogy	________
f.	Research	________
g.	Library operations	________
h.	Any other (specify)	________

37. What is the total annual cost of operating the Computer system ?

____

38. What is the cost of running the computer centre as a percent of your organization's total operating budget ?

____

39. What is the computer centre's annual capital (equipment) budget ?

____

40. What percent of computer centre's budget spent on maintenance of computers?

____

41. How do you meet the cost of operating the computer system ?

1.	Fees
2.	Government grant
3.	Internal funds
4.	Any other (specify)

42. What is your maintenance arrangement ?

1.	In-house
2.	Vendor maintenance
3.	Third party
4.	No maintenance contract

43. What is the type of maintenance contract in case your unit has vendor/ third party maintenance ?

1.	Regular maintenance including preventive maintenance
2.	Per call maintenance
3.	Others (specify) ———

44. Is your library system computerized ?

No( )/Yes( )

If yes, give details.

45. What changes are planned with respect to your library system and why ?

46. How do you manage and co-ordinate all computing activities on campus ?

47. Do you plan to separate the computing centre into an academic centre and an administrative centre ? Why ?

48. Have your views changed over the years on the role and the importance of computer ?

No( )/Yes( )

If yes, explain.

49. What do you see as the major advantage(s) of computer in the academic enterprise ?

50. What do you see as the major disadvantage(s) ?

51. What do you see as the greatest impact of computer on the academic enterprise ?

52. Has there been any problem arisen between employees and management with regard to computerization ?

53. What efforts the Government/UGC/Management has made to encourage the use of computer in your institution ?

54. What are or where are the major obstacles related to introduction of computer in the institution ?

55. What are the difficulties you face in providing the facilities of computer to various users ?

56. Does your institution face any resistance in the use of computer ? Indicate, if any.

57. What are the difficulties you face in keeping the various items of equipment operational ?

Part-III Questionnaire

APPLICATIONS AND SOCIAL IMPACT OF COMPUTER TECHNOLOGY IN HIGHER EDUCATION
(A DESIGN MODEL FOR A COMPUTERIZING UNIVERSITY)

Opinion Questionnaire (Part-III)

1. Name of the respondent __________
2. Name of the Institution __________
3. Postal Address __________
4. Telephone No. __________
5. Designation __________
6. Sex __________ 7. Age (Completed years) __________
8. Educational Qualifications __________
9. Faculty __________ 10. Subjects__________
11. Experience Teaching(Undergraduate) ______ Research ______
(years) Teaching(Postgraduate) ______
12. Have you ever used any computer for teaching/research? NO( )/YES( )

If 'NO', would you like to use computer ?
NO( )/YES( )

If 'YES', for teaching __________
for research __________
for M.A./M.Phil. research __________
for Ph.D. research __________
for other research __________

13. Do you have any hands-on experience of using computer your self ?

NO( )/YES( )

If 'NO', would you like to have some experience ?
NO( )/YES( )

If 'YES',
for using available software __________

for writing/using own programmes __________

for report/dissertation preparation __________

for class room use of computer __________

A. Many educational/research institutions do not use computer as much as they could or should. We are interested in finding out the reason for the same. Some of the possible reasons are listed below.Please indicate your own opinion regarding each possible reason by tick mark in one of the appropriate boxes against each reason.

	Reasons for inadequate use of computer	Very Certain	Fairly Certain	Doubtful
1.	Lack of technical skills and expertise for the use and maintenance of computer			
2.	High cost of hardware, software and maintenance			
3.	Ignorance about the potential use of computer			
4.	Feeling that those who work with computer have a hold over others because of their specialized knowledge			
5.	Teaching/training does not require computer technology			
6.	Fear of role change			
7.	Fear of loss of power since all the information will be centralised			
8.	Computer requires change of work habit			
9.	Introduction of computer may require reorganization of the educational system			
10.	Reduction in the importance or power of some people who are taking decisions			
11.	Fear that computer may go wrong and the mistakes may not be detected			
12.	Changes in the social and cultural environment due to computer and the problems to adjust with these changes			

B. We would like to ask you some general opinion questions concerning the role and impact of the computer in higher education and the society as a whole.Please be reassured that the data will be treated as an aggregate and no individual responses will be identified. Your opinion regarding each statement has to be indicated by a (tick mark) in only one of the five boxes (Strongly agree, Agree, No opinion, Disagree, Strongly disagree) which closely correspond with your opinion. Please indicate your opinion regarding all statements.

No.	Statement	Strongly agree	Agree	No opinion	Disagree	Strongly disagree
1.	Computer can help to increase productivity in the educational process					
2.	Computer can help achieve higher quality of learning					
3.	Computer can help to individualize instructions to the needs of particular students					
4.	Computer helps to lay the foundation of basic education					
5.	Computer motivate students					
6.	Computer can prevent social isolation					
7.	Computer can help the students of weaker sections by repeated exposures					
8.	Development of computer based pedagogical modules are very time consuming and costly and hence not worth the efforts					
9.	Computer will widen the gap between rural and urban students					
10.	Computer will reduce the gap between poor and better standard universities					
11.	Introduction of computer is just a "political game" for higher education					
12.	Computer will bring about a revolution in the pedagogy of higher education					
13.	Computer can be used only in science and technical education					

No. Statement	Strongly agree	Agree	No opinion	Disagree	Strongly disagree
14. Introduction of computer will increase malpractices in the examination and admission of higher education					
15. Computer will help improve university administration					
16. Introduction of computer will lead to fair and equitable admission and evaluation					
17. Computer is neutral for learning by men and women					
18. Computer will adversely affect students' analytical abilities					
19. Computer will increase creativity of the teachers, researchers and students.					
20. Computer will make humans machine-dependent					
21. Computer will widen the gap between rich and poor students					
22. Computer is an expensive toy					
23. Introduction of computer in pedagogy will become a threat to teachers					
24. Adoption of computer will create new jobs					
25. University administrators implement computerization to make their jobs easier					
26. Computer can represent a threat to workers' health					
27. Computer studies will ensure a higher paying jobs					
28. Computer will widen the gap between men and women					
29. Those with power in the university make all major decisions about computer					
30. Adoption of computer will lead to loss of jobs					

APPENDIX-B

TRAINING PROGRAMMES AT COMTAL

This report aims at documenting the experiences of training courses given at Gujarat University under this collaborative project on the pedagogy of Computer Applications in Higher Education. A Computer Laboratory named as "Computer Training and Applications Laboratory" (COMTAL) was set up for this purpose at Gujarat University, Ahmedabad, in 1991. The Digital Equipment India gifted a Micro VAX-II Computer System for COMTAL. The University of Regina collaborative research team played a crucial role in persuading the Digital Equipment in India through their headquarters in United States for donating the computer. COMTAL though became operational in April 1991, was formally inaugurated by Professor S. K. Khanna, Vice Chairman, University Grants Commission on December 11, 1991. Professor Larry Symes, Project Director, Regina Team specifically flew in from Canada to attend the inaugural function of COMTAL. Since then COMTAL is fully operational and is being used for training purposes. Besides Micro Vax-II, six PC/XT computers and two dot matrix printers have been installed during 1991-92. Efforts are being made to procure a full fledged AT/486 with GIST card and a laser printer.

1. Objectives of Training

There has been a great deal of discussion among the computer professionals about the distinction that needs to be made between "learning about computer" and "learning with computer". Learning with computer accelerates one's ability to apply the tool for solving any research, teaching and administrative problems related to higher education. Due to the lack of adequately computer trained college and university teachers, it is extremely difficult to utilize the potential of computer in higher education, research, and administrative activities. Hence, the most important task is to set up computer training facilities for college and university teachers. At the same time, it is essential to continue to provide refresher courses also, to upgrade the knowledge and to keep up with the fast changing technology and developments, both in hardware and software areas. Keeping this in view, a broad outline of the proposed training programmes (reproduced below) was prepared in a joint meeting of Indian and Canadian Research team members, held during August 1990 at Gujarat University.

TRAINING PROGRAMME AT GUJARAT UNIVERSITY

OBJECTIVES OF THE TRAINING

1 To familiarize the teachers with potential uses of computers in educational environment.

2 To develop skills in use of available software for different academic and administrative activities.

3 The participant should be able to use the available software in the teaching activities of his/her discipline.

PRE-REQUISITE

1 It is assumed that the teacher trainees will have a computer available/accessible in his own institution. This will facilitate immediate use of the machine soon after the training.

2 The training will be as far as possible subject-specific i.e. exercises, examples will be drawn from the subject area of the trainee in which he/she is involved in teaching at the undergraduate/postgraduate level.

3 The software to be demonstrated will also be subject specific.

DURATION

The training programme will be of 4 weeks duration.

TYPES OF COURSES

The following will be the sequence for subject specific training courses :

a. Mathematics

b. Economics

c. Social Sciences

d. Chemistry

e. Physics

PARTICIPANTS

Participants will be drawn from colleges and universities for the subject in which training is to be imparted. It is assumed that participants have no previous experience of computers.

CURRICULUM FOR THE COURSE ON MATHEMATICS

WEEK 1	Introduction to Computers, OS Commands, file creation and editing, Word Processing, use of the subject specific packages.
WEEK 2	Use of Spread Sheet, EMAIL, Presentation software.
WEEK 3	Use of Computers in examinations and admissions, subject specific assignment.
WEEK 4	Work on subject specific assignment.

The training contents, therefore, cannot be the same for all the teachers. The curriculum should consist of two components : general introduction and orientation, and subject-specific training. In the first part, the participants should be acquainted with the computer as a system, its components and functioning. This part should be common for all the participants of computer training. The second part of the training should be specific for teachers keeping in view their discipline, background and subject matter of academic teaching and research. In it, the participants should be exposed to some of the available software packages and their uses in subjects like Physics, Chemistry, Statistics, Mathematics and Social Sciences. The use of these packages in teaching and research would be of immense help to the participating teachers.

Therefore, it was decided to organize subject-specific training programmes rather than general short-term programmes. However, the software useful for teaching of a subject needs to be made available for hands-on experience to the teachers in the laboratory. In addition, they would also be given exposure to some administrative packages which would be of great help to the teachers in managing admissions, examinations and such other related administrative functions. It was expected that the teachers, after undergoing such a training programme, would become equipped to use the computer technology advantageously in their own institutions.

The University Grants Commission has given grants for computers to several colleges and universities in the country. Hence, it is assumed that the teachers, after the training, will have access to computers in their institutions for teaching, demonstration and hands-on experience in the use of various available software. This will help to bring awareness of potentialities of computers in higher education.

2. Training Activities of COMTAL

2.1 Subject Specific Training

The first training programme was conducted for the teachers of Mathematics from April 15 to May 10, 1991. That programme was well received by the participants. Encouraged by this, the project team conducted separate training programmes for teachers of Economics, Social Science, Physics, Statistics, Library Science and Chemistry (See Table 1). All these training programmes except for Library Science were of four weeks' duration. These training programmes met the objectives satisfactorily, and were also well received by the participants. Each programme had fifteen to sixteen participants. Each participant completed a small project in the use of the computer in his/her own subject discipline. In addition to these seven programmes, a programme for Research Scholars was conducted during November-December 1992, which was coordinated by Mr. D. J. Divraniya and Mrs. Jyotika Doshi.

Table 1 Training Programmes Conducted During 1991-92

	Programme for the faculty of	Duration	Co-ordinator
1	Mathematics	15.04.91 to 10.05.91	Dr. Sarla Achuthan
2	Economics	17.06.91 to 12.07.91	Dr. C. H. Thacker
3	Social Science	05.08.91 to 30.08.91	Dr. V. P. Shah
4	Library Science	14.10.91 to 26.10.91	Mr. Kalpesh Parikh
5	Physics	11.11.91 to 06.12.91	Dr. S. P. Bhatnagar
6	Statistics	09.12.91 to 04.01.92	Dr. Sarla Achuthan
7	Chemistry	24.02.92 to 18.03.92	Dr. Y. K. Agrawal & Dr. Neesha Shah

The seven training programmes conducted upto March 1992 had 104 participants (See Table 2). The sex ratio of male to female was 4:1. This ratio is no different than what exists in the university system today in India. In the training programmes for Mathematics and Chemistry, there was only one female participant each, and in statistics all were male.

As far as age group is concerned, majority of them were in their forties or in early fifties. Two-third of the participants were master degree holders, 16 had M. Phil and 19 participants had done doctorate in their respective fields of specialization. The overwhelming majority was of college lecturers and professors. Professionals from research institutes and university departments accounted for only 30 percent of total participants. The remaining 75 percent included lecturers, professors, readers, researchers, librarians and a principal of a college. Almost 59 percent of the teachers had more than five years of teaching experience but only 20 per cent participants had research experience of more than five years. Almost half of the participants lacked any research experience. There were many participants without any previous exposure to computers. However, total number of such participants is less than those having some or reasonable exposure to the working of computers.

The pattern of lectures in various training courses was designed keeping in view the discipline of the participants and hence was not the same. This is presented in Table 3. Both PCs and MicroVax machines were extensively used for laboratory work. The programme for Librarians was mainly conducted using MicroVax where the CDS/ISIS package was installed.

2.2 Pre-Training Orientation

In addition to the subject specific programmes, three training programmes one each in 1990, 1991 and 1992 were conducted for the participants selected for the training organized at University of Regina. These programmes were conducted for a week immediately prior to the departure of the trainees for Canada. All the twelve trainees came to Ahmedabad and participated in the training programme for one week. During the training they were given general orientation about computers and popular PC packages. They were also given some hands-on practice on Vax machine and the facility of electronic mail. Each team leader gave general information to the participants about the country, the city and the university they were visiting. The first batch was led by Mr. R. P. Soni, second by Dr. Sarla Achuthan and the third was led by Dr. Binod Agrawal.

2.3 Training to Participants of Courses Conducted by Academic Staff College

A one week training was arranged for the participants of each of the programme conducted by the Academic Staff Training College of Gujarat University. The training included general introduction to computers and popular packages. Practical training was also arranged for about three hours every day during the week.

Table 2 Background Characteristics of the Participants

VARIABLES	PROGRAMME NAME MATHEMATICS	ECONOMICS	SOCIAL SCIENCE	LIBRARY	PHYSICS	STATISTICS	CHEMISTRY	TOTAL
1. GENDER								
Male	15	10	8	7	14	15	14	83
Female	1	3	8	6	2	–	1	21
2. SUBJECT	Stat. 2 Maths. 14	Eco. 13	Eco. 8 Soci. 5 Geo. 2 Psy. 1	Edu. 2 Gen. 8 Sci. 3	Phy. 16	Stat. 15	Chem. 15	
3. AGE								
Upto 40yr.	3	3	8	4	13	7	10	48
40+yrs.	13	10	8	9	3	8	5	56
4. HIGHEST DEGREE								
Graduate	-	-	-	1	-	-	-	1
Master's	8	8	10	12	11	11	8	68
M.Phil	4	2	4	-	2	3	1	16
Ph.D.	4	3	2	-	3	1	6	19
5. INSTITUTIONS								
College	14	10	9	6	13	10	12	74
Research Inst.	–	1	3	5	-	4	-	13
University Department	2	2	4	2	3	1	3	17
6. POSITION								
Lecturer	12	9	11	3	10	10	8	63
Reader/Principal	2	2	3		1	-	5	13
Professor	–	1	2	-	4	-	-	07
Researcher	2	1	-	-	1	4	2	10
Others	-	-	-	10	-	1	-	11
7. TRAINING IN STATISTICS								
Nil	-	-	3	-	-	-	-	3
Introductory	N.A	N.A	11	N.A	N.A	-	N.A	11
Advance			2			15		17
8. TEACHING EXPERIENCE								
Nil	1	1	7	10	-	2	–	21
Upto 5 yrs.	4	1	4	2	2	4	5	22
6 to 10 yrs.	1	2	3	–	13	2	3	24
10+yrs.	10	9	2	1	1	7	7	37
9. Research Experience								
Nil	–	6	7	13	11	11	3	51
Upto 5 yrs.	12	1	4	-	5	2	8	32
5+yrs	4	6	5	-	-	2	4	21
10. EXPOSURE TO COMPUTER								
Nil	5	10	7	6	–	1	12	41
Somewhat	6	2	4	3	–	14	1	30
Reasonable	5	1	5	4	–	–	2	17

Table 3 Topicwise number of sessions covered

Topics	Sessions						
	MATHS	ECONOMICS	SOCIAL SCIENCE	LIBRARY SCIENCE	PHY.	STAT.	CHEM.
Introduction to Computers using PCs	3	3	2	2	2	2	2
DOS commands.	1	1	2	2	2	2	2
Word Processing	1	1	2	2	2	2	2
Mathematical Word Processing	2	-	-	-	-	3	2
Lotus 1-2-3	2	4	3	-	3	3	2
Dbase III	-	2	3	-	2	2	2
Graphics	2	2	2	-	2	2	1
Overview of Statistics	-	-	3	-	-	-	-
MicroVax & Email	2	2	2	2	2	2	2
SPSS	-	4	9	-	-	8	-
General	4	6	4	-	-	3	-
Electronic Scratch pad	2	-	-	-	3	3	2
Computers in pedagogy	4	3	-	-	4	3	4
Operations Research	1	1	-	-	-	-	-
Project Selection	1	1	1	1	1	1	1
Final Session	2	2	2	2	2	2	2
CDS/ISIS	-	-	-	8	-	-	-

3. Assistance from Regina University

Prof. Symes visited Gujarat University during May 1991, December 1991 and November 1992. During each of his visit, he participated actively in teaching at COMTAL. He extensively covered mathematical applications in the course for Mathematics teachers. To facilitate the task of instructional computing, the Canadian team provided some software packages useful for demonstration as well as practice. Such packages were for mathematical and statistical applications and VT-100 terminal emulation. A package known as CALLGEN has been provided for academic use by the University of Calgary. The CDS/ISIS package for Library functions has been obtained from NISSAT and installed on MicroVAx. Efforts are being made to procure specific software useful for training activities and make available to the participants of future training programmes. The SPSS package donated by Regina University, will be shortly installed on MicroVax.

4. Future Activities

The training given to more than 100 teachers had the objective of familiarizing them with potential use of computers, providing exposure, and developing skill for computer usage. Based on the experience gained during the training programme of seven courses it is felt that some modifications in the course content will be required in the future. Advance programmes may be designed for the teachers who have already undergone basic or introductory course. These programmes must include the latest developments in the field, computer languages and techniques of using computers as an aid to teaching.

4.1 Programmes for Administrative Staff

Keeping in view the crucial support provided by administrative staff in higher education, it is suggested that there should be separately designed regular training programmes for the different levels of administrative staff. This will lead to bridging the gap between academic and administrative staff and will also help in changing their attitude, which in the past had been one of the reasons for slow progress of computerization in higher education.

5. Likely Impact of Training

From the reports of the co-ordinators and the feedback obtained from the participants through a questionnaire, it is clear that the training programmes organized by the Project Team at COMTAL were successful.

Another achievement of these training programmes was that almost three-fourth of the participants belonged to under graduate colleges, and most of them were young lecturers having negligible research and computer experiences in the past. After this training they expressed the hope to get involved in research activities in their own disciplines. These training programmes, therefore, are likely to have a multiplier effect on the spread of computer literacy in the colleges and universities.

If appropriate and sustained support is provided to COMTAL, the experiences gained in the computer training programmes of college and university teachers can form a nucleus for the future discipline specific trainings. It can take a shape of National Academic Staff College for Computer use and application, in which pedagogical experiments in computer education and research can form the core of the total programme.

APPENDIX-C

A BRIEF HISTORY OF COMPUTERIZATION AT GUJARAT UNIVERSITY

Gujarat University was established in the year 1949 with its jurisdiction covering the areas within the State of Gujarat. Since it had the responsibility of conducting examinations for various undergraduate and postgraduate courses, the administration experienced considerable stress in managing this workload using manual methods. It was during 1959-60 that Mr. B. M. Patel, Accounts Officer initiated a proposal to introduce mechanization for handling the increasing workload of examination results processing. This marked the beginning of mechanization and later computerization of administrative tasks in Gujarat University.

1. Initial Phase of Mechanization

The University ordered a set of punch card equipments consisting of four mechanical punches, four verifiers, one reproducer, one tabulator and two sorters with the International Computers and Tabulators (ICT) Company on 14th October, 1960. This decision was later revised and a fresh order was placed on 14th March, 1961. The main machine was the ICT 853 Tabulator for which a monthly rental of Rs. 2195/- was to be paid. The number of candidates registered from 55 affiliated colleges in various examinations of the year 1960 conducted in 18 centres was around 42,000. Considering the need of increasing number of students, the 853 tabulator was replaced in the year 1967 by two ICT 903 tabulators having a speed of 100 cards per minute. The rental per month of each machine was Rs. 2840/-. The following table extracted from a report of ICT Company dated 30th March, 1966 shows the number of candidates covered under mechanization, number of colleges, number of examinations and number of centres in the years 1962 and 1966.

Table 1 Unit Record Data Processing in 1962, 1966

	1962	1966
Number of candidates	31,802	67,162
Number of colleges	55	138
Number of Examinations	6	23
Number of centres	18	50

This unit record equipment was housed on the second floor of the main university building. A separate section reporting to Controller of Examination was established.

2. Computerization Process

The existing mechanization procedure was reviewed in the year 1967 by a committee of which Mr. S. R. Thakore was also a member. This committee met on 22-9-67 and 23-9-67. The committee recommended initiation of punch operators training programme to meet the increasing workload of card punching. Another major recommendation of the committee was to start using the IBM 1620 computer available in the nearby Physical Research Laboratory (PRL). Accordingly, the university started using the IBM 1620 from March-April 1968. Gradually, the final processing of examination results was transferred to IBM 1620 for all major examinations.

It was observed that the equipment supplied by ICT (now known as ICL) had several functional problems and, therefore, a decision was taken in April 1969 to replace the ICT equipment by IBM unit record equipment. The overall monthly cost was reduced by about Rs. 1000/-. The major machine acquired from IBM was an IBM 447 accounting machine with a speed of 150 cards per minute and capable of data processing through pluggable programming. Finding the experience of using IBM 1620 at Physical Research Laboratory and the in-house IBM 447 satisfactory, more administrative and data analysis jobs such as the financial accounting and payroll processing were added immediately. Enthused by the performance and successful implementation of administrative as well as statistical data analysis jobs, a proposal of IBM for supplying an IBM 1401 on discounted rent was seriously considered. However, IBM withdrew the proposal and no progress could be made in acquiring a computer.

3. Creation of Computer Centre in the University

In order to mobilize resources for purchase of a computer, a scheme was formulated known as "Computer Club" in which all the affiliated colleges will contribute required share, which would enable the university by adding its own share to acquire a computer system for research and academic computing. Many of the local colleges had shown their willingness to participate in this computer club. At this time i.e. in 1972, an IBM 360/44 was installed in Physical Research Laboratory. The management of Physical Research Laboratory and the Electronics Commission were requested to transfer the IBM 1620 from Physical Research Laboratory at book value to Gujarat University so that a central computing centre can be created and academic computing services can be provided on the campus. This proposal was cleared by Department of Electronics on 27th December, 1972 and accepted by PRL on 5th January 1973. However, the management of PRL decided to transfer the IBM 1620 for use by Gujarat University free of cost. This IBM 1620 was housed in the ground floor of main university building and the computing centre was inaugurated on 14th March, 1973 by Dr. D. Lal, Director of PRL, under the Chairmanship of Dr. K. R. Ramanathan, Professor, Emeritus, PRL. The Vice Chancellor Shri Ishwarbhai Patel persuaded the Rollwala group who instantly agreed to donate a sum of Rs. 3.5 lakhs for a separate building of the Computer Centre. The U.G.C. also approved the scheme of central computer centre and provided financial assistance for recurring expenditure for staff and maintenance of the equipment. The foundation stone of the new building, was laid by Shri Chimanbhai Patel, the then Chief Minister of Gujarat State, in March 1974, and the computer centre moved into the new building in August 1975. The building named as Rollwala Computer Centre, was inaugurated by the then Chief Minister, Shri Babubhai Patel. An Advisory Computer Committee with representation from faculty, administration, and academic users was set up to provide guidance and policy formulation regarding computerization, expansion of training activities and selection of staff.

4. Initial Use of Facilities by Administration, Faculty and Students

With the establishment of central facility, the research scholars started getting good support for data analysis and mathematical computation. Necessary training courses were organized for the faculty and research scholars. Since there were only two computing centres in this part of the State offering academic computing facilities, many research scholars from nearby universities like Saurashtra University, Bhavnagar University, M. S. University, Udaipur, South Gujarat University etc. were visiting the centre for availing the computational facilities.

A Certificate course in Computer Programming was initiated in 1973. This was a six-month part time course, and about 30 students were enrolled in each session. The same is being continued without any interruption. The other course, Diploma in Computer Applications, was started at a later stage. Several new administrative areas were computerized and the scope of existing administrative applications enlarged. The following diagram shows the services being offered at that time by the computing centre.

To support the growing activities, a line printer was acquired from Control Data Corporation and interfaced with the IBM 1620 by the maintenance agency M/s. CMC Limited in 1979. The funds for this were provided by UGC. At the same time, the speed of card reader attached to IBM 1620 was increased from 250 to 500 cards per minute.

5. Installation of Vax 11/730

After 1980, it was becoming difficult to maintain IBM 1620 since IBM had left India in 1978. It was decided to acquire a new computer system for replacement of IBM 1620 with internal funds (the response from UGC was not forthcoming). After a careful evaluation of the available indigenous

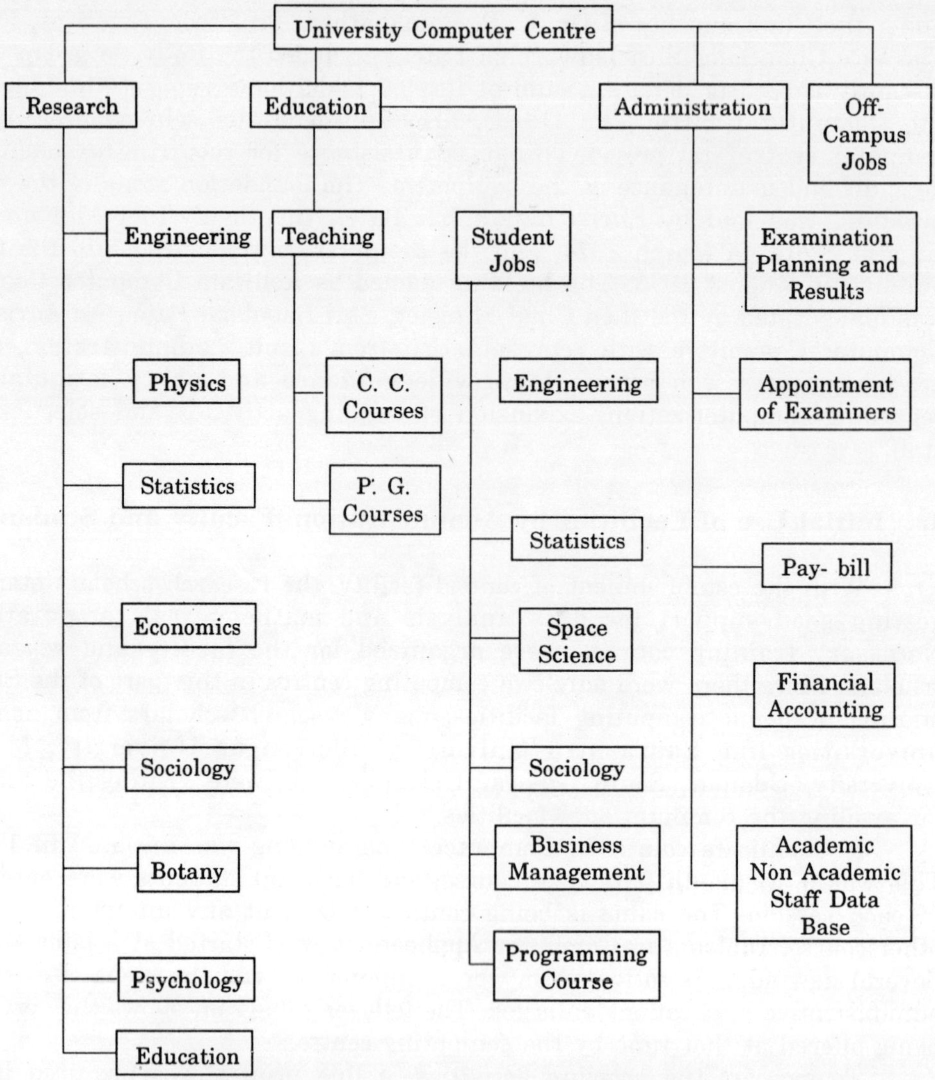

Activities of Computer Centre in 1977

computer systems, it was proposed to import a small Vax system at a cost of Rs. 5 lakhs. The Department of Electronics cleared this proposal and the Vax 11/730 was installed during August 1983. The machine had just 1 MB memory and two 10 MB RL02 disk drives. The existing line printer was connected to this system. A year later, a tape drive was added. The main data input to the system was still through the card reader. The university incurred this expenditure of around Rs. 7 lacs from internal revenues. This was probably the first centre with the building and equipments procured without the support of funding agencies.

The University Grants Commission during May 1984, sanctioned a proposal for augmentation of the system at a cost of Rs. 12 lakhs. Additional memory, disk drives, floppy drives, a line printer and a tape drive were added in March 1986. With this configuration, the system is being used for teaching computer science, training of teachers, administrative computing and research computing extensively. The following table shows various regular training programmes offered by the Computer Centre.

Table 2 Courses Offered by the Computer Centre

SR NO	NAME OF THE COURSE	YEAR OF STARTING	INTAKE	DURATION
1	Master of Computer Application	1988	30	3 YEARS
2	Diploma In Computer Science	1982	30	1 YEAR
3	Certificate In Computer Programming	1973	30	6 MONTHS
4	Data Entry Operations	1968	20-25	2+6 MONTHS

In addition, the following training programmes were offered in the last few years :

1) Training in SPSS package for research staff of Tata Institute of Social Sciences (1978).

2) Computers and Fortran programming for teachers (October-November 1982).

3) Introduction to data processing for teachers (1983).

4) Fortran programming for Engineers (1984).

5) Workshop on using SPSSX package (October 1986).

6) Introduction to programming for college teachers (1987).

7) Micro Computer Software and Programming for college teachers (1988).

8) Unesco Seminar on use of computer for Social Science data analysis and reporting (January 1990).

6. Current Usage and Services

Ever since the university started using IBM 1620 at PRL, the software for all the applications including research computing and data analysis was developed in-house. A few generalized packages for statistical analysis were developed by the programmers at the Centre. Similarly, all the programmes for payroll, financial accounting, examinations and other applications as well as for the external users were developed by the Computer Centre Staff. With the installation of Vax 11/730, the entire software was initially ported on the new machine and later on modified to broaden the coverage and take maximum benefit of the new hardware. The refinement process of this software is a continuous one and is being done internally. Though the laser printer facility could not be acquired due to limitation of finance, the administration was advised to use this facility available in the market for printing of around 30,000 degree certificates every year. It was probably the first attempt to print degree certificates in this volume on a laser printer in the year 1988.

The staff of the computer centre helps the University departments in preparing proposals for acquiring the hardware/software and operationalization of applications. It offers training to the administrative staff in using computers for various administrative applications. The staff is active in various academic and professional bodies such as Computer Society of India, Institute of Chartered Computer Professionals and IEEE. It also provides guidance to colleges and other local institutions for setting up of internal computing facilities. Though the main area of functioning is in the academic computing, it has helped industrial organizations considerably in their initial attempts of computerization of management activities. The centre has taken a lead in introducing the subject of Computer Science in undergraduate courses of Commerce, Science and recently in Arts as well as in Education. Efforts have been made by the Centre to develop text books in local Gujarati language. So far such efforts have resulted into publication of four books in Gujarati.

Since the use of the system is made by a large number of students of regular courses, research scholars and faculty members and the administrative staff, the facility is provided on an open shop working basis all days of the week except on festival days. On all working days this facility is accessible from 7.30 a.m. to 10.00 p.m.

Inspite of this, it is becoming difficult to satisfy the computing needs of the campus both in terms of hardware as well as software. Therefore, UGC has been approached to sanction a proposal for replacement of the existing Vax-11/730 by a cluster of Supermini Computers/RISC Machines with around 40 to 50 terminals and current software packages suitable for educational as well as application development needs. With the availability of new facility, it would be possible to help the researchers, faculty members and students by way of improving the level of services and making available the current software packages useful in research computing and learning of Computer Science.

With the establishment of Computer Training and Applications Laboratory (COMTAL) under the Indo-Canadian collaborative research project, special subject specific training programmes for the teachers have been initiated. So far such programmes for the teachers of Mathematics, Economics,

Social Science, Library Science, Statistics, Physics and Chemistry have been conducted during the year .1991-92. Another training programme for research scholars was conducted during November-December 1992. Support for training and practicals was also provided to the participants of teachers training programmes conducted by the Academic Staff College. Pre-training orientation programmes for the trainees going to Regina were conducted during 1990, 1991 and 1992.

In order to computerize the day-to-day activities of accounts and examinations, personal computers have been installed in these departments in the year 1988. To set up the applications initially, limited help from external agencies has been obtained for software development as well as operationalization on an experimental basis. With the availability of financial resources, such arrangement will be extended to other departments also.

7. Charging Policy

As per the charging policy framed by the Advisory Computer Committee, the following categories of users are charged towards the use of the facility:

1) External non-academic

2) External academic

3) Research projects funded by external agencies.

The use by the campus academic and non-academic users-researchers, students, faculty members and administration are provided free computing facility. Only consumables are accounted for and debited to the respective departmental budgets.

8. Equipment in other Departments

The B. K. School of Business Management acquired a Motorola based PSI Unix system with four terminals in 1988. The other departments, i.e., Statistics, Physics, Chemistry, Zoology, Geography have acquired a few micro computers with dot matrix printers.

APPENDIX-D

1. Assistance to Universities for Computers

The University Grants Commission has started providing assistance to set up computer facilities at the universities/institutions since early seventies when the computer technology was not much advanced. Slowly, as the need was realized by the Commission the programme was expanded and depending on availability of resources, it was decided to provide computer to every university/institution of higher learning. The research, education, administrative and examination workload, size of the university and strength of the staff etc. are assessed by CDC, on the basis of which the level of computer, to be given to the universities, is decided.

'A' Level

Under this category the financial assistance is normally limited upto Rs. 10 lakhs (8 lakhs for hardware & software and 2 lakhs for site preparation). This level of assistance for computer is extended to those institutions which are establishing the computer facilities for the first time keeping in view their needs and requirements.

'B' Level

The support level under this category ranges from Rs. 10 to 50 lakhs. This includes, normally, Rs. 5 lakhs for the site preparation and accessories and the balance grant for purchase of hardware and software. The university which have already used 'A' level computers for 5 years or more are considered under this category for replacement/addition of accessories/peripherals to increase memory and speed of computers. The proposal of the university should also include not only utilization of the computer for research and administrative work but for manpower development such as for courses at Masters and PG diploma levels. A few institutions had been supported in the first instance itself with 'B' level computers on the basis of their needs and requirements although they have not used 'A' level computers.

'C' Level

Under this category the financial assistance for purchase of computer is over Rs. 50 lakhs. The criteria for such support are based on the following :

a) Size of the university and strength of the staff

b) Number of research scholars

c) Number of postgraduate courses, postgraduate diploma courses and other computer related courses

d) Administrative and examination work-load

e) The university has already used 'B' level computer for atleast 7-8 years or more.

At present only 3 universities are being assisted under this category namely Roorkee, Delhi and B.H.U. Initially, financial assistance was also provided to RCCs at Jadavpur, Chandigarh and Poona.

The number of universities/institutions supported under 3 levels is as follows :

Level	Numbers
'A'	40
'B'	61
'C'	3
Total	**104**

2. Assistance to Universities for Staff

2.1 Staff and Scales of Pay

LEVEL 'A' For system upto Rs. 10.00 lakhs

Post	No. of positions	Scale of pay
Manager or Head of Computer Centre	1	Reader's Grade
System Analyst/System Programmer	1	Lecturer's Grade
Computer Operator	2	University's Senior Technical Asstt. Grade
Trainee Programmer	1	@ Rs. 1200 p.m. fixed (Tenure for one year)
Trainee Operator	1	@ Rs. 800 p.m. fixed (Tenure for one year)

LEVEL 'B' For system above Rs. 10 lakhs & upto 50 lakhs

Post	No. of positions	Scale of pay
Director, Computer Centre	1	Professor's Grade
Senior System Programmer/Senior	1	Reader's GradeSystem Analyst
System Programmer/System Analyst (2 posts for 1 shift plus one for each extra shift of 8 hrs.)	2	Lecturer's Grade
Computer Operator (2 posts for 1 shift plus one for each extra shift of 8 hrs.)	2	University's Senior Technical Asstt. Grade
Data Entry Operator	2	University's Technical Asstt. Grade
Trainee Programmer	3	@ Rs. 1200 p.m. fixed (Tenure for one year only)
Trainee Operator	2	@ Rs. 800 p.m. fixed (Tenure for one year only)

LEVEL 'C' For system over Rs. 50 lakhs

Post	No. of positions	Scale of pay
Director	1	Professor's Grade
System Manager/Senior System Analyst/Senior System Programmer	3	Reader's Grade
System Analyst/System Programmer (4 posts for 1 shift plus one for each extra shift of 8 hrs.)	4	Lecturer's Grade
Computer Operator	4	University's Senior Technical Asstt. Grade
Data Entry Operator	3	University's Technical Asstt. Grade
Trainee Operator	3	@ Rs. 800 p.m. fixed (Tenure for one year)

Besides the staffing pattern as mentioned above, the following posts and other items are also admissible :

LEVEL 'A'

Post	No. of positions	Scale of pay
Jr. Stenographer	1	University's prescribed Scale
Attendant	1	University's Scale
Stationery and Contingencies		Rs. 50,000/- p.a.
Maintenance after Warranty period		10% of purchase price p.a.

LEVEL 'B'

Post	No. of positions	Scale of pay
Stenographer	1	As per University's Scale
UDC/LDC	1	As per University's Scale
Attendant	1	As per University's Scale
Stationery and Contingencies		Rs. 60,000/- p.a.
Maintenance Charges after warranty		10% of purchase price periodp.a.

LEVEL 'C'

Post	No. of positions	Scale of pay
Assistant	1	As per University's Scale
Stenographer	1	As per University's Scale
UDC/LDC	1	As per University's Scale
Library Asstt.	1	As per University's Scale
Attendant	1	As per University's Scale
Stationery & Contingencies		Rs. 60,000/- p.a.
Maintenance Charges after Warranty Period		10% of purchase price p.a.

3. Assistance to Universities for Recurring Grant

Normally the recurring assistance from UGC is provided for the following items .

1. Salary of the staff on scaling down basis i.e. 100% in the first year, 75% in the 2nd year, 50% in the 3rd year and 25% in the 4th year.

2. Maintenance grant for computer and airconditioner to the extent of 10% of the capital cost for a period of four years after the warranty period on scaling down basis as in the case of staff.

3. Grant for stationary and consumables.

4. Expenditure on water and electricity are to be met by the institution itself.

The scaling down basis of the salary of staff is on the basis of the presumptions that the computer time will be commercialized for other agencies and the institution will become self-dependent in 4 years. However, as the use of computers as well as the availability in every institution have increased enormously, there are no buyers for the computer time. The requirement of the institution has increased at optimal level and is not sufficient to discharge in house work-load.

In view of above the CDC has now recommended assistance 100% for salary to staff for a period of 5 years and maintenance grant after the warranty period is over for a period of four years at the rate of 10% of the hardware.